XANTHUS

Cover illustration: *Xanthus, George Scharf sketching the Box Tomb.*

Xanthus, Raffaelle casting the Inscribed Stele.

XANTHUS
Travels of Discovery in Turkey

Original illustrations by Charles Fellows
and George Scharf junior

Enid Slatter

The Rubicon Press

The Rubicon Press
57 Cornwall Gardens
London SW7 4BE

British Library Cataloguing-in-Publication Data.

A catalogue record for this book is available from the British Library.

0-948695-30-7 (hardback edition)
0-948695-31-5 (paperback edition)

Printed and bound in Great Britain by Biddles Limited of Guildford and King's Lynn

Contents

List of Illustrations

Acknowledgements

I would like to thank the Society of Dilettanti for a most generous grant and the Twenty-Seven Foundation for an award which have made this publication possible. I am also deeply indebted to an anonymous donor for a handsome contribution and to Sir Jeremy Morse and others for their financial support.

My special thanks go to Sir Brinsley Ford and Miss Edith Clay and Professor Pierre Demargne, who have given me much useful advice and information and who encouraged me to pursue this project. I am also very grateful to Sir John Boardman and Peter A. Clayton in this respect and to my sister Doreen and friends, who have borne with me during the years of research and writing.

I wish to acknowledge Eric Freeman, Librarian and Director of History of Medicine, and my colleagues at the Wellcome Institute for the History of Medicine, and the staff of the Wellcome Centre Photo Library for their continued concern and collaboration in the making of this book. My thanks are also due to Mrs Valerie Batson and her staff at the Heinz Archive and Library of the National Portrait Gallery, and to Dr Susan Walker and staff of the Greek and Roman Department of the British Museum. I am much obliged to Mustafa Türkmen, Information Counsellor at the Turkish Embassy, London, for his valuable aid and to Adrian Henstock, archivist, for his interest and for kindly showing me round Fellows's home in Nottingham.

By courtesy of the Trustees of the British Museum, I have used extracts from the BM Central Archive: Minutes of Trustees' General Meetings, Standing Committee and, by courtesy of the British Library, extracts from Scharf's diaries, 1839-44 [Department of Manuscripts, MSS Collections, 36488 a-c additional]. I acknowledge Crown copyright for the quotations from letters and papers of Admiral Owen, Captain Warden, Dr Armstrong and Charles Fellows conserved at the Public Record Office, Kew [ADM 1/5530 and 5540; 12/403 and 418; 51/3637; 91]. I also thank John Murray for permission to quote from some of Fellows's letters.

For photographs and permission to reproduce them, I am much obliged to the Trustees of the British Museum for plates 3, 15, 79,

107, 114, 118, 119, 123, 126, 127, 129, 133, 135, 141, 142, 144, 145, 146, 148, 151 and cover illustration; to the British Library for plates 68, 115, and 116; to the National Portrait Gallery for plates 1, 5, 6, 25, 38, 53, 58, 72, 87, 101, 103, 117, 120, 121, 122, 125, 128, 131, 132, 139, 140 and 150; to the Centre for Kentish Studies, Maidstone, for plate 4; to The Illustrated London News Picture Library for plates 82, 111 and 152; to Professor Demargne for plate 149. All other plates are by courtesy of the Wellcome Institute Library, London.

Preface

"The acquisition of the Xanthian Marbles for
the British Museum is a subject of rejoicing for
all scholars and lovers of ancient art."

Sir Edmund W. Head Bt, FRS, KCB, 1843

In the eighteenth century, antiquarian travellers and rich tourists had journeyed to Italy and Greece, some going even as far as Turkey, to augment their Classical education by seeing for themselves the famous places of literature - Rome, Athens, Constantinople. The Grand Tour, as it was known, also offered the young men a good opportunity to disport themselves away from the restraints of the family and to return home with examples of Greek and Roman sculpture, which would enhance their properties and Cabinets of Curiosities.

By the nineteenth century, the dilettante traveller had, in large measure, been replaced by official parties, sent abroad specifically to study Classical sites and obtain sculptures for their collections. Many carved friezes, capitals and statues have thus found their way into European museums.

With regard to the Xanthian Marbles, as a result of the interest taken by the British Museum Trustees in the antiquities of Xanthus, described and illustrated by Fellows in a book about his travels in Turkey in 1838, the Government decided to mount an expedition to collect some of the sculptures, which show a unique Graeco-Persian style and date back to the 5th century BC. Fellows was glad to lend his assistance, in order to ensure that a proper selection was made, one that was truly representative of Lycian art and which would bring the wonders of Xanthus to a wide public and which would promote the study of Lycian civilization.

Until recently, Xanthus and Sir Charles Fellows, its discoverer, have remained unfamiliar to the general public. The opening up of Turkey to modern tourism has, however, put that ancient city - and many others also discovered by Fellows - on the holiday-maker's itinerary. It is, therefore, unfortunate that modern guidebooks and travel brochures seldom give accurate information regarding the

Marbles and even censure Fellows for their removal. This was not his initiative: he directed the operations on behalf of the Museum Trustees and the Government, who had full permission from the Turkish authorities for this enterprise.

With all the modern facilities of quick and easy travel, photographic technology and site conservation, from today's standpoint it may be regretted that antiquities such as these were removed, but, a century and more ago, the only way they could be seen and studied by the general public, indeed preserved for posterity, was to house them in a museum. It is certain that many fine sculptures and statues would have been lost, as the ancient places stood open to be pillaged and vandalized by anyone, not to say destroyed by natural disasters. Xanthus was no exception.

The modest number of objects transferred to England is often magnified into 'stripping' the site of 'all' its treasures, yet, at the same time, Continental collectors are praised for 'filling' their museums with rare sculptures from foreign lands. In point of fact, Xanthus today looks very much as it did 150 years ago, when Fellows first entered that long lost city of the Lycians.

The complete story of the acquisition of the Xanthian Marbles has never been told. *Xanthus* seeks to make good this omission and is based on both published works and unpublished archive material.

This book also draws attention to the important part played by George Scharf junior, Fellows's artist, who accompanied him twice, to record the appearance of the archaeological sites and their monuments. The experience and knowledge he gained furnished the bases for Scharf's later career as a connoisseur of art, leading to his being chosen first as Secretary, then as Director, of the newly-founded National Portrait Gallery.

Scharf's charming and accurately-observed sketches make delightful illustrations to this narrative. They also serve as documentation on places and works of art, in some cases being unique records of objects subsequently severely damaged or even totally destroyed.

Xanthus, Travels of discovery in Turkey, chronicles the sequence of events from the time Fellows discovered the ancient city of Xanthus, to the time when the Marbles were first shown, to great acclaim, in the British Museum. It is the story of Fellows's boundless energy, perseverance and enthusiasm in the pursuit and dissemination of knowledge of a lost culture from a vanished world.

xiv

INTRODUCTION

I The Xanthian Marbles

The Xanthian Marbles. How many visitors to the British Museum today know of their existence, much less enquire where they may be seen? Yet 150 years ago, when the first of the sculptures were placed on display, they soon became a familiar and popular sight. "There in the Saloon", it was said, "may be daily seen multitudes gazing up in wonder at the mysterious Harpy-Tomb." Eighteen months later, in August 1844, sculptures and casts from the Second Xanthian Expedition arrived and, like the Elgin Marbles before them, had initially to be left lying in the courtyard, where they created a similar sensation. "Hither antiquarians, historians, artists, come with eager curiosity to examine, to compare, to investigate."

In 1848, the whole collection was housed in the specially built 'Lycian Room' in the newly-opened West Wing of the Museum. The Lycian treasures were considered to be "one of the most interesting collections of antiquities in the British Museum." Indeed, it was agreed that "the appearance of the Room on entering is more striking and impressive than any other in the Museum." This must truly have been the case. The magnificent tombs of massive construction, Ionic columns, statues, sculptured slabs, bilingual inscriptions - even casts, some coloured in facsimile of the originals - were all gathered together in one large hall.

The Ionic Trophy Monument, now called the Nereid Monument, has been partially reconstructed and is beautifully displayed in the 'Nereid Room', with elements of its several friezes round the walls. The rest of the Xanthian Marbles - four great tombs, sculptures from the Xanthian acropolis and a few casts - are, however, distributed in four other locations. Thus the impact of the collection as a whole is lost. The visitor can still 'examine', but can no longer 'compare'. Furthermore, he may, quite easily, miss seeing all of them - even confuse the Xanthian antiquities with those from quite different places altogether.

Most of the original casts have disappeared, but there was a time when the interested public could purchase plaster casts[1] of their own of the Lion Tomb; the Horse Tomb; the Harpy Tomb slabs; and all four of the Nereid Monument's friezes. Twenty years ago, postcards were available of the Xanthian treasures, now only a photograph of the Nereid Monument is on sale, though admittedly, for those carrying a suitable camera, photography in the galleries is allowed.

But private photography of objects of specialized interest is generally based on previous knowledge, which today's visitor may not possess. In his perambulations through the Museum, he may well be struck by these splendid tombs and sculptures, but even if he can assemble them together in his mind, he is unlikely to be aware of them as a collection from Xanthus[2], the outcome of the perception, energy and perseverance of one man - Sir Charles Fellows - whose initiative and learning led him to make the discovery of Xanthus, and whose zeal enabled the British Government to acquire these magnificent relics from a vanished world.

II Sir Charles Fellows, traveller, cartographer, and pioneer archaeologist

"His name has of late been less prominently before the world of art and literature, but the services he rendered to the antiquarian world, by his discoveries in Lycia, are not likely to be forgotten." Alas for these brave words written in an obituary to Sir Charles Fellows in 1860.

1. Sir Charles Fellows by William Brockedon, 1845.

It was just over twenty years since 'the antiquarian world' had first heard of his discovery of Xanthus in southern Turkey, and, a short time later, had been able to gaze in wonderment at the unique sculptures, brought through two Government expeditions to the British Museum. Although the excitement they caused had by then died down, Fellows's name and the Xanthian Marbles, as these treasures were called, were still much discussed in scholarly circles.

Charles Fellows (1799-1860), the fifth son of John Fellows, a wealthy silk-merchant and banker of Nottingham[1], had long been devoted to travel and adventure. Blessed with a robust, if slight, physique, enormous energy and resourcefulness, his enquiring mind sent him to study at first hand the topographical features and cultural heritage of the places that aroused his curiosity.

As a young man, in 1827, he had undertaken a walking tour of the Rhine and Switzerland with a friend and neighbour, to study the geology and natural history of those regions. Finding themselves at the foot of Mont Blanc and the weather in their favour, on an impulse, they decided to attempt the climb to the summit. Theirs was only the thirteenth successful ascent in the history of the mountain[2]. Their new route, called 'the Corridor', subsequently became the preferred way to the top. Mont Blanc had first been climbed in 1786, forty-one years earlier.

His Classical education led Fellows to travel in Italy and Greece, adding a growing appreciation of Roman and Greek antiquities to his fundamental interests of geology and natural science. He had friends amongst the intelligentsia everywhere, on the Continent as well as in England. He was very well read and possessed an extensive library[3].

2. Fellows's bookplate.

His wide range of personal experiences made him a welcome participant in discussions on a multiplicity of subjects. For nearly thirty years, Fellows regularly attended the sessions of the Royal Institution, where he held office as Vice-President on several occasions. He was at a meeting there a few days before his death. As a Member, Fellows also attended the annual conferences of the British Association for the Advancement of Science [BAAS], travelling to wherever the Meeting was held.

Sir Charles Fellows died in November 1860, aged 61. He is buried in Highgate Cemetery, his grave marked by a simple stone bearing just his name and dates upon it.

Fellows made his first journey to Turkey in 1838, as a private individual and purely to gratify his love of travel. He wished to experience life in the mysterious world of the Orient, but knew in advance that there were many Classical remains to be seen in the easily accessible area between Smyrna [İzmir] and the capital of the Ottoman Empire, Constantinople [İstanbul].

A tour in Turkey was not to be considered lightly, however. In the first decades of the nineteenth century, the attempt at reform within the Turkish Empire and the revolt in Greece against its rule had brought much bloodshed and general unrest. Turks were given the reputation for extreme cruelty and for a fierce hatred of Christians. For all that, times were changing, and Fellows had heard through his friends that a European might now travel through Asia Minor without fear of attack, robbery or murder. In fact, it was safer to travel in Turkey itself, than in the Balkans or in Egypt, which were still under Turkish domination.

At first, Fellows kept to the well-trodden routes of earlier travellers, then, gaining in confidence, his enterprising spirit induced him to attempt to cross the whole country from north to south, passing through an area which was nothing but an empty space on the maps. He was to take great delight in this journey, which he achieved without mishap. As an amateur geologist, he found the terrain unusually interesting. He also had the satisfaction of examining a number of remarkable ancient ruins, rarely - if ever - viewed by a European.

On his return along the southern coast, circumstances forced Fellows to take an inland route, leading to his discovery of "the extensive and highly interesting ruins of Xanthus", the ancient capital of Lycia. Shortly afterwards, he was to discover a second ancient Lycian city - Tlos. The remains of both date back to the 5th century BC, the sculptures and monuments having strange and distinctive characteristics. Fellows knew at once, that it was his duty to publish an account of his travels in this antique land, and so bring to the notice of the scholastic world its rich treasury of ancient art. He also resolved to make a second, more exhaustive tour of the province, as soon as was practicable.

Back in London, Fellows carried out his intentions of attracting the attention of antiquarians to his discoveries, and soon the Trustees of the British Museum became aware of the unusual qualities and special beauty of ancient Lycian sculpture. In consequence, it was decided to send a naval vessel to Xanthus to carry away examples of this art for conservation in the Museum. Fellows was greatly pleased by the prospect and put forward many useful suggestions. He drew a plan of the site and marked the positions of the objects he recommended should be collected as the best expression of Lycian style.

Meanwhile, he made preparations for his second personal tour. He proposed to make a detailed survey of Caria and Lycia, the old Roman provinces to the south of Smyrna. The results of these investigations far surpassed even his wildest dreams. Astonishingly, he discovered "13 other cities in Lycia", visiting as many as twenty-four of the thirty-six places mentioned by Pliny, the Elder, in his *Historiae naturalis*, AD 77, as still in existence at that time.

Fellows produced a new map showing the positions of cities old and new, villages, mountains and rivers, "traced for 200 miles, 2 lakes found and all on a white space on the Maps." He collected bird-skins and plant specimens for the Museum and compiled a list of plants of Lycia, which included four new species. He gathered together coins of the region, many of them unique examples, and made stamps (impressions) of Lycian letters, which, with the copies he painstakingly took of bilingual inscriptions, he was confident would provide sufficient material for experts to decipher the strange and fascinating language, which looked akin to ancient Etruscan and Zend, ancient Persian.

Fellows published his second book the following year, 1841. It was his profound hope that others might then follow his lead and visit that lovely land. During the next decade, Lycia did, in fact, become a focus of study for European geographers, naturalists and archaeologists, some of whom were sent specifically by their governments to seek out ancient sculptures to put in their museums.

Glad that his efforts to promote research into ancient Lycia seemed to have borne fruit, Fellows intended to return to the quiet of his private life, which he held so dear, and to his hobbies of collecting coins and antique watches[4]. But this was not to be.

When the Government expedition to Xanthus was about to get started, in October 1841, Fellows heard that it was to be sent without any experienced person to guide the naval men in their search for 'Marbles'. In his concern that no mistakes should occur, Fellows hastened to volunteer his services to supervise the selection. In the event, he had to assume complete management of the excavations, even funding the operations, as that important detail had been overlooked by the organizers. Luckily his health and energy were boundless and his wealth allowed him to pay his own expenses on this, his third journey to Xanthus.

Skilfully, Fellows turned what must surely have been a failure into a partial success and, when the first Xanthian Marbles were seen by the public, they received great acclaim. The merits of the enterprise could now be fully appraised, so, in 1843, a second Xanthian expedition was accordingly mounted to continue the excavations. The value of Fellows's participation the previous year was duly recognized and he was officially appointed to direct the work at Xanthus, thus making his fourth visit to that city of such absorbing interest.

Once more, Fellows gave liberally of his time and knowledge, to ensure that his country's collections would be enriched by the most representative examples of Lycian sculpture. The Xanthian, or Lycian, Marbles demonstrate rare Graeco-Persian features, characteristic of Lycian culture. Fellows's dream that they should be preserved, not only for the edification of artists and Classical historians, but also for the instruction and delight of the general public for future generations everywhere, was now an assured reality.

On 7 May 1845, Fellows received the honour of a knighthood from Queen Victoria at St James's Palace, "in acknowledgement of his services in the removal of the Xanthian antiquities to this country," a fitting reward. Nobody could have done more in the interest of his nation, or for archaeology. "A part in the drama of the world was assigned to him, and he fulfilled it thoroughly."

In an obituary, Fellows was hailed as "the first of the modern Asiatic explorers and by the success of his operations to have induced others...to lay bare the wonders of Assyria, Lycia and Halicarnassus." Amongst the first to benefit from the groundwork done by Fellows in Lycia were some naval officers led by Lieutenant Thomas Spratt, who made a survey of the province in 1842, and a German scientific party, who went there in consequence of reading translations from Fellows's book.

Young Henry Layard, whose uncle lived near Fellows and knew him well, acknowledged his advice and encouragement to travel in Asia Minor without fear, even to penetrate deeper into unknown parts of Asiatic Turkey, if he so desired. Thus inspired, Layard started on the journey that was to culminate in the discovery of the Assyrian palace of Nimrud, then believed to be Nineveh, near Mosul (in Iraq). In 1846, with funds from the British Museum, excavations went ahead. Sculptures[5] from the site began to arrive in England at the end of 1848.

With the successful acquisition of these new treasures, the Trustees decided to finance the search for more antiquities from Turkey. For the past ten years, Charles T. Newton had been working on the coin collections, where he must have frequently met Fellows and seen his coins from Lycia and elsewhere in Asia Minor. Newton was Consul at Rhodes in 1853-54. Then in 1857-58 he succeeded in excavating the site of the Mausoleum at Halicarnassus [Bodrum], one of the Seven Wonders of the World, obtaining for the Museum many valuable statues and elements of this famous tomb[6]. Ten years later, J.T. Wood was to discover another of the Seven Wonders, the great Temple of Diana [Artemis] at Ephesus[7], excavated in the 1870s.

Not only the world of archaeology, however, owes a debt to Fellows, that of art and architecture do also. When the landscape painter, William J. Müller, met him and heard at first hand of the beauty of the Lycian scenery and the picturesqueness of Turkish costume, he thought Lycia would prove a new source of inspiration and subject matter for his talents. He decided to go there at the time when the Second Xanthian Expedition was at Xanthus, taking his 17-year-old pupil, Harry J. Johnson[8] with him.

Müller's Turkish paintings were very well received when he showed them at the British Institution in January 1845, and he would certainly have used his sketches to further advantage, but alas, he was not able to profit fully from his sojourn in Xanthus, as ill health overtook him and he died, aged only 33, the following September.

On his second and fourth journeys to Asia Minor, Fellows had employed both an architect and an artist to assist him. In 1839, he had taken young Robert Hesketh as architect and George Scharf junior, son of the lithographer, George Scharf, as artist. On the way out to Turkey, and again on the way back, Fellows treated the young men to a long cultural tour, spending three months in Italy, not to mention five days in Paris, a week in Athens, and ten days in Venice, giving them ample opportunity to learn from the masterpieces of the past.

For the Second Xanthian Expedition in 1843, Fellows again chose George Scharf junior as his artist, but this time his architect was Rohde Hawkins, younger son of Edward Hawkins, Keeper of the Antiquities at the British Museum. He was to join Fellows and Scharf in Naples for another long cultural journey. They made excursions to the Vesuvian cities of Pompeii and Herculaneum and also went to Paestum to see the great Greek temples there. Hawkins returned to England separately, via Athens, Venice and Munich, no doubt the route advised by Fellows.

Robert Hesketh was able to call on his experiences with Fellows when designing municipal buildings for London. During the bombing of the Second World War, his buildings in the City of London disappeared, but his fine marble Staircase Hall (1871) of the Goldsmiths' Hall can still be admired. Hesketh lived at 13 Arundel Street, off The Strand, and also occupied a house in Bermondsey, where he was District Surveyor. He died, a wealthy man, in 1880, aged 63.

Rohde Hawkins first built in the Neoclassical manner, but later changed with the fashion to the Gothic-Revival style. His Hunt's House (1851), part of Guy's Hospital, looks somewhat Bavarian in character, whereas his Royal Victoria Patriotic Asylum (1857-59) in Wandsworth, recently converted into studios, flats and offices, has an Italian Renaissance appearance. Hawkins also became very wealthy. He died in 1884, aged 64.

Finally to the artist, George Scharf junior, Fellows's protégé. His subsequent career owed everything to the groundwork he gained through his association with Fellows. It was through Fellows's generosity in taking him on those four cultural journeys through Europe, that Scharf acquired the knowledge and skills that were to lead to his becoming the first Director of the National Portrait Gallery, a situation which was ultimately to be of benefit to the whole nation. This aspect of Scharf's career is not generally known.

One hundred and fifty years after its discovery, Xanthus is being visited again - by the modern tourist. Sir Charles Fellows is now usually named in guidebooks, but his work at Xanthus is seldom accurately reported, yet it receives adverse criticism; his explorations in Lycia are completely ignored. Viewed in the context of his time, however, and with knowledge both of the course of events and of his aims, Fellows's exceptional achievements in the years 1838-44 deserve far greater recognition. He was an explorer and cartographer of merit and had the foresight and skill of a pioneer archaeologist.

III Sir George Scharf, artist and art historian; first Director of the National Portrait Gallery

The career of George Scharf junior established him not so much as a painter, but as a connoisseur of paintings, portraiture and costume.

The journeys Charles Fellows arranged for his young protégés took in all the major cities of Europe, and many lesser towns also, which possessed some special cultural feature. Nor did Fellows neglect to introduce his companions into society, taking them to meet the *bon ton* and to visit artists and sculptors in their studios. Although at times overawed, young Scharf was determined to make the most of his good luck and, from the very beginning, he made copious notes and sketches of everything he saw. These records were invaluable to him in later years.

For Fellows, young Scharf proved an ideal draughtsman and assistant, his easy-going temperament making him, in Fellows's own words, "everything I could wish as Artist and Companion." His illustrations clearly show his talents for depicting Classical subjects. Using his own sketches, Scharf produced the woodcuts for Lord Macaulay's *Lays of Ancient Rome*, published in 1847. Macaulay describes the drawings as having "very great grace and spirit", a far cry from the "vulgar" illustrations, which were his pet aversion. This 'grace and spirit' can be appreciated when looking at the four plaques on the façade of White's Club in St James's Street. They represent the seasons and were made after Scharf's designs.

His expert Classical knowledge was also called on when the Greek, Roman and Pompeian Courts were created at the Crystal Palace in 1854. Scharf published descriptions of them in three pamphlets. He also produced the official catalogue of the casts, antique figures and busts, and attended the opening ceremony by Queen Victoria on 10 June, at which there were 45,000 persons present.

11

3. George Scharf junior by George Scharf senior, 1854?

On his return from the Second Xanthian Expedition, Scharf began to prepare illustrations for a proposed publication by the British Museum, and for various articles relating to ancient Greece and the history of art. He became one of the principal artists for John Murray, the publisher of Fellows's books, illustrating the third edition of Kugler's *Handbook of Painting; The Italian Schools,* 1855. On his journey of 1843, Scharf had carried the first edition of this vade-mecum to help him in his studies; he could now supply detailed outlines of many of the paintings, after his own sketches from the originals.

Apart from such commissions, Scharf earned his living as a portrait painter and by teaching drawing at home to pupils, mostly ladies, at about one guinea a lesson. For a few months, he made weekly trips to Brighton to teach Lady Annabella King-Noel, the 18-year-old grand-daughter of the poet Lord Byron.

Scharf also gave public lectures at evening institutes and workingmen's clubs in London and up and down the country, on the science of ancient art. His style of delivery, the uncommon subject matter, and the illustrations he brought with him, proved extremely popular. He used enormous diagrams, big enough to be seen from the back of the hall. These were assiduously prepared for him by his father, the drawings enlarged by four or five times, some measuring up to ten feet in length by six feet high. It took father Scharf as long as three weeks to do one relief of nine figures.

With the arrival of the Assyrian sculptures, Scharf began lecturing on the art of Nineveh in particular, and would lend the diagrams to Layard when he himself lectured on his discoveries. Layard's journeys and discoveries also became the subject of 'Panorama' entertainments, a type of theatrical spectacular much in vogue at that time. Fellows, never the showman, gave neither lectures nor Panorama productions of *his* travels: he was no match for the young, flamboyant Layard. Thus, public enthusiasm for Nineveh soon outshone that for Xanthus. In addition, at that period, the biblical connection with Assyria had a much more powerful pull on Victorian sensibilities, than had the paganism of the antiquities from Lycia.

During the 1850s, Scharf returned to his favourite environment, the theatre, assisting the actor-manager Charles Kean by supplying him with designs for correct Classical costumes and scenery for his revivals of Shakespearian plays at the Princess's Theatre.

A precise awareness of details of costume and physiognomy was Scharf's forte, and in 1864, on the occasion of the tercentenary of Shakespeare's birth, he made a special study of the portraits and busts of the Bard, publishing his findings in a short account. The more complicated issue of which portraits of Mary, Queen of Scots, were actual likenesses, merely doubtful, or wholly spurious, occupied him until his death. His edited conclusions were published posthumously in 1903.

In 1856, the idea of creating a collection of portraits of British royalty and national figures was discussed under the Chairmanship of Philip Henry, 5th Earl Stanhope, a distinguished historian and antiquarian. A Board of Trustees was set up, which included Lord Macaulay. Early in 1857, when considering a suitable person for Secretary, John Murray suggested to Macaulay, that George Scharf junior would be a worthy choice. "He is a clever artist, a well-read man and accustomed to good society," Macaulay informed Lord Stanhope.[1]

4. Scharf's pastiche of portraits from some of the first paintings in the National Portrait Gallery, 1859.

In 1854, Scharf had failed to obtain a similar post at the National Gallery; now his talents were recognized. His chief charge was to select genuine and meritorious portraits for the collection, travelling about the country to examine pictures offered for inclusion. Thenceforth, Scharf devoted most of his time to this pursuit. During his forty years of service, he built up the collection from an initial two dozen pictures[2] to nearly one thousand.

Scharf's affable personality ensured that he was always a welcome guest at Chevening, Lord Stanhope's home (now a Government residence), and at the other mansions he visited, to view a painting or to catalogue a collection. His private cartoons[3] reveal him to have had a lively sense of humour and to have joined the noble families in their amusements.

The many sketches he made of his own home above the Gallery, then at 29 Great George Street, near Westminster Bridge, disclose his industry and preferences. His study and library walls are literally covered with books and framed prints, family por-

Possible situation of G.S. at the critical hour of Midnight between the years 1869–1870.

IN THE MIDDLE OF THE STREET

5. The NPG moves house.

15

6. *George Scharf junior, Daguerreotype by William Edward Kilburn, 1847* [4].

traits and photographs. In his bedroom, statuettes of Classical figures look down from the tops of his wardrobes and cupboards. A huge bust of the Apollo Belvedere dominates the dining-room and a portrait of Shakespeare presides over the study from above the fireplace. A Collard and Collard piano (six octaves and one note) was also somehow squeezed into the room for his relaxation and the entertainment of his frequent guests. Scharf was a good pianist and musical evenings were a feature of his life.

In 1882, on the twenty-fifth anniversary of its foundation, George Scharf was accorded the title of Director, a post he held until, at the age of 74, he resigned through ill health, a few months before his death in April 1895. Shortly before, he had been honoured by the award of the KCB. He was unmarried. Sir George Scharf (1820-95) is buried with his parents in Brompton Road Cemetery, but unfortunately the graves have become obliterated.

In an obituary, it was declared that Sir George Scharf "had not the making of an artist in him, though in respect to minute accuracy he had...hardly a compeer." He was "gifted with a keen eye for the analysis of features and costume, great shrewdness and diligence in archaeological research, and a remarkably retentive memory," which stood him in good stead in his work for the NPG.

"His industry and devotion gave new life to a branch of historical study," it was rightly claimed. His thousands of sketches in over one hundred tiny pocket-books are annotated with observations on colour, forming "a pictorial record of the portraits offered the Trustees [of the National Portrait Gallery] or examined by their Secretary in many parts of the country." They are a valued possession of the Gallery and are still in use today.

It is a great pity that the majority of visitors to the NPG know nothing of the man who first gathered the portraits together, still less of his connection with Sir Charles Fellows and the Xanthian Marbles at the British Museum.

PART ONE

I Fellows plans his excursion in Asia Minor

"To the traveller who delights in tracing vestiges of Grecian art and civilization amidst modern barbarism and desolation, and who may thus at once illustrate history and collect valuable materials for the geographer and the artist - there is no country that now affords so fertile a field of discovery as Asia Minor."

So wrote Lt-Col. William Martin Leake in his *Journal of a tour in Asia Minor*, 1824, about his travels in 1800. What a tempting prospect for someone like Charles Fellows, whose deep interest in topography and nature combined so aptly with a love of the Classics and of antiquities! This was just the incentive he needed to make such a journey himself. The Greek War of Independence had come to an end in 1833, so travel in Greece and Turkey could now be contemplated. Leake's commendations were corroborated by others whom Fellows knew, who had also made excursions to Turkey, enjoyed her people's hospitality and returned with exciting new scientific and cultural data on that antique land.

The annals of the ancient Greek settlements along the Aegean coast of Asia Minor, the later conquests by the Persians and its colonization by the Romans, were familiar to every reader of Classical literature in the eighteenth and nineteenth centuries. These provinces - Ionia, Lydia, and Caria - are rich also in Christian history. They include the sites of the Seven Churches of the Apocalypse[1], all within easy reach from the metropolis of Smyrna [İzmir]. The ruins of famous Ephesus, where both Saint Paul and Saint John lived, lie only fifty miles to the south. Farther south had stood Halicarnassus, the city of King Mausolus, where the great historian Herodotus was born. Smyrna claims the poet Homer, and, amongst many other notable personages of this region, can be named the immensely wealthy Kings, Croesus and Midas, both associated with the province of Lydia.

One of the first to write about this part of Turkey was the Rev. Richard Pococke, who travelled there in 1739-40. Twenty years later, the antiquities were thoroughly examined again by the Classical antiquary Dr Richard Chandler, who had been sent out with an architect and an artist by the Dilettanti Society, specifically to explore and investigate. During the years 1811-12, the whole of the southern coastline was surveyed by Captain Beaufort, the naval hydrographer, later to become Rear-Admiral Sir Francis Beaufort, famous for his *Scale of Winds*. He took particular care to study any ruins accessible from the sea. The young architect Charles Cockerell, who had voyaged on from Greece, where he and his friends had just made the important discoveries of temples at Aegina[2] and at Bassae (Phigaleia)[3], joined him for a time.

In the first half of the 1830s, more scientific and archaeological investigations were made in Lydia and Ionia by scholars known to Fellows, and the French Government sent the eminent archaeologist Charles Texier[4] to Asia Minor, to search out antiquities to add to the collections of the Louvre.

Fellows, as yet unmarried, had the leisure, the health and the resources to make an archaeological journey himself. His purpose was clear: he would follow the footsteps of these earlier travellers, to examine and comment on the ancient ruins, and would assemble scientific information on the natural history, topography and geology of the area. He would have the experience of travel in an Eastern country, and would learn about the people and their way of life, making his own judgment on their temperament and habits.

Given favourable circumstances, he might even explore territories not yet known to Europeans. Even before setting out, Fellows had in mind the possibility of getting as far as mysterious Lycia, the southernmost province of Asia Minor, scarcely known to the modern world, but alive in the chronicles of the ancients and in the myths about the equally mysterious beast, the Chimaera.

The legends and history of Lycia and the Lycian people appear in the texts of Homer and Herodotus, Plutarch and Pliny. The geography and mythology are described in detail and the sites of some of the places were well known. The location of Xanthus, its most famous city, however, still remained a secret. It was supposed to have been situated somewhere in the valley of the river Xanthus, yet nobody had attempted a search for its actual location.

Charles Fellows was to make that discovery. Although he could not have imagined it at that moment, this discovery was to set in motion a chain of events which would take him there three more times, and would change the lives of many others, besides his own destiny.

II Travels in an antique land; Xanthus, 1838

In his book, Fellows does not divulge the date when he left England, but he was not one to delay once his mind was made up, and on the analogy of his subsequent journeys, it was most likely to have been the early autumn of 1837, soon after he had attended the August meeting of the BAAS in Birmingham. He would first have taken a leisurely "lounge", as he called it, through Europe, no doubt stopping for a while in Florence and wintering in Rome. He may well have called in at Athens on his voyage to SMYRNA [İzmir], where he arrived on MONDAY, 12 FEBRUARY 1838.

The metropolis of Smyrna ran along the waterside and rose up the hills behind in a way that reminded Fellows of a lakeside town of Switzerland, the wooden, single-storey houses not unlike Swiss chalets. Unfortunately, they presented a serious fire risk and frequently went ablaze and were burnt down. Since there was no wheeled traffic in the town, small fire-engines had to be carried to the scene on men's shoulders through the narrow, crowded streets. All too often, they arrived to find the house well alight, which was then left to its fate.

From CASTLE HILL [MOUNT PAGUS[1]; 607 ft], a superb view of the whole Gulf can be had, and Fellows made it his daily walk. Here, for the first time, he experienced the neglect and indifference local people showed for their historic past. The medieval walls of the Castle [Kadifekale, Velvet Castle] had been allowed to crumble into decay and the recently unearthed Roman columns and mosaic pavements excited no curiosity save as potential building materials, or, the marble reshaped, as a headstone for a grave in the adjacent Turkish cemetery[2].

From the tops of the buried columns, Fellows calculated that the ground level must have risen by twenty to thirty feet, under which, in all probability, lay many more lovely works of art. The site was excavated in 1966-69, but by then little of value remained.

Fellows spent an instructive week in Smyrna, getting a measure of life in Turkey and buying the stores and equipment he needed for his travels. At the recommendation of Mr Brant, the British Consul, he engaged Demetrius Scufi, a smartly-dressed, intelligent and much-travelled Greek leech-dealer, to act as his dragoman and servant.

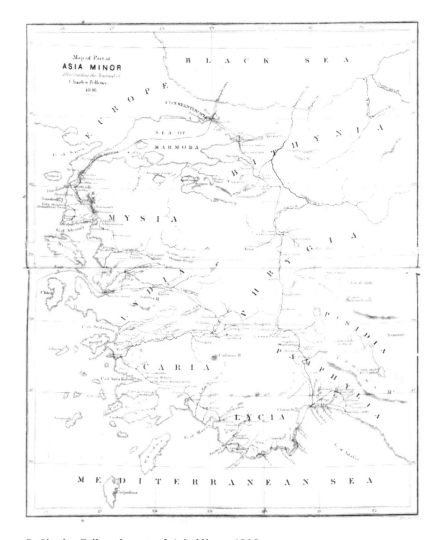

7. Charles Fellows's map of Asia Minor, 1838.

THURSDAY, 22 FEBRUARY - The start of Fellows's Turkish adventure. At half past eight in the morning, to the shrill cries of "*deh! deh!*" - gee-up - Fellows's party moved off. He had hired a cavalcade of four horses at four pence a day, rather less than one shilling in the exchange rate of that time. He paid Scufi four shillings a day, a generous wage, but Fellows believed this to be more economical than to pay a lesser amount for an inferior person.

The owner of the horses, "a black-looking, surly Turk", headed the procession, sitting atop a pile of rugs and cloaks. Then followed a skinny baggage-horse, nearly buried under Fellows's requirements - a tent, folding-bed, hammock and mattress, Levinge's special mosquito-net[3], collapsible bath, canteen of cutlery, toilet articles and medicines, a carpet-bag and saddle-bags. Scufi rode next, his horse likewise weighed down by his baggage, including an umbrella and his chibouk [*çubuk*[1]], the traditional long-stemmed pipe carried in a decorated leather case. Fellows himself brought up the rear, sitting an English saddle with long stirrup-leathers.

The first day took them as far as MANSER [ancient MAGNESIA-AD-SIPYLUM, now Manisa], about 25 miles north-east of Smyrna, a ride of six to seven hours, along a track busy with caravans of camels and heavily-laden donkeys. As was usual, the streets were covered over with vines and matting as protection against the strong sun. The public buildings here were more numerous than at Smyrna and of superior construction, though the houses were only made of adobe. That night, Fellows slept for the first time in a khan [*han*; pls 27,28], a caravanserai, the dome-topped rooms set over stables and store-rooms round a central courtyard, as in an English coaching-inn.

Fellows's first real objective was ACSÁ [Akhisar, White Castle], some 35 miles farther on. It had been built from the spoils of ancient THYATIRA, one of the Seven Churches. Of its 15,000 inhabitants, 5,000 were Greeks and Armenians, the rest being Turks. Fellows describes Acsá as a town teeming with "relics of a former splendid city, although there is not a trace of the site, of any ruin or early building. In a portion not exceeding one-third of a burial-ground", he recorded, "I counted one hundred and thirty columns; and upon measuring them, and noticing their orders, I found that seven or eight distinct temples or buildings must have contributed." Six ancient columns stood forlornly amongst the houses; the streets were paved with fragments of carved stone.

Doubling back towards the coast, Fellows arrived next at the large town of BERGAMA, consisting of 2,500 houses, built amongst the ruins of ancient PERGAMUS[1], with "several mosques and khans now occupying the buildings of the ancients." Once again, the walls of the Turkish houses incorporated marble ornaments "of the richest Grecian art". Through travellers' accounts, Fellows had been made aware of this deplorable habit of the Turks, but actually to see for himself how ancient buildings had been demolished without a thought for their historical or artistic value, greatly shocked him and, as his journey unfolded, he was to become increasingly dismayed by this wanton destruction of antique art.

He had been in Turkey only two weeks, but was already lamenting: "The Turks take you round, and show all they have not themselves built, calling every ruin by the simple name of 'old walls'." Even Scufi with his experience as dragoman to Europeans used this vague term or, more often, 'old castle', *eski hisar*. "I could not have imagined to what variety of uses columns may be applied," he continued. "They are to be had for nothing, and are therefore used for every purpose."

Fellows drew attention to the fact that antiquities were also being collected by foreign powers. "The marbles...are continually taken off for the museums of Europe. The French sent a vessel last year [1837] for a bath and statue, which had been for years unnoticed," and he was shortly to see friezes that would be following them to Paris. Forty years later, the greatest treasure of Pergamus, the Altar of Zeus[4] [2nd century BC], was removed to Berlin by the German engineer Karl Humann. Since then, there have been numerous excavations, and today's tourist has much to admire through reconstructions.

In Fellows's day, no archaeological work had been done at all. The acropolis theatre [78 rows], the steepest in the world, was half buried in earth, its vertiginous 118-foot gradient undisclosed; other wonders of this city were, likewise, covered over. Pergamus lies north of the river CAYCUS [Bakır Çayi], which flows down a broad valley to the sea, some twenty miles distant. There, in the tranquillity of a bygone age, Fellows was able to approach the bold eagles so close that he felt the current of air when they at last took wing.

24

He now turned north and headed for BEHRAHM [Behramkale], a village on the Gulf of Edremit. About 6 miles inland, the remains of ASSUS, or ASSOS, are to be found. Here, there was even more to study. "Immediately around me were the ruins, extending for miles, undisturbed by any living creature except the goats and kids. On all sides lay columns, triglyphs, and friezes, of beautiful sculpture, every object speaking of the grandeur of this ancient city. In one place I saw thirty Doric capitals placed up in a line for a fence. I descended towards the sea, and found the whole front of the hill a wilderness of ruined temples, baths and theatres, all of the best workmanship, but all of the same grey stone as the neighbouring rock."

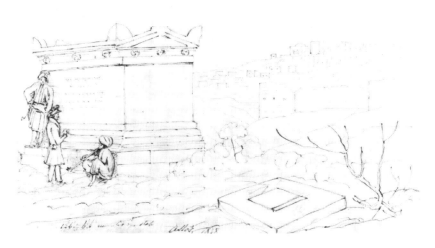

8. *Assos: Fellows studying a tomb.*

He goes on to observe: "The circumstance that the material has not the intrinsic value as marble, has preserved these remains from the depredations committed on other towns near the coast...This town is perfectly open to the antiquarian, and seems preserved for his examination," he concludes with obvious satisfaction. But not for long, for, shortly afterwards, many sections of frieze from the Temple of Athena[5] [c. 530 BC] were carried off by Texier for the Louvre, where Fellows was to see them again some years later.

9. Assos, the Triton frieze.

Other reliefs from Assos may be seen in Boston, USA, and at İstanbul. In recent years, some columns of this Temple have been reconstructed.

Continuing north a further 35 miles, Fellows arrived at the site of **ALEXANDRIA TROAS** [Eski (Old) İstanbul], "a place whose antiquity outstrips history." It had become a forest of oak trees, amongst which hundreds of broken columns and other fragments were scattered about, rendering the land useless for agriculture and confusing for the archaeologist. Fellows could recognize its ancient port, but the best of those ruins were about a mile out to sea. Of the ancient city itself, he only found what he thought to be the bases of two temples.

More interesting by far were the inhabitants - a woman and a boy, an ancient character who called himself 'Consul' and claimed to have been at the Battle of the Nile [1796], and an old man who lived in the recesses of the Roman baths and said he was more than a hundred years old. He showed Fellows what he asserted were a new set of teeth just breaking through his gums.

Fellows then made excursions to **OLD TROY** and to **NEW TROY**, but of Homer's **TROY** [Truva] he could find no trace. There were no signs of Achilles or of Alexander, of Menelaus or of Paris, much less of Helen herself, only water-buffalo lazing in the swamps and a multitude of tortoises picking their way gingerly towards the next bunch of tempting herbage.

The site was first excavated by Heinrich Schliemann in the 1870s and 1880s. Since that time, scientific operations have revealed the remains of as many as nine settlements at this place. Alexandria Troas is now too near a military zone to be much visited.

26

"Time glides away most rapidly on the tide of pleasure," Fellows wrote, or, as the Turks have it 'like a river' - *zaman nehir gibi akıyor*. Reluctantly bringing his investigations to an end, Fellows set off for the coast at CHANNAKALASY [Çannakkale, Pot Castle] on the Dardanelles to wait for a steamer to take him to the Capital.

WEDNESDAY, 7 MARCH 1838 -*Kurban Bayramı*, the Feast of the Sacrifice. The day began with a military parade, but the ill-fitting uniforms of the soldiers and their clumsiness with their muskets, carried at all angles, spoilt the overall effect. Afterwards, there was an impressive display of cannon-firing across the Straits from the pair of fortresses on either side. The balls were rounded pieces of ancient column and they bounced six or seven times on the water before sinking, just like the 'bouncing bombs' of the Dam-Buster raids of 1943. This was followed by the sacrifice of a sheep by every household, before general rejoicing and feasting began.

Fellows stayed in CONSTANTINOPLE [İstanbul] for a whole week of sight-seeing. One day he had the good luck to see the Sultan, Mahmud II, on a progress through the city. A few years earlier, to stare at the ruler would have been punished by summary execution. This modern Sultan, however, was all for reform, wishing to bring his Empire into line with the Western Nations. He no longer wore the costly *kaftan* and jewelled turban of the old rulers, but dressed in a simple blue 'French' uniform with a scarlet fez. He sported a short, trim, black beard and sat upright on his horse using an English saddle. By his own command, his portrait was displayed in every barracks, and was to be seen in many shops.

By decree, all government officials wore a similar uniform, the people, however, especially the older generations, still clung to their traditional robes. Many Europeans too adopted a type of Oriental dress, which was even recommended by doctors as invalid wear. The folds of the shalwars, [*şalvar*], baggy trousers, confining a large quantity of air, prevented chill. They were also considered very desirable attire for persons of a delicate constitution. Enveloping the loins in a long cashmere shawl provided protection against dysentery and lumbago, whilst the open, collarless Turkish shirt allowed for ease of breathing. The loose slipper, giving free use of the toes, secured the Turk from corns and bunions.

The turban shaded the eyes from the sun and protected the head from the heat - and from sabre cuts. Traditional headgear [pl. 21] proclaimed the wearer's status, like the conical *külah* of the *derviş* or the fur *kalpac* of the *tatar* (courier). Now all must wear the plain *fes*. When Kemal Atatürk came to power, he banned its use and ordered men to wear European cloth caps or hats. The brim, however, prevented worshippers from touching the floor with their foreheads, so caps were universally worn back-to-front.

Fellows made several official and social calls. One was on Dr Julius Milligen, Court Physician, who had earlier been in Greece and had attended Byron at Missolonghi. He had made various antiquarian excursions and gave Fellows details of a beautiful Ionic temple [pls 10,11], discovered as recently as 1825, in an isolated position a considerable distance to the south. This set Fellows thinking. Could he not go to see this temple and then continue on, over the Taurus Mountains, and so into Lycia? His own experiences had been so easy, pleasant and instructive, there seemed no reason why he should not strike out boldly and plot a course to gain the coast at Adalia [Antalya], even though this meant crossing an area left entirely blank on the maps.

With his spirit of adventure and resourcefulness, and with the comfortable assurance that his servant, Demetrius Scufi, was totally capable, Fellows prepared to risk both the unknown territory and its inhabitants.

SATURDAY, 17 MARCH - Fellows now began the second stage of his Turkish adventure. To start with, he followed the trade route along the north coast of the SEA OF MARMORA [Maramara Denizı], at that time, the only road in Asia Minor. It had been designed by Austrians and was to run to İzmit, sixty miles away. After 35 miles and three sets of horses, Fellows crossed the Sea by ferry and headed south to the great LAKE OF ASCANIA [Iznikgölü] four miles wide and ten miles long. At the southern end lie the ruins of "the many times famous" NICAEA [İznik]. The city, dating back to the 4th century BC, had been the meeting-place for the First Ecumenical Council in AD 325. The Nicene Creed of the Christian faith was drawn up here and, in AD 787, at the Seventh Meeting, iconoclasm was condemned.

28

"Seldom have I had a harder day's work than in attempting to see and comprehend this ruin of ruins," Fellows wrote of this extensive site. The remains - Greek, Roman and Christian - are well preserved[7] and much of the marble is highly finished and polished. The edges of the blocks fit tightly together and are grooved, showing that the joints had originally been covered by strips of metal, perhaps even of gold.

Fellows's next destination was the large town of KOOTÁYA [Kutahya, ancient COTYAEIUM], 120 miles south, steering by compass bearings with the aid of Colonel Leake's map. Leake had produced a map of the routes taken by the Romans and by later travellers, but, as he himself admitted, "five-sixth's of Asia Minor are still a blank." The journey took five days. Nothwithstanding, Fellows found the geology and natural history so fascinating, that he made a special plea for scientists to visit this area for their researches. As a guide, he wrote detailed accounts of the terrain, its vegetation and wild life.

From Kootáya he made a long excursion to the south-east, looking for the MIDAS TOMB [c. 600 BC], near Yazilikaya, meaning 'Written Rock', which he knew of through Leake's book with the plate by George Scharf senior, but, sadly, he failed to locate this Hittite monument. He then embarked on the shorter detour to see the ruins at Aezani [Aizanoi].

Here, he stayed the night in the odoor [*oda* or *köyodası*], a village room for strangers, in fact a little mud-brick house, lit by slips from the turpentine tree. The single room was swept clean and a carpet and cushions provided, as well as a very good meal, each dish brought in by a villager from his own supper. Soup was followed by various egg dishes, brain fritters, *pilav*, sweets of honey-pastry, *baklava*, and large Smyrna raisins. Between each course, the carpet was scrupulously brushed to avoid any crumbs being stepped on, that being against religious Law.

After the meal, a ewer of rose-scented water and a richly embroidered towel were brought in for the guest to wash his hands. He noticed that sight of the dirty water was prevented by a perforated cover to the basin. A man of fastidious habits himself, such cleanliness and dainty manners much impressed and pleased Fellows.

AEZANI is situated in the Karlık Dağı, the Snowy Mountains, on an exposed position, 8,000 feet above sea-level. True to the name, snow lay thick on the ground and more fell in a raging blizzard. In spite of these appalling conditions and the intense cold, Fellows persevered in his investigations of the ruins, even drawing a plan of the site. He marked the positions of 3 temples, a theatre, a stadium and 3 bridges, all "so little plundered or defaced", that he fancied some buildings could have been reassembled.

The beautiful Ionic Temple of Zeus and Adrianos Panhellenios [Jupiter and Hadrian Panhellenius; c. AD 125] had 18 columns still standing. Inside the portico are some of the earliest capitals of the Composite Order. Alas, 4 columns from another temple had lately been removed to build the Governor's house at Kootáya, leaving only one, appropriated by a stork for its nesting place. As at Yazılıkaya, the worship of Cybele, the great Mother-Goddess of Phrygia, had also taken place here.

The ride back to Kootáya, into the teeth of the blizzard, took ten hours. When Fellows finally got back, wet through and frozen to death, for once he risked offending his host by begging to be left by himself, to change out of his sodden clothes in private. It was the custom, kindly meant, never to leave a guest alone, that he might not feel lonely, an annoyance that the reserved Englishman only bore with the utmost stoicisim.

On TUESDAY, 27 MARCH, Fellows left Kootáya, the line of his route now directly south to cross the "dreary" plain of PHRYGIA. Struggling forward in snow or icy rain, combined with a cutting wind, made for a cheerless journey. Scarcely a tree grew on the volcanic tableland, blown by choking winds of tufa, a greyish-white pumice-dust, almost as thick as that lethal cloud which had engulfed Pompeii. To add to the prevailing feeling of death, Fellows had frequently to skirt round sad villages, isolated by the scourge of plague.

In the belief that the disease spread through touch, villages and the afflicted were kept apart, fumigation was practised, and furniture covered with a 'non-conductor', such as wood or coarse goat-hair cloth. The clothes of the dead were, nevertheless, sold in bazaars. Depopulation of large cities was considerable. Fortunately, precisely the years of Fellows's journeys, 1839 to 1844, plague vanished from the Levant.

10. Aezani, Temple.

11. Aezani, Temple portico.

31

Four days on, he was greatly surprised to come across "extensive remains of a superb city" on top of a mountain, 1,500 feet up. The wild grandeur and serenity of the scene gave it an awesome dignity. Fellows counted 7 or 8 temples and 3 other buildings, which he took to be market-places. There was "one of the most beautiful and perfect" theatres he had ever seen, with the greater part of the proscenium still standing. This rich city was wholly Greek, without a vestige of Roman or Christian architecture. From its situation, Fellows determined it to have been SAGALASSUS [Ağlasun; 2nd century BC to 5th century AD].

SUNDAY, 1 APRIL 1838 - This bleak, yet historic, place was about three-quarters of the distance across the interior and the lonely, snowy uplands were soon to give way to a milder and much pleasanter district. Miraculously, it seemed, spring was waiting in the next valley, with the wheat in the fields already six inches high.

Hearing that there were some ruins not far from the village of BOOJAK [Bucak], Fellows made yet another detour to look for them. Even though he might waste time and energy on what could turn out to be worthless rubble, Fellows resolutely followed up every archaeological hint and, this time, on a promontory at about 3,000 feet, at the end of a ridge of mountains, Ak Dağ, White Mountain, composed of shining white marble, he came on what he considered to be one of the finest cities that ever existed.

Riding for at least 3 miles through a part of this huge site, he counted 50 to 60 columned buildings, the remains of temples, theatres and market-places. They were splendid marble structures of the early Greek period, though the general style of the temples was Corinthian. Always lost in his unfortunate maps, Fellows ascribed these ruins to the city of SELGE. They are now considered to be those of CREMNA. Excavations began in 1985.

The descent through these mountains from this elevated position was by an ancient paved road, the stones showing the grooves made by Roman chariot-wheels. Then, suddenly, "a view burst...through the cliffs, so far exceeding the usual beauty of nature as to seem like the work of magic. I looked down from the rocky steps of the throne of winter, upon the rich and verdant plain of summer, with the blue sea in the distance, and on either side, like outstretched arms, ranges of mountains bounding the bay of

Pamphylia." But this wondrous view "passed like a dream", as the road wound on downwards towards the coast.

Fellows was to spend one more night in his tent in this wild, unmapped country, before arriving, late the following day, at his goal, Adalia. It had taken seventeen days to cross the entire country from north to south, a distance of some 400 miles, relying only on his far from accurate maps, his compass, and his innate sense of direction.

Now began the third stage of Fellows's tour of Asia Minor - the exploration of the southern provinces of Pamphylia and Lycia.

ADALIA [Antalya, ancient ATTALEIA] was a town of considerable importance, the seat of a Pasha [*paşa*]. Lieutenant Spratt, in his survey, estimated the population at about 13,000 inhabitants, of which 3,000 were Greeks. In large towns the population was mixed, but in country villages Greeks and Turks lived separately[6]. The town was enclosed by a double wall, parts of which are still standing today. For about a mile outside, the ground was cultivated with vegetables and sugar-cane. The wild flowers were those of an English hothouse. Fellows collected and drew some unfamiliar plants: *Anagallis, Astragalus, Fumaria, Gladiolus, Muscari, Pyrethrum, Salvia* and *Scilla*. "The nightingales in the evening were almost an annoyance."

Here, Fellows lodged with a rich Greek, the Pasha's banker and far wealthier than he. The women of the family all wore head-dresses made completely of gold coins. Fellows estimated the mother's as worth £150, no less. Two black slaves formed part of the household and Fellows was urged to buy one for himself at a cost of £6-8 only. Unlike previous 'milords' travelling in the Orient, he declined this opportunity.

The Pasha was a cultivated person and invited Fellows to an 'audience'. He was a fine-looking man, proudly dressed in the new 'French' uniform, rarely seen so far from the capital. He offered Fellows a European chair and they spent two hours conversing in Italian, the lingua franca of the Levant, on many subjects of mutual interest. The Pasha was particularly concerned with the geology of his territory and its mineral resources. He sought Fellows's opinion regarding the possibility of finding coal, iron and copper, showing him the specimens he had collected. Nedgib Pasha was trying to improve his domain and was constructing roads out of Adalia. Unhappily, a year or two later, he was dead and his successor allowed the work to lapse and the roads to deteriorate through neglect.

Leaving his baggage with his host, Fellows made an excursion to the east, along the coast of PAMPHYLIA, first to PERGE [Murtana], then on to SIDE [Selimiye], both sites boasting enormous Roman theatres. The theatre at Perge was almost complete, but in the 1920s, it was used as a quarry to create the modern town of Murtana, leaving little but the rows of seats.

12. Pamphylia, shield decorations on a tomb.

He had read glowing accounts of the ruins at Side in Beaufort's work, but when he got there, Fellows found the place so overgrown, that the full extent of the city was hard to judge and the remains, Hellenistic and Roman, far inferior in scale, date and age to any he had yet seen. Expecting this city to have formed the climax to his wanderings, the ruins turned out to be amongst the least interesting for him. The site was excavated in 1947 and 1967, and the theatre cleared to reveal its huge size, the tiers rising to a dizzy 70 feet above the stage, making Side a great tourist attraction.

Little suspecting that the real climax to his journey was to come quite soon, Fellows retraced his steps, sadly disappointed. By taking a different route, however, the richness of the scenery easily dispelled his sombre mood. He studied the types of rock and gravel peculiar to that area and noted down the varieties of wild life, the cultivated plants, and even shot some birds, the skins of which he sent to the British Museum[8].

MONDAY, 9 APRIL - Fellows spent some time examining the "extensive and heavy-looking ruins" of ASPENDUS, which he had glimpsed by moonlight, on arriving at the village of BOLCAS [Belkıs]. Like the other Roman ruins, they were not to his taste. He was quite frankly prejudiced against architecture "of a base age", comparing it adversely with the "chaste purity" of Greek style, in conformity with the opinions of his day, based on the writings of the German critic and Classical art historian, J. J. Winckelmann, the arbiter of Classical taste.

Describing the huge buildings, the stadium, aqueduct and theatre, Fellows wrote: "The scale is vast, but there is an absence of the most beautiful of all qualities, simplicity. Some of the cornices are elaborately rich, and of Greek workmanship; but arch rising above arch, niche above niche, and column supporting column, plainly indicate the influence of the Romans."

In several places, he found traces of patterns in red and a beautiful light blue applied to the stucco. He comments favourably on the excellent state of preservation of the theatre [2nd century AD] and, although dismissing the exterior as in the worst taste and looking like a factory building, he praised the interior as the most perfect he had ever seen. "The whole might be now used for its original purpose," he opined and, after recent restorations, this is the case.

Fellows had been hoping to find Aspendus, but alas, not realizing that this was, indeed, that ancient city, he believed his search had been fruitless. "The maps are all so extremely incorrect", he bemoaned, "that I am unable to trace my situation upon them. Having sought in vain for a considerable lake...I have no definite clue by which to discover the ruins." Unknown to him, Lake Capria had long ago dried up and completely disappeared. In Classical times, however, it had provided Aspendus with commerce in a fine powdery salt produced by evaporation of its waters in summer. Without it and without the evidence of a name from inscriptions or coins, he reluctantly conceded that this city must, after all, be PEDNELISSUS, as indicated on the maps.

The lack of interesting antiquities to keep him here longer was the first in a series of unscheduled changes, which ultimately led Fellows to the discovery of Xanthus.

Returning to Adalia, he was much distressed to find that one of his host's children had died. With his usual consideration for others, Fellows packed his bags, leaving the bereaved family to their grief, unmolested by his presence. This caused him to curtail his visit to the town, which he preferred to any other he had stayed in, and he prepared to set sail to the west, along the coast of Lycia.

It was FRIDAY, 13 APRIL. Fellows was superstitious and he recalled several misfortunes which had occurred on a Friday. This was to be no different. When it came to sea voyages, he always seemed to be plagued by bad luck. "I never was at sea", he lamented, "without forming a resolution in future to travel by land."

First his start had been delayed, leaving him without a place to sleep that night; then, during the next day or two, he had to suffer adverse weather, compounded by a timorous crew, monotony and mounting frustration. In consequence, when he went ashore to see the ruins at KAKAVA [Kekova], about halfway along the Lycian coast, Fellows decided to hazard a route along the mountain tracts, no matter that all previous travellers had been deterred from attempting it.

"I had no sooner resumed my land travels, than objects of interest appeared," he wrote with real pleasure. "Around me were nameless ruins [and] many strong, heavy sarcophagi of the ancient inhabitants." He was captivated by the bold crags and lovely valleys, thick in plant life, to be seen on every hand. "Ascending many thousand feet above the very striking coast, forming with its islands, bays, and promontories a perfect map, but differing materially, I am sorry to say, from any map that I have with me," he found to his amazement that the 'Meis' he had been making for - the port of Macry [Fethiye] as he thought - was, instead, the important island known since the Middle Ages to European traders as CASTELLORIZO [Megisti], but, apparently, called MAIS or MEIS locally. Macry, on the other hand, was more than sixty miles away to the west.

On the mainland, he saw the singular ruins of ANTIPHELLUS [Kas]. The cliffs are cut into typically Lycian rock-tombs of highly

13. *Antiphellus, tomb.*

ornamental design and, scattered thickly along the beach, there were hundreds of 'Gothic' sarcophagi, standing like huge, deserted sentry boxes. All had been broken into and they remained forlorn and forgotten, their surfaces corroded by the damp sea air.

Turning inland again, and stumbling up sheer tracks against a wind so strong that leaves were torn from the trees and the sea was whipped into a fury, covering the shoreline, by the afternoon of THURSDAY, 19 APRIL, Fellows and his little string of horses had struggled as far as the village of FORNAS, near Patara, the former outlet of the river Xanthus [Eşen Çayı].

In Roman times, PATARA had been a thriving port and was the centre of the cult of the God Apollo, whose Oracle was here. The history caught the fancy of Captain Beaufort, who identified the site in 1811, while on his survey of the coast. He came ashore to search for the Oracle and believed he had found it, but this has been discounted. He drew the triple-arched Gate [pl. 87], a well-known feature of the Lycian coastline, and, like Fellows, devoted some paragraphs in his *Journal* to deploring the destruction of the site by the inhabitants in their search, not for culture, but for building materials. He had just as harsh words for the European tourist, who, he said, "knock off a head, a hand, a leaf or a volute without comprehension and merely to show to their equally inconsiderate friends at home."

The port of Patara had long since silted up, the former harbour now rich in vegetation, not ships. The river Xanthus has moved to the north and west of the city, which seemed to Fellows in danger of becoming completely buried by dunes. Excavations began in 1986, but the theatre remains obscured under a mound of light sand.

"Colonel Leake and other writers having mentioned that the valley of the Xanthus has not been explored by Europeans, and that cities may probably be traced near its course, I have determined to seek a route to Macry up this valley, instead of by sea or across the range of Cragus."

So saying, the next morning, FRIDAY, 20 APRIL, Fellows and his servant Scufi, began their journey north, up the river. By noon, they had got as far as KOONIK [Kınık], no more than a collection of tents, where they left the baggage, before riding on to some ruins, just discernible, on the top of an escarpment overhanging the river, two miles away. This was XANTHUS [Xanthos].

14. Xanthus, the Harpy Tomb and a "Gothic" tomb beside the theatre.

"We had no sooner entered the place of tombs," which date back to the 5th century BC, "than objects of such high interest to the antiquarian, sculptor, and artist appeared, that I determined to send for the baggage, and pitch my tent here for the night," Fellows wrote in a state of high excitement. Indeed, he got so carried away, that his next diary entry is dated the 19th - the previous day. He must, in fact, have spent all the afternoon and evening on the first day [the 20th] and all the following morning [the 21st] at the ruins, before moving on.

Fellows filled several pages of his book with drawings and detailed descriptions of the antiquities, as he quickly realized that the unique Lycian style, epitomized by these tombs, had an importance far beyond that of his early intention, only to pin-point the position of Xanthus on the map. He also knew that he must return as soon as possible, to make a proper survey and investigation of the site, bringing an architect and an artist with him for that specific purpose.

39

This was the start of a dream, at times to turn into a nightmare, that was to fill his mind and his days for the next ten years, and was to change his whole life.

The city had obviously been destroyed by earthquakes, but so far it had remained relatively untouched by human hands. No town had risen at this place, robbing it of the stone, the ruins had simply become obliterated under a forest of trees and scrub. Earth had piled up to such an extent, that Fellows mistook the grave-chamber of a pillar-tomb, the 'Lion Tomb', which was actually on top of a 9-foot monolithic pillar [pl. 129], to be the entrance to a rock-tomb. 'Pillar'-tombs are a feature of Xanthus and unique to Lycia. The grave-chamber is placed high up under a cap-stone on the top of a square pillar. They are recognized as the earliest of the Lycian burial types.

The grave-chamber of the Lion Tomb is carved with lions and warriors. Another pillar-tomb, standing near the theatre, has curi-

15. Xanthus, the Lion Tomb.

ous reliefs, in archaic style, of female figures and, at the corners, strange bird-like creatures, thought to be Harpies. This 'Harpy Tomb' was to become very famous and the topic of much speculation as to the meaning of the sculptures. A third pillar-tomb is

40

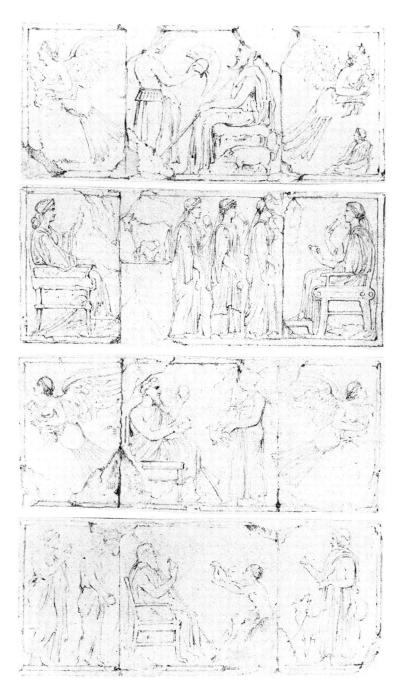

16. Xanthus, the Harpy Tomb figures.

covered in Lycian words, beautifully incised, yet completely unintelligible to Fellows. This, the 'Inscribed Stele' [pl. 148], was to be a constant source of work for him, as he endeavoured to copy its long inscription.

The tomb which most appealed to Fellows was the 'Horse Tomb'. Unable to see the carvings clearly, he first called it the

17. Xanthus, the Horse Tomb.

'Winged-Chariot Tomb'. Now it is known as the Payava Tomb. It is typical of its type, having two grave-chambers, one on top of the other, under a curved lid resembling an upturned boat, with a ridge or 'keel' along the top. This he named the "hog-mane" as it reminded him of the short-cropped bristles of Classical horses, a style then fashionable in England for carriage and riding horses. He called this type of tomb, "Gothic", from the shape of the arch.

The Horse Tomb is highly ornamented with carvings on the sides and the lid. There is a succession of figures and horses along the hog-mane. Each side of the lid has a Classical *quadriga*, a four-horse chariot, in ancient art symbolizing apotheosis. The heads of the horses are unusual in being turned in two directions. The warrior wears a Greek-style helmet, whilst the charioteer wears a soft Persian, or Phrygian, cap. The lower chamber is also decorated with figures, and, at the ends, there are men in Lycian dress. The whole tomb was an impressive 20 feet high.

Fellows felt quite overwhelmed by the importance of his discovery and very conscious of his own limitations. "It is now noon," he sighed, "and I regret that I have not had time, and do not possess sufficient talent, to examine completely the objects here, which alone afford inducement to the man of taste to visit this country, even from distant England." Reluctantly, he had to ride away, overcome by the unique beauty of this most ancient city in its wild, lonely setting.

Continuing up the river valley, two days later, Fellows made a second discovery - the ancient city of TLOS. It is situated near the village of DOOVEER [Duvar, Wall], at the foot of an escarpment. The principal ruins are perched on the top, whilst the sides of the cliff are pitted with rock-tombs in a most spectacular way.

According to his maps, this place was 'Pinara'; an inscription, however, told Fellows that it was, in reality, the city of Tlos. He rightly conjectured that the true Pinara must lie somewhere in this vicinity, but having already decided to return to Lycia as soon as he could, Fellows did not stop to search for it at this time. He made the discovery two years later.

For this journey, there were still the well-known ruins of several more ancient cities for him to investigate, including those at

18. Tlos, rock-tombs.

TELMESSUS [pls 55,56], near the misleading 'Meis', or Macry, to which he found a way through the Cragus Mountains.

From here, Fellows set his return route, the final stage of his round-tour, in a north-westerly direction, into CARIA and LYDIA, following in the footsteps of Richard Chandler and the Dilettanti party. On his second journey to Asia Minor, he repeated this part of his itinerary in the reverse direction, entering the province of Lycia at Macry.

One of the most important places to visit, on this stage, was EPHESUS [Efes][9] owing to its Classical and Christian associations, but "the memory of the past may perhaps have led [travellers] to indulge too freely their imagination whilst contemplating the few silent walls which remain" was Fellows's view, as he looked at the gigantic, but nameless piles of buildings, without ornaments or

44

inscriptions. The stadium remained "tolerably entire", but the famous theatre was recognizable only by its shape, "every seat is removed, and the proscenium is a hill of ruins." Fellows felt great disappointment "at not seeing realized all the ideas associated with it," but the glory that was Ephesus, had been plundered in the Middle Ages to build the adjoining town of AIASALOOK[9] which had, in its turn, crumbled into ruin.

As always, the countryside outshone the pillaged remains. "My time was fully employed", he explained, "in admiring the great variety of beauty of the trees and other features of the natural history of the spot." The Turkey oak [*Quercus cerris*] with fern-like leaves, and the aromatic terebinth tree [*Pistacia terebinthus*[10]], which gives a sweet gum-resin, were new to Fellows. The air was also perfumed by the oleaster [*Elaeagnus angustifolia*].

He goes on to describe the brilliant beetles, the gorgeous butterflies, "strangers to northern Europe", and the enormous cicadas, mentioned in the works of Homer, Anacreon and Virgil. "I thought England in my younger days a rich and beautiful [field for study], but here the insects, like man, assume a far more gay costume," Fellows declared.

He followed the valley of the MAEANDER inland as far as LAODICEIA, over a hundred miles from the coast, then made an about-turn to travel along the COGAMUS to see PHILADELPHIA and SARDIS, completing his visits to the sites of the Seven Churches, before arriving back at SMYRNA, on SATURDAY, 12 MAY 1838, after an "excursion" lasting exactly three months.

45

Back again in SMYRNA and comfortably settled in the Navy Hotel, Charles Fellows began to review his journey. "I quite enjoy to be sitting on a chair, with a table before me," he confessed, "and shall spend this day of rest [SUNDAY, 13 MAY, 1838] in thinking over the interest and pleasure of the past three months. My first feeling on making the retrospect cannot but be gratitude that I have escaped even the slightest accident, on a journey of three thousand miles, through a country little travelled, and in which there are neither carriages nor roads."

Previous travellers had turned back on hearing of an outbreak of plague, others had not risked venturing along unmapped tracks through sparsely populated regions, but Fellows, with only Scufi and local guides, had bravely journeyed on, regardless of the dangers of robber-bands, wild animal attacks, illness, or becoming irredeemably lost.

Of his achievements, Fellows wrote nothing, though he had every right to be proud of his success in discovering two ancient cities, dating back to the 5th century BC, their relics, in a good state of preservation, displaying a particularly beautiful and unusual style, apparently of Greek workmanship, and yet showing distinct Persian influence.

Fellows's immediate concern was to write a book of his travels, to bring to the notice of the antiquarian world and the public in general, the delights of a journey in Asia Minor, stressing the attractive features of the countryside and giving details of its antiquities. Here, indeed, was a land richly rewarding to travellers and artists in search of the picturesque, and worthy of investigation by historians and scientists too.

Fellows returned to England via Greece, Trieste and the overland route through Europe, arriving home in early summer 1838. After consulting his publisher John Murray, he set to work to write up his diary notes and prepare his drawings for publication. Within a year, the book, *A Journal written during an excursion in*

Asia Minor, 1839, was out, his drawings[1] lithographed by the printer Charles Hullmandel.

The book at once attracted the attention of scholars both in England and on the Continent. Edward Hawkins, a numismatist, Keeper of the Department of Antiquities at the British Museum, was quite fascinated by the Lycian sculptures and when, in MARCH 1839, Fellows presented some engravings of the tombs and sculptures at Xanthus to the Department, Hawkins immediately showed them to the Trustees. They were greatly impressed and, at first, seemed eager to mount an expedition to Xanthus to acquire some examples for the collection.

In MAY, Fellows was able to write in the preface of his book: "I hear that on their recommendation, the Government has given directions for having these monuments of ancient art brought to this country; we may hope therefore to see them among the treasures of our National Institution." The Trustees applied to Lord Palmerston, Secretary of State for Foreign Affairs, to obtain permission from the Sultan for the removal of the sculptures. The practicalities of their transference to England were discussed with Captain Thomas Graves, Commander of the survey-vessel *Beacon (6)*[2].

This was to be an enterprise undertaken by the British Government on behalf of the British Museum. Fellows himself would not be involved in any capacity. Nonetheless, he was extremely glad of this unexpected outcome to his travels and furnished the Trustees with what information he could, to assist the scheme.

Meanwhile, he was preparing for his second journey to Turkey. This time, he planned to remain longer in Caria and Lycia and possibly make a further foray into Pamphylia. He intended to fix the positions of all towns and archaeological remains, and chart the rivers and mountains, correcting the current maps and extending the information they contained. This survey-work he could do himself, but detailed drawings and measurements of the antiquities needed the expertise of an artist and an architect. His choice fell on two young men: George Scharf junior, aged 18, who lived just round the corner at 14 Francis Street[3]; and Robert Hesketh, aged 22, who was completing his apprenticeship under the architect, Philip Hardwick[4], whose residence, 60 Russell Square, was opposite Fellows's home, number 30[5].

Charles Fellows has never received acknowledgement for the essential rôle he played in the fortunes of these lucky young men. Under his patronage, his generosity not only took them to Turkey, but enabled them to spend six months on the Continent studying the paintings and buildings of international renown, and learning from the artists and art critics, whom they would meet.

George Scharf junior had scarcely begun to make his way in the world since leaving the Academy Schools. In November 1838, he had met the actor-manager Charles Macready, who put him on the 'free list' at Covent Garden Theatre, allowing him to sketch there. Thus encouraged, he began to draw Macready's famous productions with the exciting scenic effects created by the Romantic theatrical artist, Clarkson Stanfield[6]. Father Scharf helped him to etch his sketches on copper and they were published as a little book[7] in monthly parts, distributed to subscribers by Henry[8], George's younger brother.

Fellows evidently perceived latent talent in his drawings, so like his father's - clear, animated and covered with notes on colour, and he must surely have known Scharf senior, encountering him busily sketching in the streets and squares of London, especially since the artist enjoyed having onlookers around him. They also had many mutual acquaintances, not least of whom were Colonel Leake, John Murray and Edward Hawkins. Nevertheless, when Fellows was looking for a suitable artist to take with him to Turkey, it was the printer, Charles Hullmandel, who put them in touch.

Regrettably, neither Fellows nor the Scharfs[9] reveal the exact nature of their agreement. Fellows refers only once to young George, acknowledging that he was everything he could wish for "as an artist and companion". George himself, on one occasion, calls Fellows "my Guardian", and several times he expresses his desire to please him, grateful for the opportunities put in his way, and anxious to be worthy of such kindness and faith in his ability.

The arrangement made was probably similar to that agreed between the poet Goethe, and his young artist C.H. Kniep, when they travelled together in Italy in 1787[10]. Goethe was responsible for all Kniep's expenses, and his drawings were Goethe's by right. Goethe was, however, going to buy a certain number of his own choosing, allowing the artist to keep the rest. Kniep could use these as he liked - to form bases for exhibition paintings and commissions, or to sell. This type of patronage was quite usual at that period, and a similar contract was settled between the artist W.J. Müller and Benjamin Johnson, the father of his pupil Harry J. Johnson, when they travelled to Xanthus in 1843.

On THURSDAY, 29 JULY 1839, father Scharf called on Fellows, to discuss details; next day, young George took tea at Fellows's home. A few days later, he was introduced to Fellows's sister, Mrs Pearson, who lived close by. Thereafter, there was a regular coming and going between the Scharf family, Charles Fellows, and Mrs Pearson. Throughout the time of their travels, father Scharf and Fellows's sister would exchange news and letters, and show each other tracings sent home in the manner of today's holiday snaps. They would consult together regarding replies, letters to Europe taking only one or two weeks, but those to Malta and beyond needing three weeks to two months to arrive, which necessitated considerable forward planning.

PART TWO

I The journey out

On SATURDAY, 19 OCTOBER 1839, Fellows went round to 14 Francis Street to help young George with his packing. It took all day. As well as clothing and artists' materials, Scharf took art and travel guides, a small Shakespeare, and, very wisely, an extra pair of steel-rimmed spectacles.

At half past six in the morning of TUESDAY, 22 OCTOBER, George Scharf junior left his home to walk the short distance to Fellows's house. By 8 o'clock, the three travellers, Charles Fellows, George Scharf junior and Robert Hesketh, had boarded the steamer *Calpe* at London Wharf, Tower Bridge, for the passage to BOULOGNE and thence to PARIS.

The galleries of the Louvre were first on their agenda. The pictures were arranged alphabetically within their different Schools. "Their collection is amazingly fine, especially of their own school," young George declared, but thought that modern works should have been placed well away from the Old Masters. "For large important originals of the Italian and other schools, I think we at least equal them," he was proud to assert.

Fellows's itinerary then took them across FRANCE and SWITZERLAND, over the Cenis Pass and on south to GENOA. The sunshine of Italy encouraged the tourists to attempt to walk along the Ligurian coast as far as LIVORNO. After three days, Scharf, the youngest of the party, but unlike the others not used to long walks, could not go on, so Fellows hired a hackney carriage to complete the journey. They finally arrived in PISA at midday on MONDAY, 18 NOVEMBER 1839, where they rested for two days. They put up at the Albergo dell' Ussero where the host spoke English and was an agent for Messrs Barclay and Co., bankers.

The exotic architecture of the Duomo and Baptistry and the celebrated Leaning Tower enchanted Scharf. He relished, in particular, the rich and varied colours of the marble. While he drew their peculiarities, Fellows went off to draw the house, where his hero Byron[1] had lived in 1822.

FLORENCE was their next objective, where they were to spend five days. "As a city, Florence is a place of the greatest interest and elegance, abounding in antiquities and loaded with gems of art." Scharf could scarcely "conceive" of such a wealth of artistic treasures. On the other hand, "the shops have a mean appearance and want style," he opined. "They appear like recesses in the street wall with little glass cases attached to their sides, containing the sorts of goods they profess to vend."

They had been away a month and Scharf began to consider what progress his studies were making. "I cannot yet pretend to *see* the beauties of several masters," he confessed, "but I feel *convinced* of the existence of the highest and most consummate finish and perfection. The portraits of Raffaelle [the preferred spelling of the artist's name at that time], and there were several, are exquisite and their excessive fidelity to nature and perfect drawing much captivated me."

Fellows took the trouble to introduce his protégés to artists and sculptors in their own studios. Lorenzo Bartolini, a good-looking 62-year-old, specialized in portrait busts, including one of Byron. Tourists could sit for him quite cheaply and, for as little as £22, carriage paid, he would also reproduce in marble, casts sent to him from London. There they met Aubrey Bezzi[2], a very clever and intelligent sculptor and connoisseur of art. He had met Fellows at the BAAS meeting in 1838. He became their cicerone and taught Scharf much - how to look at pictures and how to appreciate fine workmanship.

They also met the philanthropist John Kenyon, whom they were to meet again in Rome. Within a few days of their return to London, in August 1840, he invited Fellows and Scharf to his home at 4 Harley Place, to discuss their discoveries in Lycia and to see their sketches. Kenyon took a lively interest in all Scharf's work and, from that time, he became a frequent visitor and a life-long friend.

At Kenyon's home in Florence, they met the aging actor Charles Kemble, whom Scharf described as "quite broken; his voice has left him." He thought this might have been due to his recent illness, coupled with the death of his wife and a financial loss through the failure of an American bank. He became almost totally deaf, the beginnings of that affliction perhaps already showing in his lack of voice[3].

Fellows now took his friends to VOLTERRA, specifically to see the Etruscan Museum there. The objects were viewed by torchlight, a method often used for sculpture, the strong artificial light intensifying the pose of a statue and accenting the depth of reliefs on friezes. Fellows pointed out the similarities between Etruscan and Lycian art. Both peoples cut their tombs into the rock itself - the Etruscans painting the 'death banquet' on the walls inside, whereas the Lycians carved the scene on the outside of the grave. Both painted their figures. Lions, panthers, dogs and horses are other features in common. The letters too are similar [pl. 46], indications of cultivated yet obscure civilizations in some way connected.

On SUNDAY, 1 DECEMBER 1839, they passed from the Grand Duchy of Tuscany into the Papal States and, in the early evening of TUESDAY, 3 DECEMBER, the travellers entered ROME in the traditional manner through the Porta del Popolo, on foot. A gratuity to the customs men obviated a baggage search. Scharf was overwhelmed. "I felt all the sensations as I approached, which I had pictured to myself; the atmosphere, effect of sunset, and distant sight of our object long before approaching it, powerfully assisted our feelings. I look forward with great pleasure to our two months' sojourn. We shall seek lodgings as soon as possible."

A comfortable apartment was found at 42, Piazza di Spagna in the heart of the English quarter. In 1814, Byron had lived in the Piazza, opposite the house where John Keats[4], the ill-fated poet, spent his last days. Fellows had many friends in Rome with whom he spent most of his time, leaving the young men to pursue their own activities. The weeks flew by in a whirl of sight-seeing and serious study. The Roman Forum, in particular, fascinated Scharf and he took to revisiting it again and again, especially on moonlight nights. By daylight, the long grass and the trees, not to mention the women's washing laid out to dry on the old stones, took much away from its magic.

The enormous size of St Peter's Scharf found hard to comprehend. "It must require a long time to understand its size. The Dome is quite lost unless you are at a great distance from it," he observed. "The first thing that would strike the spectator would be the very conspicuous appearance of the windows, like so many great holes...Everything is proportionately colossal and can only be seen by comparison with persons near it." He often returned there too, in an effort to come to terms with its vast proportions.

Next to St Peter's, of course, stand the Vatican buildings and Scharf was determined to get the necessary permission that would allow him to draw the sculptures and other treasures kept in the Vatican Museum. An English artist residing in Rome had warned him that there was more trouble and difficulty in getting into the Vatican Museum than into any other gallery in Europe, and it took persistent effort over a period of three weeks, going from one office to another, being told to return the following day, only to be sent to apply again through a different official, before Scharf finally received his permit.

MONDAY, 16 DECEMBER - "My birthday! How different my situation, thoughts, sentiments and prospects are to those of last year!" Scharf exclaimed, pondering the great changes in his life since that time. He spent the day in the Forum and the Museum of the Capitol, meeting his friends, as usual, for dinner.

One of the highlights of their stay was attending High Mass in St Peter's on Christmas morning. By wearing full evening dress, they were able to stand very near the Papal Throne, allowing them to get a really good look at Pope Gregory XVI. "His head is very fine, his nose large," reminding Scharf of Raphael's portrait of Pope Leo X. "His face looked bronze from being surrounded by nothing but gold and silver," he commented, but the sallow complexion might have been because, earlier that month, the 75-year-old Pope had been ill, and the progress through St Peter's, carried high on the Papal Chair, always made him feel giddy and sick.

Afterwards, the tourists enjoyed a real English Christmas dinner of roast turkey and plum pudding amongst their friends, accompanied by much seasonal hilarity. For young Scharf, however, thoughts of home would intrude and, next day, at the Puppet Theatre, he kept wondering whether his family were not likewise enjoying a theatrical production in London.

The puppets were large wooden figures with extremely ugly faces, but their costumes were rich and the scenery excellent. The dolls were moved with wonderful grace and ease - even if, at times, their feet did rise several inches off the ground. There were some capital combats between knights dressed in clanking armour, and the performance ended with a ghost and a castle, blown up in a most spectacular manner. All this had cost only 2½d. The Christmas dinner had cost 13 pence, and Scharf's total expenses for meals, wood, candles, laundry, etc., amounted to 108 *scudi*, or 4s.8½d. a day.

One day he was invited to go on a jaunt to OSTIA ANTICA, the former port of Rome at the mouth [Latin, *ostium*] of the River Tiber, fourteen miles south-west of the city. This was to be Scharf's first experience of a true archaeological site, the temples and arches in Rome itself, not exactly coming under that category. No excavations had as yet taken place and its ruins were so unimpressive as not to be included in the itinerary of the average tourist at all. The beautiful 'Townley Venus'[5] was found here in 1775; excavations began in 1909.

The site was deep in long grass and tangled brambles, trailing ivy covering fallen masonry and nondescript walls. Miscellaneous pieces of marble, capitals and broken shafts of columns, tiles and bits of mosaic pavements were simply scattered about everywhere. Only the brick walls of the Baths of Neptune could with any confidence be named. There were lots of souvenirs to be picked up, however, in the shape of coins, Roman glass, lamps and pieces of pottery, so the friends spent the afternoon collecting whatever they could find, making it into a game of 'Hunt-the-Slipper'.

Another day, the companions took an omnibus to the site of the Basilica of S. Paolo fuori le Mura, about a mile 'outside the walls', where Saint Paul is buried. The fourth century church had been almost totally destroyed by fire in the night of 15/16 July 1823. Rebuilding was started at once. "The building is at present in a very unfinished state," Scharf recorded. "The bases of the pillars with the marble shafts are all that is erected, with the exception of part of a transept, which has the ceiling and panelling gilded." That part was completed the following year; the finished church was consecrated in 1854.

The site was filled with "marble blocks, masons, workmen, convicts, painters' scaffolding, and the dust, noise of sawing and clanking of chains intolerable." Picking their way carefully, they inspected the shrine, mercifully little damaged, and then retreated.

The sojourn of two months quickly passed, every day filled with activity. Then, all too soon, it was time to prepare for the voyage to Malta and thence to Smyrna, the starting-place for their tour of Asia Minor. They had spent ten full weeks in Rome and had been away for almost four months. In Italy, it was still only early spring, but farther south in Turkey, the season was advancing rapidly and Fellows could not delay their departure any longer and risk illness through the hot, moist climate there.

MONDAY, 3 FEBRUARY 1840 - After an early breakfast, Fellows's party took their places in the coach for the ten-hour journey to CIVITA VECCHIA, a busy port, 50 miles north-west of Rome. Five lines of steamers, running between Marseilles and the Italian Tyrrhenian coast, called in here, as well as the French government packets for Malta and the Levant. The Englishmen were to have embarked on one of these early the next morning, but, as they neared the coast, they could see a raging sea from the storm, which had buffeted the coach all day long. Fellows was not sorry to learn that their steamer had been delayed in port at Livorno.

He took rooms at the Hôtel de la Poste, where the three settled down to wait out the time by making up their diaries and getting out their portfolios to retouch their sketches and add a little colouring.

THURSDAY, 6 FEBRUARY - "Was woke in the morning by a discharge of artillery from the fort, in honour of the day, being the anniversary of the Pope's ascending the Papal Chair[6], and after breakfast, we were entertained by a very good military band playing in the piazza, into which some of the windows of our hotel looked. This was followed by a petty sort of review and the soldiers went to the church. News was brought that the vessel (long looked for) was in sight." The travellers went on board at once. The steam-vessel *Tancredi* moved out of the harbour at 4.30 in the afternoon. The first stage of their adventure into the unknown Asia Minor had begun.

II Malta; Smyrna, preparations

The wind had lessened somewhat, but, nonetheless, the sea was still very rough, which did not augur well for the crossing. The next forty-eight hours had, in fact, to be endured in bed, "rolling, jolting, fasting, dozing and grumbling". Thankfully, they arrived none the worse in VALETTA Grand Harbour at 7 o'clock in the evening of SATURDAY, 8 FEBRUARY 1840, and went ashore at once for supper.

The party were conducted into the old town to Mrs Morrell's Hotel in Strada Forni [Old Bakery Street], a tiring walk since many of the streets are just flights of steps. "This is tedious, and in such a climate, very provoking," Scharf complained, thinking of his dinner, after all those hours without food. The only vehicles were the *calèches*, a carriage without fore-wheels, drawn by a horse, the driver running beside the animal.

The very distinctive dress of the women, naturally, attracted Scharf's attention. They "are all very dark," he noticed, " and wear black silk hoods, which gives them the appearance of nuns or mourners at a funeral." The *stamina* is a uniquely Maltese garment, being the back of an overskirt drawn over the head and stiffened in front. "Upon the arms, the mantle is often disposed in very beautifully arranged folds." This hood served as good protection from the sun - and the gaze of men.

Another relic of their Moslem past is the covered balcony. "The lattices, which first appear like so many boxes hung outside the walls, are in fact, delightful places, affording shade and, from their projection, commanding a general view of the street. Ladies may be frequently seen sitting in them, and in many houses, they are of considerable length."

SUNDAY, 9 FEBRUARY - This was to be a day of delays and irritations. It began badly with one of the Fellows's cases going missing, and over an hour went by in a frantic search for it. Only then could they disembark from the *Tancredi*. After an English breakfast at Mrs Morrell's, Fellows went to Admiralty House [now the National Museum] to call on Captain Graves to learn if there had been any further developments in the proposed expedition to Xanthus. It was agreed that, on arrival in Smyrna, Fellows should write to Lord Ponsonby, the British Ambassador at Constantinople, stressing the importance of obtaining as quickly as possible the Firman, or Permit, from the Sultan, and requesting that it be sent to Rhodes for the Captain to pick up. He and Fellows would then meet later in Lycia.

This matter of business apparently satisfactorily concluded, the three tourists hastened to take a look into the Co-Cathedral of St John, before going back to the quay to be rowed over to another vessel bound for the Levant, then moored in the Quarantine [Marsaxett] Harbour. The boatman, like many another 'taximan', took them round the longest way, making Fellows nervous that they might miss the sailing, and the whole party thoroughly vexed, when they learned that it would have been quicker and easier to have walked across the headland and taken the ferry.

The French packet *Rhamses* was steamed up in readiness for departure, when the machinery was found to be defective. A considerable delay ensued, while the boilers were cooled and then pumped out, in order to discover the fault and effect repairs. It was evening before the boilers were proved to be in too bad a condition for the ship to leave port that day. Since the ship was in quarantine, having come from the Levant, the unfortunate passengers had been forced to remain on board all day under a scorching sun.

The following morning, MONDAY, 10 FEBRUARY, the passengers were woken by the discordant clanging of church bells, announcing the Festival of St Paul, the Shipwrecked. The night before, the town had been lit up by flaring torches and hundreds of candles and tiny oil-lamps, placed on window-ledges and over doors, giving the town a quite magical aspect as it rose up, tier after tier, to the Cathedral.

Disappointing news then came that the *Rhamses* would not sail, and all must return to the *Tancredi*, which would now continue on to Smyrna. This was a great pity, as the food and accommodation of the *Rhamses* was greatly superior, a not unimportant factor in a voyage lasting for several days. By 10 o'clock, all baggage had been transferred, and the *Tancredi* steamed majestically out of harbour.

For the first day, the wind was in their favour, and the *Tancredi* made good way, but, with Fellows on board, this could not last and the wind soon veered and set full ahead. The vessel now lurched and groaned in tune with her passengers as she battled forward. Two days later, they put in at SYRA, [Siros], where Fellows and his party would spend a period in quarantine on their way home. Here, all the other passengers disembarked, leaving them alone on board.

The following day was utterly boring, passing through barren, featureless islands, and the increasing cold, with even a hint of sleet, sent the party from deck, to sit frustratedly in the stuffy saloon. At last, the vessel entered the GULF OF SMYRNA [İzmir Korfesı]. As she chugged by the ships of the French and Austrian navies riding at anchor, excitement took over again, and the Englishmen strained to see the shoreline with its rows of houses

19. Smyrna, Bay with shipping.

58

and wharfs. Their baggage ready, there was no hesitation on disembarkation, Fellows taking his companions straight to the Navy Hotel in Frank Street [Atatürk Caddesı], his previous lodging on the foreshore. This was the fashionable quarter where the Consuls and foreign (Frank) merchants had their houses.

Turkish houses had projecting upper storeys like the Tudor houses of England, the ground floors used for storage or as a shop. Only the living quarters above had windows, and many of these were shuttered or had latticed balconies [*kafes*, cage], similar to those of Valetta.

FRIDAY, 14 FEBRUARY - Their suite of rooms, consisting of a sitting-room and three bedrooms, all communicating with one another, was over a café. That evening, the owner, Salvo, provided the weary travellers with an English tea, set before a bright fire of English coal, a great comfort against the keen north wind, blowing down from the snow-covered mountains behind the town. The following morning, after a good English breakfast, the tourists sallied forth to examine this fascinating Oriental city. "All my ideas of an Eastern city were realized," Scharf exclaimed with satisfaction.

"The Bazaars are to me always a pleasing lounge, [which] offer ceaseless novelty to an European. By the assistance of my companion, Mr Scharf, I hope to possess many sketches, to call to mind these scenes," Fellows confided, and soon his young artist had drawn their hotel on the quayside, and would later add the

20. Smyrna, the Navy Hotel.

various khans and private dwellings, where they were to put up in the course of their Turkish peregrinations.

Smyrna was very cosmopolitan. Of a population of 150,000, only half were Turks, the rest comprised 40,000 Greeks, 15,000 Jews, 10,000 Armenians, and over 5,000 Franks (Europeans) - mainly English, Italians and Russians. The port, bazaars, and cafés were thronged with merchants discussing business, while the streets pulsated with the movement of the white-veiled women and their children, often accompanied by their black slaves, the urgent scurry of the donkeys and the stately plodding of the camel-trains bearing bales of merchandise - corn and cotton, wood and iron - on their way to and from the Caravan Bridge.

Needless to say, Scharf was much fascinated by the appearance of the Turkish women, shrouded from head to foot in a veil [*çarşaf*] of gauze, embroidered with gold thread, leaving only one kohl-ringed eye exposed. He noticed that they decorated their fingers with dots of henna [*kına*] and, had he known it, the soles of their feet were reddened too. Greek women did not cover their faces and so he could see that they wore their thick, black hair braided round their heads like a turban, a flower placed at one side.

Greek men were very sombrely clad in tight jackets and knee-length, full trousers. Only Turks were allowed to wear green, their holy colour. In spite of the recently imposed New Regulations from the Capital, most Turkish men still wore their traditional turbans, long, full shalwars and rich, fur-lined robes. Their jackets were highly decorated in gold and silver thread and their thick sashes were stuffed with chased-silver pistols and the curved *yatağan* (cutlass). These weapons, and the general bulkiness of their clothing, made them all look exceedingly fat.

European dress of the period with its tight lacing, even corsets for dandies, the men wearing 'drain-pipe' trousers and 'stove-pipe' top hats made them, in contrast, all look tall and slender. Fellows confessed that custom had prejudiced him in favour of the "compressed waist", but by the time he had returned from his travels in Turkey, he had a different opinion. "How soon is a new habit acquired," he declared. He now saw European clothes as "deformities compared with the natural, easy, and graceful costume" of the Turkish people.

The British Consul, Mr Brant, welcomed Fellows back to Smyrna and made him and his assistants honorary members of the Casino Club, open each evening at eight. There, they could read newspapers and periodicals, play cards or billiards, and could attend the weekly balls. The first they went to was only a modest affair, disappointing Scharf, who, "expecting to see the beauty of Smyrna assembled...found but few ladies, and scarcely any Greek girls in their proper costume." The second ball, however, was a much grander occasion.

This ball was given by Prince Friedrich, Archduke of Austria, a cousin of the Emperor. He was a Commander in the Austrian Mediterranean fleet[1], then at anchor in the Bay. The Casino was now gaily decorated with sails and flags covering the terraces to form extra rooms, and adding a colourfully nautical flavour. This time, "the assemblage of ladies was very great and the costumes superb. Great profusion of diamonds, gold embroidered fezzes and velvet bodices with Mameluk [puffed] sleeves were seen everywhere." The Governor of Smyrna, several Consuls, members of the Turkish Court, naval and military officers and all the *bon ton* of the European community were present. Fellows and Scharf came away at one, but even when their friend Hesketh left at five in the morning, the dancing and carousing were still in progress.

The travellers began their archaeological studies by Fellows taking the young men to see the recently excavated ruins on Castle Hill. Since his last visit, nothing more had come to light and possibly some stones had already been purloined. A more entertaining walk was to the Roman CARAVAN BRIDGE over the river MELES [Melez], the gate to the city, where a government toll was levied on merchandise. There were always groups of Turks to be seen taking their ease, smoking their long chibouks, or sitting in the cafinet [*kahvehane*], drinking coffee and smoking the hookah [*nargile*]. Fellows painted the general scene with a camel-train passing over the Bridge; Scharf drew the many types of headgear. Not so long ago, he would have been pelted with stones and driven away, as the depiction of the human face was against Mohammedan Law. But times were changing fast and many Turks invited the Englishmen to produce their likenesses.

21. Smyrna, types of headgear:
a) Dragoman; b) Armenian;
c) Courier (Tatar) wearing a
fur kalpak; d) and e) Jewish
money-changers (sarraf); f) Jew;
g) Seller of simit (bread ring);
h) Mevlevi, Dervish wearing a
külâh; i) Government official
wearing a fez; j) Scribe wearing
a muslin turban; k) Tailor.

22. Smyrna, Caravan Bridge.

Before they could set off on their journey, Fellows had several purchases to make, not least of which was to lay in a supply of arrowroot and good English tea. He also bought a stock of English patent wax candles with a twisted wick, to use for their own comfort as they gave a smokeless flame. These were likewise the best for illuminating the interiors of tombs and for casting a raking light on inscriptions, to make them easier to decipher. All three men needed English saddles. Fellows converted sufficient bills-of-exchange into low-value coin for local purchases, lodgings and tips, and applied to Mr Brant for their Firman [ferman]. This document, freely translated, stated: "Dear Sir, This gentleman, accompanied by three others, has arrived from the island of England, in order to investigate ancient civilizations."[2]

Fellows also sought out Demetrius Scufi to act as dragoman as before. He, however, was away in pursuit of his own business, so, at Mr Brant's suggestion, Fellows engaged Pagniotti Mania, another Greek, who was to prove himself just as capable as Scufi. Mania would serve Lieutenant Spratt in 1842, and Fellows again in 1843, at the time of the Second Xanthian Expedition. Mania was less sophisticated than Scufi, his manners were not so refined and he had a quick temper. He had, however, a fund of anecdotes and folklore, which were both entertaining and instructive.

THURSDAY, 27 FEBRUARY should have seen the commencement of their great journey. The Englishmen had risen at 6 o'clock, in the expectation of making an early start. By four in the afternoon, however, the horses had still not appeared. Mr Brant sent to enquire the reason. It seemed that all post-horses would be engaged for days to come, on account of the movement of the district Governors, brought about by new annual elections and, whereas before the town had abounded with them, few horses were now kept for the service of the post, this due, in part, to the recent establishment of steam-vessel communications with the Capital.

Fellows had expected to be able to hire horses at the post-station [menzil], as he had done last time, but the New Regulations were now in force and the postal service had been disbanded. This put Fellows in considerable difficulty, but he was, at least, able to hire a string privately for the next few days. The cavalcade was made up of riding horses for the three travellers and their dragoman, with two baggage-horses for their belongings. There was a riding and a baggage-horse for the owner, who would be going with them. Fellows paid him about 8 shillings, calculated at the exchange rate of 95 piastres to the pound sterling.

Eager to get started, instead of waiting for the baggage to be loaded, which would take a considerable time, the party set off to walk the comparatively short distance of 4-5 miles to the next place. The bad luck of the morning, however, still dogged them and, by missing a turn shortly after crossing the Caravan Bridge, they took much longer than expected to get to BOOJAH [Buca], a pretty village, where the European merchants and the British Consul had their villas.

It was 7 o'clock and quite dark by the time they arrived, very tired, with sore feet, but thankful to be able to enjoy 'home' comforts in a second Navy Hotel, run by Salvo's father. The hotel was newly opened and had a beautiful colonnaded terrace looking on to a formal garden in the Italian style, with gravel paths, ornamental urns, tall cypresses and large, shady trees.

When he presented his bill the following morning, like his son, the proprietor had made exorbitant charges, demanding nearly £1 for the tea of ham, eggs, fruit and cheese, their rooms and an English breakfast. After much haggling, high words and extravagant gestures, he finally accepted 10 shillings with smiles and bows.

The horses with the baggage arrived with Mania at 8 o'clock. Mounting their scraggy nags, the party rode off, their tour of exploration in Asia Minor now well and truly begun.

III Lydia

The first stage of their journey was to take a south-easterly route through the province of LYDIA.

The routine followed was to rise at about 6.30, travel for six to eight hours and, at the end of the day, put up in a khan. After a meal cooked by Mania, they would discuss the day's events, write up their diaries, retouch their sketches, read a little, until settling down for the night at about ten. A good day's journey would cover about 30 miles, an hour's ride calculated at 3-5 miles, depending on the pace of the baggage-animals.

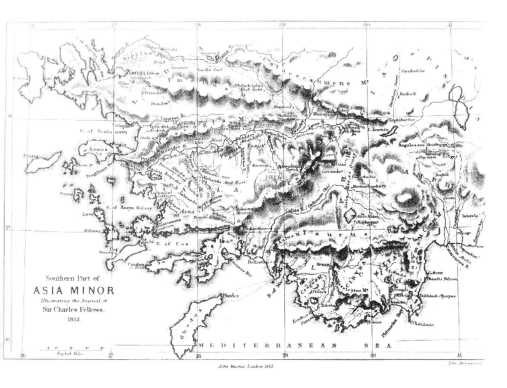

23. Map of southern Asia Minor, 1840.

Turks rode at a sort of amble, called 'chack-bin' [*çikbiniş,* parade pace], with no rising in the saddle. A Turkish saddle was high at front and back, with short leathers and a shovel foot-iron, used as a goad. It was perched on top of a mound of rugs and cloaks. Most Europeans found the motion difficult and the saddles uncomfortable, preferring to use an English saddle with long leathers and the trotting action. Travellers would often ride in advance of their cavalcade, but it was inadvisable to lose all sight of it, in case an animal stumbled and lost its load, bringing the whole train to a halt for an hour or two.

FRIDAY, 28 FEBRUARY 1840 - The first day was a particularly long one, getting as far as BIENDEER [Bayındır], some 50 miles from Smyrna, at eight in the evening. The party repaired at once to the khan and were taken to a square, empty room with a low bench [*peyke*] set round the sides, to sit and sleep on. Each

24. Turks sitting around a brazier in a khan.

traveller was expected to bring his own carpets and cushions and to prepare his own food. The advantage of a bare room was that a good sweeping kept it quite clean and free from the bugs, which infested the inns of Europe. On departure, there was no fear of leaving anything behind. A tip to the khanjee [*hancı*] was all that it cost.

Mania cooked fresh boiled bullock's tongue and eggs, with well-seasoned rice for their meal, finishing with dried grapes. These were the large Smyrna grapes, sold at 2 pounds for a penny and exported to England as raisins. Large bunches were twined and plaited together into a rope, which were steeped several times in boiling water to sterilize them, and then left in a cool place to dry out. Breakfast was simply toast and local honey, with tea from their own stores.

25. *Hoozumlee, departure from the khan.*

The local Governor, or Aga [ağa], sent to express his regret that the party had not gone to his house, where, as strangers, they would have been treated as honoured guests. Fellows, however, preferred his independence and chose to avoid such obligations when he could.

Next day, they rode to THERA [Tire], only 11 miles along the CAYSTER, or SMALL MAEANDER [Küçük Menderes], the valley richly cultivated with corn, cotton, olives, grape-vines, and mulberries. The large town, with a population of nearly 75,000, occupied the site of ancient CAYSTRUS, of which no trace remained. Thera boasted several mosques, their minarets, shining out white against the hillside, could be seen from some distance away. The streets and bazaars were crowded with Turks, who looked at the Englishmen with curiosity and some small boys shouted insults and threw stones. There were only twenty-five

26. *Thera, mosques and minarets.*

Greeks in the town and the people were quite unused to seeing Europeans wearing Frank clothes.

But a few years earlier, no European would have dared to travel in Turkey without donning the disguise of Turkish costume, usually with the pretence of being a medical man. Was it foolhardy to have followed the example of recent travellers and kept their European attire so far from the cosmopolitan north? Notwithstanding this unpleasant experience, Fellows and his friends boldly continued to wear their own clothes. In the event, they only once more met such animosity. Curiously enough, right up to the 1870s, it remained advisable to dress in Turkish robes in all Turkish controlled territories in Europe, and in Egypt, though not in Turkey itself.

Here, Fellows had to hire fresh horses and another guide. This new string was composed of ten animals - mounts for Fellows and his party; for two Zoorigees [*sürücü*; drover, groom]; one for a Kezann [*kazan*][1], an Officer of Police, sent by the Governor; and three baggage-horses. Though richly armed and ostensibly for their protection, the Kezann was entirely unnecessary. In any case, he was often very drunk and the cause of frequent embarrassment and annoyance. When a horse fell on the rough road, scattering its baggage, he would lean back against the rocks, smoke his pipe and drink arrack [*rakı*, raw spirits], shouting abuse and instructions to the Zoorigees, as they struggled to get the animal back on its feet and the bags reloaded.

As the cavalcade neared the next town, IDIN [Aydın, formerly GÜZELHİSAR, Beautiful Castle], the road improved and levelled out The Kezann now took the opportunity to make an impression on the inhabitants by screaming "*deh! deh!*" at the top of his voice, urging the horses into a brisk trot and clattering with much show into the great khan.

The town, was - and still is - a place of considerable importance, ranking second to Smyrna. There were nearly 8,000 Turkish houses and at least 300 Greek ones. Its bazaars were superior to those of Smyrna and the khan had three floors, the rooms approached by an arcaded gallery at both levels. The building was of wood, under a tiled roof. There was also an octagonal kiosk [*kösk*] in the central courtyard.

*27. Idin, the great gate
of the khan.*

*28. Idin, kiosk in the
central courtyard of
the khan.*

70

Idin had always been a military town and there were numerous groups of soldiers of the Nizam Djedid [*Nizam Cedit*], the New Army, lolling about, all looking miserably uncomfortable in their New Regulation uniforms. They wore a short blue jacket with cross-belts, shapeless white trousers, slipshod boots and the scarlet fez, pushed well back from their foreheads. Many had, in fact, concealed their traditional clothes under their uniforms, ashamed at having to wear 'Infidel' attire.

The Pasha, on the contrary, was very proud of his new *setre* (frock-coat) [pl. 117], enhanced by a pair of white kid gloves. He smoked cigars and drank wine, but still enjoyed the more traditional Oriental entertainment provided by dancing-boys, painted and dressed like girls. When the Pasha went to the Mosque - by coach - he was surrounded by a retinue of thirty to forty guards.

Tahir Pasha a youthful-looking man of 60, was described as a tyrant, yet enlightened. He was universally hated for the way he oppressed the large region under his rule as chief Pasha of southern Asia Minor. A few months later, there was to be an uprising and he was taken prisoner to the Sultan, relieved of his rank and forced to retire into private life. In less moderate times, he would have paid with his head.

Before the travellers could continue their journey, Fellows had to get a *tezkere*, a local passport, from him. Tahir Pasha could speak Italian and badly wanted the prestige of talking to Fellows. He sent twice to invite him to his residence, but Fellows declined, suspecting his motives, not wishing to waste time in idle conversation and ceremony. He made the excuse that his travelling wardrobe did not include suitable clothes for such an august presence, but proffered polite acknowledgements for the honour. The Pasha, feeling aggrieved, purposely delayed issuing the Pass and the Englishmen had to leave the town on foot.

The modern town had been built out of the 'quarry' of ancient TRALLES, the modern Üç Göz (Three Eyes), so called from the great arches of the Roman gymnasium [3rd century AD], which, with some pieces of broken columns and cornices, were all that was left of the ancient city. It had long suffered from despoliation by the garrison town and many pieces of Classical sculpture were incorporated into domestic buildings, none very interesting to the Englishmen, however, as all were of a 'base age'.

71

Built in on either side of the Pasha's doorway were some "gladiatorial" figures, of which he was inordinately proud, but these probably dated from the Crusader period. He had more 'worthless' statues in his garden, which a tip of nearly £1, greedily taken by his servants, gave the English travellers the 'privilege' of viewing. The site was excavated in 1902-03.

WEDNESDAY, 4 MARCH 1840 - The party now turned in an easterly direction, to follow the northern banks of the LARGE MAEANDER [Büyük Menderes], which winds east/west across the country, between the provinces of Lydia, on the north bank, and Caria on the southern side. Thirty miles from Idin, the travellers came to SULTANHISAR, Sultan's Castle, called by the Greeks, HELIOPOLIS, Sun City, situated near the site of NYSA, an ancient Greek city of the 3rd century BC, where Strabo, the Greek geographer had studied.

He describes Nysa as a double city, divided by a gorge. The ancient bridge over the Maeander, joining the two parts, had only recently collapsed. The torrential waters passed through an underground passage, much of which had also fallen in. An amphitheatre, built over the gorge, had been used in the ordinary way in dry weather, and for water spectacles, when flooded. It was, appropriately, pouring with rain, when Fellows and his friends were there.

Scharf could count only 8 rows of seats, but the theatre has now been excavated, exposing 49 rows. As was usual with Greek theatres in Asia Minor, it was more than a semicircle and commanded wonderful views over the valley, the river meandering [Greek, *maiandros*] in an incredible number of turns "like a bright, white thread, for at least 50 miles."

Near the theatre, they looked for a mysterious cave connected with the legend of Charon, who ferried the Dead to the Infernal Regions and had to be paid in gold. The river here is, indeed, yellow - but with sulphur, not gold. Enormous fish, a sort of conger eel, were caught in its waters. They were smooth-skinned, nearly 12 inches in thickness and up to 6 feet long. They could weigh anything from 100 to 400 pounds and were considered to be very good eating.

72

In spite of the bad weather, the three antiquarians persevered in their search of the ruins, "crossing several walls and breaking thro' underwood." They were able to distinguish the huge, square market-place, gymnasium and library buildings [2nd century AD]. It was all tremendously exciting for Scharf, who had never seen anything remotely like this site before, with buildings, well preserved and easily identifiable. And to be able to enter the very city where Strabo had lived! Scharf had read his Classical texts, and with Fellows's scholarship to fill in the details, the dead past had suddenly come to life, bringing reality to the existence of the ancient Greeks.

The site was excavated in 1907 and again in recent years, uncovering much more of the city, although, sadly, many columns were appropriated for stone when the railway was built.

Another 12 miles or so farther on was NASLEE [Nazilli]. Here, they obtained a room in the small, but comfortable khan and, thankfully, changed out of their wet clothes. It was pleasant to warm themselves in front of a cheerful fire, with a cup of English tea, whilst Mania prepared a hot meal. The Kezann also relaxed in his fashion - by getting loudly drunk. Fellows, a strict Unitarian, was very shocked by his behaviour, noting that he drank three bottles of spirits a day, in spite of the Prophet's Laws against alcohol. When he sobered up, the Kezann would become tearful and pathetic. He was not the only Turk, however, to get stupidly intoxicated, "industriously learning of the Europeans their vices," Fellows was sorry to have to acknowledge.

As usual, to Scharf's initial amazement, as the evening progressed, the room became crowded with onlookers. The visiting Turks would watch their every action, fascinated to see the Englishmen eating with a knife and fork instead of with their fingers, as was customary amongst themselves. They were surprised to discover their clothes contained pockets - Turks used their sashes [kuşak] and turban cloths [sarık] to hold small items - and everywhere he went, Scharf's spectacles always caused astonishment, then merriment, leading to the whole assemblage wanting to try them on.

In Turkey, it was considered impolite to leave a guest on his own, so the Englishmen found that all the men of the village would come in with their pipes and, though "saying everything that is kind and hospitable," made it impossible for the travellers to write up their journals, or do anything requiring attention. It was also embarrassing for them to change their clothes in front of a concourse of curious eyes. Mania could, of course, have been asked to put the villagers out, but that would have been very uncivil on the part of the strangers. Fellows, who was always reluctant to join a large social gathering, was especially irritated by this well-meaning Turkish tradition.

The travellers had intended to leave the following day, but they were again hindered by the general shortage of horses, some soldiers having commandeered theirs. There was nothing to do but wander round the bazaar, where they noticed a Dervish going from shop to shop, asking for charity. He carried a basket, shaped like a Roman galley, into which people placed scraps of food. He wore a white felt cap, rounder and less high than the conical *külah* of the Mevlevi sect. Fellows had witnessed their characteristic whirling dance, when he was in Constantinople. This *derviş* had a light blue robe and carried a clean lamb-skin over his shoulder. His hair fell in ringlets round his swarthy face.

In the town, storks were nesting on every chimney-top, rattling their bills together in the courtship ritual. In the country, the little screech-owl was much in evidence. They look exactly like the ones depicted on ancient coins of Athens. According to mythology, this bird, called 'Minerva's owl' [*Athenae indigena*], denotes wisdom and always attended the Roman Goddess Minerva [the Greek, Pallas Athene]. She is often portrayed with the owl, perched on her helmet.

Fellows also found a chamaeleon basking on a sandy path. He picked it up to show it to his companions, who had never seen such an animal before. The chamaeleon quickly changed colour from a yellowish to a greyish shade, getting even darker when placed on a red handkerchief. It soon resumed its original colour, however, on being returned to its place in the sun.

This surprise natural history lesson was not yet over. On the way back, they noticed some little frogs sitting on the branches of a bush. Scharf was greatly intrigued by this unlikely habitat and

74

poked them with a stick, whereupon the frogs jumped higher up, and clung to the tips of the twigs, with all their legs together, "as the bears sit upon their pole in the Zoological Gardens in London." He made a rapid sketch of the creatures. As it happened, in 1835[2], his father had painted a charming picture of bears on their pole, in just such an attitude, as one of his series of scenes of the Zoological Gardens. Tree frogs [*Hyla arborea*] are bright green and normally live in small trees, as their name implies. They have suction pads on almost unwebbed feet to enable them to cling to branches.

Fellows was in his element in this sylvan glade. He picked more wild flowers and savoured the warmth of the spring sunshine. For him, even the gnats, by their dancing, were expressing their happiness, and the birds with their universal song were proclaiming aloud peace and harmony to the world.

FRIDAY, 6 MARCH 1840 - Fellows was still unable to obtain post-horses, the Post-Masters either professing that they had none, or demanding double the official rate. On applying to the Governor, a string was at last assembled, but the party had been delayed until nearly midday.

Continuing east, they crossed the Maeander into the province of CARIA. The province is bounded in the south-east by the Dollomon river and the Taurus Mountains; in the west, it extends to the coast, with its many inlets and islands.

Fellows was making for ANTIOCHEIA, the home of Hegesander, the sculptor of the Laocoön[1] group and, according to some authorities, of the Venus di Milo[2]. She had been rescued from a lime-kiln on the island of Melos, only twenty years earlier. Having gone out of their way to examine these ruins, discovered in 1826, they proved to be nothing more than rough stones of a late date, with scarcely a piece of worked marble to be seen.

Fellows now conducted his party south, along the pretty valley of the MORSYNUS [Dandalus Çayi]. The weather was agreeably fine, the crocuses, scillas and hyacinths just coming into bloom. The way was enlivened by many flocks of Karaman[3] sheep, being taken to the hills for the summer. They have black heads and large flat tails of rich marrow-fat, which could weigh as much as 6-8 pounds. The Zoorigees assured them that these sheep produced lambs twice a year, but Mania boasted that those of Corfu lambed three times.

The little village of YEHNEJAH [Yenice], their *menzil*, stopping-place, for the night, was far too small to have a khan, so the party put up in the Aga's *konak*, official residence, though he himself was absent. As Governor, he would have been responsible for the comfort of strangers, and it was customary for them to stay in his house. A flight of steps led to an open loggia, the tiled roof supported on tree-trunks. It was a fine example of Turkish domestic architecture, the *divanhane*, or main hall, on the upper floor

29. Yehnejah, the Aga's konak.

having large windows nearly to the ground, with a rug [*kilim*] on the floor and expensively embroidered cushions [*minder*] all round the walls to recline against. The women's quarters were behind the *perde*, a rich hanging.

Mania lit a fire in the fireplace, which had a typical repoussé, copper cowl [pl. 65]. He prepared rice with sugar, while chickens were cooked for the party in another person's house. These arrived, along with all the men of the village, who proceeded to sit round in their usual way to watch the strangers at their meal. They all finally left, except for the Aga's secretary, who courteously remained with the party all night.

The next day brought a different type of scenery, the road winding through forests of cultivated fir [*Abies cilicica*] and pine trees. They were grown partly for their timber, but also for other products. The Aleppo pine [*Pinus halepensis*] gives the wood and pitch used in ship-building; the Umbrella, or Stone pine [*P. pinea*] produces the large seeds used in cookery; the Maritime pine [*P. pinaster*] gives both timber and turpentine. An important use of the resinous wood was as slips, cut and lit to make torches, and to illuminate Turkish houses. They give a bright, but very smoky flame.

30. Turkish boy holding a turpentine torch.

Cones are used to flavour wine, like the Greek Retsina (resin). Fellows remarked that in ancient times the staff [*Thyrsus*] of Bacchus, the God of the Vine, was a pole wreathed in vine-leaves with a fir-cone at the end.

The view before them to MOUNT CADMUS[4] [Baba Dağ, Venerable or Father Mountain] was superb, but the east wind blowing down over the snows was bitterly cold. As they drew near the village of KARASOO [Karacasu, Black (clear) Water], the soil of the ravines became very red in colour and the many streams of good (black) water were channelled through clay pipes from the pottery trade. Local conditions also favoured a dyeing and bleaching industry, profiting from the limey soil and the sulphurous springs. Fellows picked up some fine specimens of pure lime, sulphur and mica to add to his collection of minerals.

78

SUNDAY, 8 MARCH - Keeping the Morsynus to their left (east), the group now entered a wide plain, 1,000 feet above sea-level and the Englishmen began to make out the ruins of APHRODISIAS, named for Aphrodite, the Greek Goddess of Love [Roman, Venus]. In the distance, the white marble columns of her Temple were silhouetted against a darkening sky. It was late in the afternoon, however, before they actually got there, but, as they rode slowly along, they were able to see more and more of the ruins, which cover an area of about 1,300 acres.

"After passing the ancient Gate, the prospect of a rich harvest of remains burst upon us. The whole ground was covered with sculptured fragments and the modern houses of the village are built in among the old walls, most of which are still standing." That was more than could be said of the ruinous village of YEERAH [Geyre], most of the houses being deserted, the sole inhabitants seeming to be the little Minerva owls, which peered out from their holes with interest as the cavalcade passed. A few storks stood "like monuments to melancholy" on the tops of ancient pillars, nothing else stirring in this sad desolation.

When Yeerah, a corruption of Caria, the name given to the place in Byzantine times, was destroyed by an earthquake in 1956, the new village was built away from the ancient archaeological site.

The Aga had apparently just left, so Fellows and his party again took possession of an empty house. Its steps were of the finest marble, pillaged from the site; the rooms were large and handsomely decorated, with texts from the *Kuran*. The stabling was good and dry. Here, the travellers made themselves comfortable for a stay of four days, to make a thorough study of these extensive ruins.

Aphrodisias is about 150 miles from Smyrna by modern road. Its location in low ground is unusual for a Greek city, most of which were built high up a mountainside, or crowning the top of a hill. Indeed, the buildings all date from the Roman period, the earliest remains being of the late 2nd century BC. The city has long been known to antiquarians and travellers and has been excavated several times. Work has been going on continuously since 1961, with reconstructions, making Aphrodisias today one of the major tourist sights of Turkey.

31. Aphrodisias, the Temple.

The first building to claim the attention then, as now, is the Temple of Aphrodite [c. 100 BC], extended in the 5th century AD to form a Christian church. There were 15 columns still standing, others were lying where they fell, the result of earthquakes. They are fluted and of the Ionic Order. Some have tablets with dedicatory inscriptions, indicating the importance temple columns held for the ancients. Fellows and Scharf attempted to copy some of them, one calling out the letters to the other. They also took impressions of the letters by rubbing a mixture of soap and black soot on to paper placed over the words. 'Squeezes' were made by beating wet pulpy paper into the incised letters and letting them dry naturally to produce a kind of cast.

In swampy ground to the south of the Temple, the Roman market-place can be seen, and, a little beyond, are the huge blocks of stone, which had once been the enormous Baths of Hadrian [2nd century AD]. The stadium [1st century AD] is to the north. Although completely overgrown by bushes, it was still in an excellent state of preservation, one of the best in the world, nearly every seat being perfect. The stadium is about 860 feet long and could accommodate 30,000 spectators.

The whole area was buried deep in soil and brushwood, obscuring the theatre, which appeared as a small hill. Diligent use of spades and bare hands brought to light many fine sculptures, including one frieze, which much intrigued them, showing fighting between animals and men, some of whom were winged, others having double fish-tails, instead of legs. The blocks were 1 foot, 3 inches high and from 2 feet, 6 inches to 4 feet in length.

The city wall and fortifications, about 2 miles in circumference, were built by the Romans. They are constructed out of miscellaneous stones, carelessly mingled and turned all ways, reminding Scharf of a bill-stickers' wall in London. This very wall

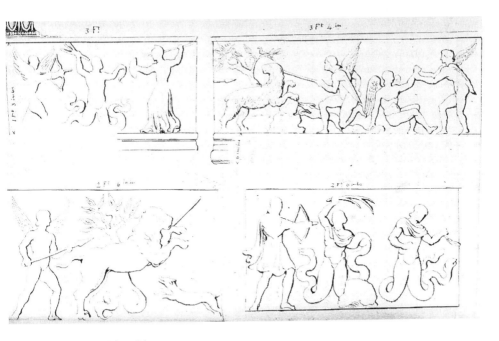

32. *Aphrodisias, friezes.*

has recently been excavated and is now known as the 'Archive Wall'. The inscriptions date from the 3rd to the 1st century BC.

WEDNESDAY, 10 MARCH - After spending most of the day at the ruins, each in his own way, the companions met at the North Gate, near the stadium to return to Karasoo. Before leaving, Fellows took a box-sextant and altitude thermometer to fix the position of the site.

Back at the khan, they were pleased to spend a quiet evening in conversation with a Greek priest, who called on them and stayed to enjoy a cup of tea in their company.

33. Karasoo, Greek priest in the courtyard of the khan.

The following day, there was the recurring problem of obtaining horses. What had begun as a simple annoyance was fast becoming a real anxiety. At the outset of their journey nobody had appreciated that the difficulty they had experienced at Smyrna was the forerunner of a completely new order of things, which would adversely affect their progress from now on. A whole new system, including tax reforms and conscription, had come into force that very weak, leaving everyone confused and worried. Some peasants, in fear of having their young men taken for soldiers and their land and goods confiscated, had even abandoned their homes and fled to the mountains. Police-soldiers were out scouring the country to impose a passport on anybody leaving his village.

As far as the postal service was concerned, the Post-Master no longer had a salary, but could, instead, charge individuals with a *tezkere* 2½ piastres [6d.] an hour for the use of a horse. He was obliged to carry government dispatches free of charge. Where, as here in Karasoo, there was almost no call for horses, the Post-Master was likely very soon to be out of pocket.

The travellers could now understand the reason for the absent Agas. Under the New Regulations, instead of electing an Aga locally, an official was sent from the Capital. Many had yet to arrive, leaving the villages temporarily without a Governor.

Sultan Abdul Mecit, a young man only 17 years of age, had been in power for just six months, since the death of his father, Mahmud II, whom Fellows had seen riding through Constantinople. He was continuing the reforms begun by Mahmud to try to bring his country more into line with the Western World.

The dilemma of how to continue their travels was finally resolved when the erstwhile Post-Master, the Menzil-khanner [*menzilhanci*], offered himself and his string of ten or eleven horses, plus two Zoorigees, for their use for a month. The bargain was struck, Fellows only too glad to accede to his demand of TL14 [14 *Türk lirasi*, lire], about 10s. a day, which he considered quite reasonable. The party were all prepared to set off, when the Aga sent to request Fellows to allow the Menzil-khanner to complete his last postal duties, by carrying letters to Naslee, thereby delaying the party by yet another day.

FRIDAY, 13 MARCH - The newly-formed cavalcade moved off in great state, headed by the Menzil-khanner attired in a splendid costume of "crimson satin, black, blue, white and a profusion of braiding and gold embroidery. He also sported a very rich pipe and tobacco-bag, which is an indispensable part of their personal travelling establishment with every Turk." In his broad sash, he carried two silver-embossed pistols and a *yatagan*. His horse was also richly caparisoned and trained to the "prancing gait of such an officer in Turkish processions", putting on a show for the benefit of the farewell deputation of villagers.

Behind him came a Zoorigee, leading a spare horse, then three baggage-horses for Fellows's party and another for the Menzil-khanner. After them rode Fellows, Scharf and Hesketh, with Mania and the other Zoorigee bringing up the rear.

Heading back north, passing the pottery-kilns of KARASOO, they re-entered the pine forest, where many trees were smouldering. To bring down the turpentine, trees were cut at the bottom and fired; others were left burning to fell them, both highly dangerous procedures, the cause of many a forest fire.

By nightfall, the cavalcade had got as far as the tiny village of ARRACHIFLEE [Aga's Farm, now Çiftlik-köyü, Farm Village], near the relics of ANTIOCHEIA, which they had examined a week earlier. Hesketh returned to look again at the site, while the others stayed in the peasant's hut, which had only one room besides a kitchen and stables. This detour of nearly 200 miles to see the extensive ruins of Aphrodisias, illustrates Fellows's determination to get the absolute maximum from his enterprise and to travel no matter how far to inspect anything of possible archaeological interest. His resolve of purpose was only matched by his phenomenal energy and scholarly zeal.

The next two days were spent riding back along the MAEANDER, but on the south bank, to its confluence with the river CHEENA [Çine Çayı], the ancient MARSYAS. Across the plain, they could see Sultanhisar and Idin. Fellows was now steering his party to an area where several cities of antiquity were situated fairly close together. The region had been explored in the eighteenth century, but the true identity of certain places still remained in doubt. Fellows determined, if possible to establish their exact names and positions.

V Caria, the south-west

On SUNDAY, 15 MARCH 1840, they arrived at ZHUMARLEE-COOE [Çumalı], a village [köy], and were accommodated in the Aga's *konak*. All around lay fragments of broken columns and cornices, obviously taken from ruins somewhere in the neighbourhood. In the courtyard, they were excited to find a little pedestal with an inscription to Apollo 'the Liberator, the August', epithets seldom applied to that God. They were informed that the 23

34. Zhumarlee-Cooe, the Aga's konak.

ancient columns used to support the stable roof had been carried off from an 'old castle', 8 miles away. Indeed, all the houses were made of stone appropriated from that inviting site.

Typically, the houses were of a single square room, under a flat roof, on which earth was piled to form a seal. A piece of a column served as a roller to keep it compacted. Long grass grew at the corners. Seeing this, gave Fellows the idea that this could be

85

the origin of the Greek *acroteria*, leaf-like ornaments placed at the corners and apex of a pediment. On summer evenings, the menfolk would congregate on their roof-tops to smoke.

The whole village was made noisy by courting storks, established on every roof. They are highly regarded by Turks, who construct a special platform for them to nest on. Storks are known as the 'Turkish' bird - allegedly never nesting on a Greek house. They are called *leylek*, or 'Hadgi laklak'. *Hacı* is a pilgrim to Mecca, in this case, a migrant; '*laklak*' (clack, clack) is the noise they make with their bills; also chatter, idle talk.

The following morning, the explorers went in search of the 'old castle'. They crossed to the west bank of the Cheena and, by late afternoon, found themselves at the miserable hamlet of ARAB-HISSAR [Araphisar, Arab Castle], just a few huts built into the remains of clearly a very ancient city. All round were enormous sarcophagi made of coarse granite, much weathered by time. Inscriptions had probably been engraved on metal plates, long since vanished, set into the sides of the tombs. Coins determined the name of this place. It was ALABANDA.

This important discovery confirmed Colonel Leake's conjecture and proved that Pococke and Chandler had both been mistaken in assigning these relics to 'Alinda'. The terminations '-anda' and '-inda' denote great antiquity; the absence of any marble dated the city to the pre-Greek era. The Carian name, according to the grammarian Stephanus of Byzantium, means 'horse victory' - Alabanda.

The enormous theatre on the hillside is more than a semicircle; its façade measures over 270 feet. It is constructed of massive stones, rendered the more conspicuous by virtue of their bulging 'cushion' form. Between each double row, there is one of narrow stones, giving a horizontally fluted appearance. "The proscenium was very imperfect, but we could trace the Doric columns of its doorways, half-buried in the soil." The Doric Order and its giant size both spoke of great age.

They found the basement of a Doric Temple, dedicated to Apollo Isotimus, a God peculiar to Alabanda, 'Isotimus' - equal in honour - gave him the same status as Zeus Chrysaoreus (of the Golden Sword) at Stratoniceia, a site they would soon see. A large, oblong council-house [84 ft x 117 ft] has the unusual features of windows. The walls were 30 feet high, yet, by the end of the century, they had become completely buried. The companions could trace the basements of some other buildings too and the city walls, which extend well into the plain.

Although the city had come under Roman rule, they could find no examples of Roman architecture. The site, which dates back to the 5th century BC, has not yet been thoroughly excavated, but in 1905, some Roman remains were uncovered.

The party now proceeded westwards, up a fertile valley, where farmers were busy ploughing, using pairs of oxen with short, thick horns to pull the simple wooden shares of former ages.

35. Ploughing with oxen.

Turkish cattle are all short-horns, grey or black, and no bigger than a large donkey. The countryside was covered in great carpets of lavender, perfuming the air and providing food for the bees from the neighbourhood apiaries. The hives were hollowed-out trunks of fir trees, laid one on top of the other, much like beer barrels in a cellar.

In some places, women were treading olives, their heads and faces closely covered with the white veil, but their legs were bare to the knee! This extraordinary reversal of values was quite startling to the Englishmen, perfectly accustomed to seeing a woman's face - and even bare shoulders at the theatre or a ball - but for whom the sight of an exposed ankle, let alone a leg, was an extreme immodesty.

The method of obtaining the oil was to crush the olives and steep them in brine. They were then tied in a bag and put in a sloping trough with hot water. The juice ran into a pail and the oily matter floating on top was separated off.

TUESDAY, 17 MARCH - After crossing the KARPUZLU-CHI [Water-melon River], the travellers came to the foot of a mountain, on the top of which, Fellows had been assured, was an 'old castle'. In spite of a tremendous downpour, they pushed on for another five hours (about 16 miles), up a steep, narrow track, to arrive at a shabby collection of houses called DEMMERGEE-DERASY [Demirci-Deresı, Blacksmith's Brook], situated just below the ruins. This was their *menzil*, halting-place.

They put up at the "best" house, but it had only one room with a raised area at one end, the *bir oda* [pl. 48], which Fellows and his party occupied, the Menzil-khanner insisting on stabling his horses at the other.

Above the village, the Englishmen discovered an ancient city, but were in total ignorance as to its name. Fellows noticed that its situation, high up on a mountain, was "perfectly Greek", yet the tombs were quite unlike any he had seen before, except for those at Alabanda. The tombs are huge, wider at the top than the bottom, and elevated on three or four steps. Some are hollowed out of the rock, the lids resting directly on the ground. As at Alabanda, they are of coarse granite and bear the marks of tablets. Three or four lines of these tombs and a road, 17 feet long, composed of giant paving-stones, 8-9 feet across, lead up to the acropolis, 500 feet above.

Here they found a wall, 330 feet long and 50 feet high, of beautiful masonry. This, they thought, might have been the market-place, with shops below as in a bazaar. Above, there are two storeys of terraces, supported by Doric columns. As at

88

36. Alinda, tombs.

Alabanda, the stones of the small but very perfect theatre (only 35 rows) are cushioned. It does not, however, exceed the semicircle. Other curiosities are a well or grotto of excellent groined Greek brickwork and, right on the top of the mountain, a two-storey Hellenistic tower of enormous stones.

All the signs of a city of great antiquity are present: immense stones, but no marble; the Doric Order; coarse, unadorned surfaces. Fellows judged the city to be of the 4th century BC, but, for all their searching, the Englishmen could find not a single inscription. As to the name, there was the evidence of coins found by the peasants and sold to Fellows to add to his collection.

That evening, there was great excitement in the 'best house', the coins laid out on the floor and each minutely examined and commented on by Fellows. The assembled Turks, raising their hands and exclaiming "*Allah!*" and "*fevkalâde!*" marvellous! indic-

89

ated their pleasure at the obvious appreciation shown for the 'worthless' money found in their gardens and fields. "*Görenedir görene, köre nedir köre ne?*" - a person with sight sees what a thing is, but a blind man has no way of understanding it - they quoted, pointing out the truth of the proverb.

Out of twenty copper coins, five of them bore the name - ALINDA. "In the absence of better authority," Fellows wrote with caution, "I should consider this as sufficient to mark these ruins as the site of the ancient Alinda." Earlier travellers had confused it with Alabanda. The truth of Fellows's assertion has now been established. Before leaving, as was his usual practice, he carefully fixed its position on his new map.

The melancholy grandeur of this lost city of distant antiquity quite overwhelmed the sensitive Fellows. He contemplated the simple massive tombs and considered that as monuments to the dead, they were more fitting than the highly decorated tombs of Lycia, a true example of the "perfection of taste amongst the early Greeks", whose works he so much admired. The wild, bosky land gave them an aura and fascination that stirred the spirit and imagination to wonder what manner of people could have lived here, leaving behind them these colossal yet elegant structures. In Britain, only the enigmatic stone circles can evoke a similar emotion.

THURSDAY, 19 MARCH - Fellows's route now turned to the south-west, to bring them into another area of conflicting opinions. The steep track was plentifully strewn with bright spring flowers, giving the ground the appearance of being spread with a true Turkey carpet. The yellow and white of narcissi, jonquils, asphodels and crocuses mingled with the crimson of cyclamen and the large Oriental anemones [*Anemone coronaria*] with blooms 2-3 inches across of many shades, set off by the brilliant blue of *Muscari* (grape hyacinths), a flower new to Scharf. In the more open areas, wild lavender, sage and thyme gave off their fragrance as the horses brushed through them. Firs and Stone pines clad the upper slopes, brightened by the occasional vivid splash of yellow broom; dull green-grey olives softened the lower slopes.

Fellows considered the scenery to be the most beautiful he had ever seen and, as a much-travelled man, that was no idle statement. He devoted several paragraphs of his book to extolling the charms of these craggy mountains, their bright green mossy banks, sparkling rills and precipitous ravines, ending his 'purple passage' with a scientific account of the geology and vegetation of the region. This wooded mountain range stretched for thirty miles, until it dropped to the coastal plains, beyond which the sea appeared as a placid lake, the island of Kos, just a grey shape in the far distance.

About 12 miles north of the town of Mellasa [Milâs], they discovered some unexpected ruins, the remains of an oblong building with a side portico. In Fellows's day, it was known as the Temple of Jupiter Strator [Zeus Stratus], the Warrior, also given the epithet, 'Labrandus'. It is now identified as an *andrion* (a Greek meeting-house for men), dedicated to Zeus [4th century BC]. The fluted columns are of the Doric Order. There are also some Ionic columns of the actual Temple. Nothing else remained, except extensive sections of the city wall and a few tombs outside it.

Fellows had been in touch with Colonel Leake before setting out to discuss the problems of these various Carian sites and now, as with Alabanda, he was in agreement that this must certainly be the true LABRANDUS, the name then applied to remains some eight miles to the north-west of Mellassa. The site was excavated in 1948, 1953 and again at present, and this hypothesis confirmed.

Descending the mountain, they crossed and recrossed several times the ancient paved road, a *Via Sacra*, which led from this city to another, MYLASA, on which the modern MELLASSA had been built. The journey took two days. This town was well known to travellers, since it lies only about eighteen miles from the coast, thus easily accessible from the sea. It boasted a large khan and, as was to be expected, "many beautiful fragments of cornices, mould-ings, capitals and friezes were built into the Turkish houses."

Mylasa (the suffix '-asa' denoting great age) had been the capital of Caria, until it was superseded by Halicarnassus [Bodrum], the city of Mausolus [4th century BC], situated on the coast about thirty miles to the south-west. About a quarter of an hour outside Mellassa, on the west side, stands the well-known Roman Tomb [2nd century AD], now given the name 'Gümükesen', Silver Purse. It was loosely designed on the celebrated Mausoleum[1] and has, in

37. Mylasa, the Roman Tomb.

its turn, served as a model for the reconstruction of that tomb. It is typically Carian in style and almost perfect.

Twelve Corinthian columns carry a stepped pyramid of five courses, the underside of which was decorated in red. Beneath is an unadorned burial chamber with a door, the whole tomb raised on a stepped base. There is a hole in the floor of the upper chamber, through to the lower section, which has 4 supporting square pillars, and was once painted in blue. Relations of the deceased were supposed to have assembled in the upper storey to pour libations down through the hole to the dead below, a custom, Fellows claimed, still prevailing amongst the Greeks in Turkey.

Greek graves were only outlined by stones, but a wooden or earthenware pipe, rising a few inches above the ground, communicated down to the corpse. The bereaved family also retained the ancient custom of hiring women mourners to wail at the funeral.

Pococke[2], who had explored this part of Caria in 1740, went so far as to conjecture that the hole in the floor was connected with bull-worship. It was to let the blood of a sacrificial animal flow onto a person standing below, thus rendering him sacred. He believed the Tomb to have been a magnificent altar, of the "taurobole" kind, and compared it with others at Stratoniceia and at Ephesus, one at Eleusis in Greece, and another at Marseilles. By the time Chandler[3] came here, in 1764, it had been recognized as a Carian tomb. Both antiquarians remarked on the straight inner sides to the columns of the upper chamber, suggesting that there might once have been panels between them.

A later tourist, John Morritt[4] of Rokeby Hall, Yorkshire, describes the Tomb as "the prettiest little bijoux of a temple that you can imagine. It is most like a square summer-house...a pretty pavilion at the end of a modern garden more than an ancient ruin," and clearly wished he possessed it as a folly, to adorn his own estate.

In Mellassa itself few relics of ancient Mylasa remain. "In the centre of the town", Scharf reported, "there is yet standing a large Corinthian column, bearing an inscription in a tablet on its shaft. The letters appear to have been purposely effaced, but, tho' the outer surface is removed, they can, with a little care, be traced."

This 11-foot shaft is the sole remaining column of the Temple of Zeus Carius[5] [c. 40 BC], which once stood on a podium 5 feet high. "The column is a conspicuous object from every part of the town." This is still the case.

Another interesting relic of the ancient city is one of its Gates. "On the eastern side...is remaining a very handsome marble arch of the Corinthian Order. On the key stone is the representation of a double axe...Adjoining the arch were remains of a broken aqueduct." The double axe [Lydian, *labrys*] was the emblem of Zeus Labrandus and was used on coins. Fellows found the symbol on four keystones, all built into the walls of the modern town. From this he concluded that it was probably used on each of the city gates in ancient times. The Gate is still there, now given the name Baltalı Kapı, Axe Gate, but the aqueduct has disappeared.

38. Mylasa, the Axe Gate.

On the SUNDAY, 22 MARCH, the English party made an excursion to the ancient site near the village of IAKLY [Ayaklı], a long, wet, three-hour ride away. Fellows had visited these ruins in 1838, when he cited it as 'Labrandus', the name given on his maps. He rightly suspected, however, that, as ever, Leake was correct in regarding this place as EUROMUS. At that time, of course, Fellows had not yet discovered the true Labranda.

Unfortunately, the bad weather worsened, preventing them from exploring the site, or copying any of the inscriptions. They were obliged to stand "helpless beings in the pouring rain", their drawing-paper stuffed into their waterproof leather caps for protection. Fellows had already made copies from the tablets on the columns, which record the donors' names. There were 16 Corinthian columns of the Temple of Zeus [Jupiter] Lepsynus [2nd

39. Euromus, the Temple.

century AD], complete with entablature. Four columns lacked the flutings. The Temple was excavated in 1969 and is now undergoing reconstruction.

Given the inclement conditions, they were lucky in finding a shorter way back, crossing a swollen river by a bridge, but having to wade through water on the roads, which had turned into running torrents. "We arrived at our Khan at half past six, where we indulged in a complete change of clothes and enjoyed our dinner of roast mutton, soup and grapes."

The following day was clear and sunny, bringing out many new flowers - lilies, black and blue irises, various kinds of orchids, asters, the milk-flower, oleander, dwarf laburnum - all shining brightly amongst the dark foliage of immense evergreen Holm oaks [*Quercus ilex*], a tree sacred to Zeus. Their trunks were 7 feet in diameter, with a girth of 20 feet. Their arms spread to 25 feet across, shading a circle of some 70 feet. The villagers were busy all day, cutting and rolling the grass on their roof-tops. The women had plaited flowers into their long hair and the men and boys had added some to their turbans.

TUESDAY, 24 MARCH - Once more the party were on their way, heading in a south-easterly direction by a route that would take them into Lycia. Unlike the much explored Caria, this was an area almost unknown to Europeans. A hard ride of seven hours brought them to ESKY HISSAR, Old Castle, a few houses built into the ruins of ancient STRATONICEIA. They put up in the Aga's *konak*, which, like so many, was deserted.

"We could procure nothing but eggs and milk, on which with rice we dined well," Scharf remarked stoically. The Menzil-khanner got terribly drunk and made a great fool of himself. He complained bitterly of the high price of provender for the horses, which was his responsibility, no doubt regretting that part of the bargain. Nevertheless, he spent liberally on spirits for himself.

The Aga's house was actually within the *cella*, the main body of the Temple of Zeus Chrysaoreus [2nd-3rd century AD], the epithet being the original name of the city. It is now known to be the Temple of Serapis, an Egyptian deity, worshipped at Pergamus

40. Stratoniceia, Aga's konak in the ruins.

and in Italy. The Temple of Zeus may have been outside the city. Another Temple, dedicated to Augustus and Rome, had been destroyed sometime in the previous hundred years to make a mosque.

The courtyard was bounded by massive walls, on which the celebrated Edict (AD 303) of the Roman Emperor Diocletian was inscribed in both Greek and Latin. Leake had given Fellows a copy of a transcript[6] made in 1709 by the botanist, William Sherard, while he was British Consul in Smyrna. On his first journey, Fellows had copied it out and now, with Scharf's help, he was able to impress it on paper, "as a specimen of the most beautifully formed Greek letters" he had ever seen.

Shields had been carved at each corner of the walls of the Temple, crossed by spears, one by a sword giving credence in the name 'Chrysaoreus', the Golden Sword. These devices measured 2 feet in diameter. Fellows had seen similar shields, in Pamphylia [pl. 12], and had had a cast made of one for the British Museum. He had used the design on the title-page of his first book.

The scale and dignity of an ancient city can be measured by its theatre. Here, it had once had 40 rows of seats giving a capacity of 10,000 places, but now it was hidden under thick scrub and the

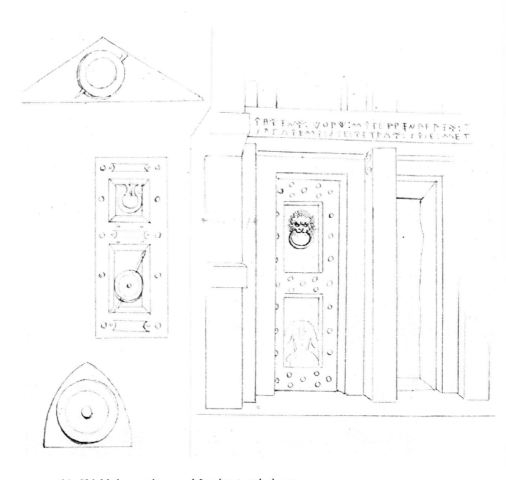

41. Shield decorations and Lycian tomb doors.

proscenium was just a heap of stones. As at Mylasa, the most striking feature of the ruins was a single Corinthian column near some arches, with a stork's nest on top. This, with a later generation of storks, is still characteristic of the site, at present undergoing excavation work.

They left Esky Hissar at half past nine next morning, to continue their journey across a high plain, about 1,500 feet above sea-level, recrossing the Cheena, which they had left at Alabanda, more than a week before.

98

On the top of a mountain, they espied their first rock-tombs, so typical of the province of Lycia. They gave evidence that Lycians may well have lived for a time in Caria. For the English party, they were an emotive indication that they were now not so very far from their goal. The necropolis is extensive, yet there is not trace of a city. The tombs may have belonged to Idyma, on the coast; Fellows's maps, unhelpfully, marked the place as 'Alinda'.

All had been broken into. It was generally believed that ancient tombs contained gold and that inscriptions held the key to hidden treasure. Every tomb and sarcophagus in Turkey has, therefore, been pillaged. Lighting their wax-candles, the Englishmen excitedly entered some of the chambers, which proved to be about 3 feet square and 5 feet high, with shelves on either side for the dead to rest on, and square niches above for lamps and offerings.

The awesome location, and the eeriness of these silent, empty graves, far from any signs of habitation, made the Englishmen shudder, yet, at the same time, the tombs powerfully suggested the mystery of the people of Lycia, whose territory they would soon enter. Their guide held the whimsical notion that the tombs were the homes of angels or spirits. They would certainly have made fitting residences for the Djinns [cin] of Oriental fairy tales.

Next day, the intrepid travellers arrived at the large town of MOOLAH [Muğla], ancient MOBOLLA, of which almost nothing remains. By chance, it happened to be a FRIDAY (27 MARCH), the Mohammedan day of prayer, so they had the highly interesting and unexpected opportunity of seeing the Pasha leaving the mosque. He was enveloped in fumes of incense and well escorted by soldiers and attendants, who scattered baksheesh [bahşiş] amongst the assembled people. The Pasha was "a tall mild-looking, elderly man with a fine white beard; he wore the fez and semi-European costume with a richly furred, dark purple cloak." He had adopted thus far the decrees of the New Regulations, but, as Fellows remarks: "A little eastern form still lingered about his suite; a white horse, saddled and covered with scarlet velvet and trappings of gold, was led in front to prance and display its attitudes, which were beautiful, as it reared and curvetted almost on the same spot."

42. Moolah, seen from the khan.

This show of grandeur demonstrated the importance of this town, the last of such a size that the travellers would find for many weeks. It possessed a fine khan, also the last they would find until they were well on their way back through the hinterlands of Lycia. For the next six weeks, they would have to put up in whatever accommodation could be had, from deserted houses to wicker huts, or their own ample tent.

The line of their route now crossed a range of mountains at an elevation of some 3,000 feet. People at these high altitudes were reputed to live to become centenarians and Fellows records seeing at least twenty peasants above a hundred years of age, apparently enjoying health and activity of body. Recent study tends to confirm this phenomenon. Before them rose the western ranges of the Taurus Mountains, crowned by MOUNT DAEDALUS[7] [Sandras Dağı; c. 7,500 ft]. Fellows reiterated his opinion that the most perfectly beautiful scenery was to be found in this part of Asia Minor, the border country between Caria and Lycia.

He had grown up in the Romantic era and again the sight of rugged mountains, backed by the lowering skies of a thunderstorm, pierced by flashes of lightning, elicited paragraphs of

100

'Gothick' description. The picturesqueness of the views was not lost on Scharf either, whose artistic eye relished contrasts of colour and texture, and he too, covered many pages of his diary in 'purple prose'.

Scharf compared the views with paintings by the contemporary Romantic artist, John Martin[8], whose enormous canvasses of biblical subjects, set in fantasized landscapes of rocks, cypress and pine trees, could easily have been painted here. The great vistas also called to mind the 'moving panoramas' and 'dioramas' created by Clarkson Stanfield for the Macready productions, which he had lately drawn at Covent Garden Theatre. These were large-scale backdrops, with dramatic sound and lighting effects, the *son-et-lumière* of the day.

From the high passes, the way gradually descended towards the coast. The terrain composed of schisty serpentine, strewn with large pieces of iron-ore, glistened with many colours in the damp atmosphere. The road finally became a swamp, the tired horses floundering in the heavy mud. At sea-level, the foliage on the trees was in its spring green and birds sang from every branch. It was a happy land. "In the evening, the nightingales hymn my vespers," Fellows wrote poetically, content in his nomadic existence.

A charming Turkish proverb says that even when given a golden cage, a nightingale still cries for its home - *bülbülü altın kafese koymuşlar: 'Ah vatanım,' demiş* - expressing the sentiment that there is nothing like freedom. In Turkey and many other countries, nightingales and finches were kept in small cages, hung outside the window, to sing for the owner. This practice has, fortunately, been discontinued in Britain, but is remembered in the music-hall ditty, '*She's only a bird in a gilded cage*', written in 1900.

Late in the afternoon of SUNDAY, 29 MARCH, the cavalcade rode into KOOGEZ [Köyceğiz], by the side of a large lake, about fifteen miles from the sea. While Mania prepared the meal, the three travellers visited an island on the lake. They were carried to a dugout canoe and punted over. They found only a few Greek houses and the remains of an early Christian church. The lake is now joined to the sea by a six-mile-long channel at its southern end, where a flourishing fishing and fish-curing trade is established. Grey mullet and bass are excellent eating, and the fish in the lake provide food for hundreds of pelicans and cormorants.

Koogez was not the usual village with an Aga, but the whole domain of a former Derebbe [*derebeyi*, despot], a kind of feudal lord, who lived in a castle, with the villagers all housed within its walls, as in medieval England. Since their recent suppression, their castles had been allowed to fall into disrepair[9]. This one had been a fine establishment of stone, with an arcaded courtyard and buildings of three storeys. There were open loggias on the first floor, which had at some time been extravagantly painted in reds and blues, but now the palace presented a sad specimen of fallen grandeur, most of the quadrangle being in ruins.

43. Koogez, Derebbe Castle.

The father of the present owner had, indeed, been a man of great power and importance. He had had hundreds of dependants, a private army, and ten ships-of-war on the lake. Those times were gone, yet the courtyard still rang to the sounds of drilling soldiers. It so happened that Fellows's party had arrived at the same time as a *Bey* from Constantinople. All the accommodation was occupied by his suite, in consequence of which, the English party were given the use of a villager's hut.

It was made of wicker, with a central tree-trunk supporting a roof of leaves and branches. Inside, bags of seed and festoons of tobacco and pepper-pods hung from the rafters. There were only a few utensils, but the most important, the coffee-pot, stood ready by the fire - *köylünün kahve cezvesi karaca amma sürece*, the villager's coffee-pot is badly blackened, but it is always in use.

44. Making coffee.

The travellers had already finished the bread bought in Mellassa and were now obliged to eat the coarser maize bread of the peasantry. The Menzil-khanner again complained of the high price of feed for the horses, which were daily growing weaker from want of barley. The poor things had not eaten for four days, because they steadfastly refused to touch maize. Oats and hay were not used as fodder for horses in Turkey, nor in other Eastern countries.

TUESDAY, 31 MARCH - The party with their long string of "fainting nags" came at last to the DOLLOMON river [Dalaman Çayı], the ancient INDUS, the natural border between the Roman

103

provinces of Caria and Lycia. It was so swollen that it took thirteen local men to get the party across. First the baggage was carried over on men's shoulders, the water reaching up to their necks and wetting the cases. The party followed on horseback with three men each to guide the animals to safety. Other men took charge of the baggage-horses. Fellows paid them well - 6 piastres (1 shilling) each for their services.

The men then swam back across the river, and when all had climbed onto the bank, they cheered and waved, shouting "Oorlah! Oorlah!" [*güle! güle!*] go smilingly, praising Allah for his goodness and wishing the strangers well on their journey - *Allah selamet versin!*

VI   Lycia, the north-west

By now the Englishmen had spent six weeks in Turkey and as many months away from home, family and friends. Their journey had already proved enormously exciting and interesting, a multitude of antiquities examined, ancient names unravelled, Turkish life experienced, and its natural beauties and resources enjoyed. Fellows expressed himself more than satisfied with the work of his two young protégés and rejoiced that he was returning to Lycia, that antique land, which had lain forgotten and neglected for hundreds, perhaps thousands, of years, its glorious cities left to crack and crumble beneath the invading trees and brushwood.

LYCIA is the southernmost of the Roman provinces of Asia Minor. It is cut off from the rest of the country by a series of

45. Fellows's map of Lycia, showing his routes of 1838 and 1840.

mountain ranges - the Taurus Mountains [Toros Dağları] rise to 11,500 feet. The province, 70-80 miles across by 40-50 miles deep, depends from them in a half-circle to the Mediterranean Sea. In the interior at over 4,000 feet there are moist, fertile plateaux.

The rugged coastline is much indented, mighty cliffs dropping into deep water, except where the three main rivers - the Xanthus [Eşen Çayi], the Demre [Demre Çayi], and the Arycandus [Aykiriçay], debouch into silted deltas and swampy plains. The chief ports, Macry [Fethiye] and Adalia [Antalya], mark the western and eastern extremes. Off the southern coast, there are two small islands, Castellorizo [Megisti] and Kakava [Kekova]; the Chelidonian Islands lie off the Sacrum Promontarium [Gelidonya Burnu], the southern tip. Rhodes lies some distance to the west, south of the province of Caria.

Due in part to its geographical isolation, in antiquity Lycia formed a separate nation with a distinctive language[1], akin to Zend, ancient Persian, and perhaps associated with Etruscan. It is

46. *Lycian alphabet compared with Greek and Zend by Daniel Sharpe.*

still not fully understood. From the 6th to the 4th century BC, Lycia was occupied by the Persians, coming under Greek rule after the conquests of Alexander the Great, followed by Rhodian control, before freedom was obtained. In the 2nd century BC, the chief cities formed the 'Lycian League'[2]. When the Romans established their provinces in Asia Minor, Lycia was not fully integrated, until, in the 1st century AD, it was joined with Pamphylia, under the Emperor Diocletian. In the 4th century AD, it became a separate entity.

In the Classical period, there were 40 cities with a total population estimated at some 20,000 inhabitants, twice as many as now. In Fellows's time, there were even fewer, the present-day towns then being little more than hamlets or, at best, modest towns of a few hundred souls. It is thought that the decline began with the Great Plague of c. AD 540, which raged over Asia Minor for more than a decade, decimating the population.

After crossing the Dollomon, Fellows's party rode on for another couple of hours through the marshes, till they came to the settlement of DOLLOMON [Dalaman], another former Derebbe

47. Dollomon, Derebbe Castle.

stronghold. When Fellows was here before, the place had been "all animation" with at least fifty people assembled to stare at his arrival. Now, all was deserted. At last, the former Derebbe's son appeared. He was a delicate-looking youth of 18, with very agreeable manners. He wore the plain fez and a scarlet jacket; older

48. Dollomon, inside the Derebbe Castle.

members of the household preferred the traditional turban and long robes. This castle was in much better condition than the one at Koogez; the ceremonial entrance was up a double flight of steps and the rooms inside still retained their elaborate painted woodwork.

WEDNESDAY, 1 APRIL 1840 - "An unfortunate date!" was the opinion of the superstitious Fellows. And so it proved, in so far as they wasted the whole day searching for an ancient city, which then turned out to be nothing more than the remains of another Derebbe fortress, an 'old castle' in the true sense. Fellows, however, could console himself with the knowledge that he had left

108

"nothing unseen" and, in any case, he deemed: "The mere act of travelling in this country is itself pleasurable; everything is beautiful and much new to an European eye."

Scharf described the view in poetic vein: "The morning was beautiful and the combinations and infinite varieties of mountain and wood scenery were beyond any attempt at description. The Myrtle[3] here grows in trees of amazing height, which, with the wild lavender, materially added to the enchantment of the scene by their delicate fragrance. At half past twelve, from the summit of barren rocks and Fir trees, we came in sight of the Gulf [of Macry] with its islands [pl. 53]. The sun shone brilliantly on the large, flat, snow top of Mount Cragus [ANTICRAGUS, Baba Dağ; 6,500 ft], supported by purple mountains and all varieties of coloured hills, the dark blue sea running in between them. The brilliancy of the atmospheric effect on the scene before us exceeded anything I had ever seen before."

Fellows also described the scene in lyrical fashion, but he added the scientific note that the Dollomon valley is about fifteen miles wide, bounded in the north by mountains thirty miles away, and in the south by the sea, "the misty horizon, broken by the mountainous island of Rhodes in the south-west." The swamps near the river were alive with plovers, quail and snipe, some of which Hesketh and Mania sought to shoot for the table. Camels and brood-mares grazed in the fields, black buffaloes wallowed in the water, and large tortoises lumbered painfully amongst the boulders.

The very next day, however, THURSDAY, 2 APRIL, they had better luck. The 'Esky Hissar' was, indeed, an interesting antiquity - their first authentic Lycian tomb - and, later in the day, they were to make their first major discovery - a Lycian city, lost for thousands of years on the top of a mountain.

The tomb is of the Doric Order, cut in a marble rock, with an entrance looking like a temple front [pl. 55]. Two pillars *in antis* (in front), flanked by pilasters, support a pediment, in which various ornaments are carved, including shields with swords behind them, reminiscent of those at Stratoneceia. "It is entirely hewn out of the solid rock and presents a beautiful variety of tones of colour, being red, white and yellow," wrote Scharf excitedly, as they stopped to gaze in wonder at this first tangible evidence of the Lycian people, whose works they had journeyed so far to see. There was something infinitely moving about this single tomb. It was as if a sentinel at the very outpost of the territory had been buried here, to keep his solitary vigil for eternity.

Fellows published two composite drawings to show the varieties of tombs typical to Lycia. The 'pillar', 'house' and 'Gothic' tombs are free-standing-the pillar type being the oldest and rarest, the Gothic, the most ornate. Rock-tombs, cut into cliff-sides, range from simple cavities to chambers closed behind a façade resembling windows or doors. The most elaborate, like the one just found, have porticoes in the 'temple' style. The pillars of these are almost always of the Ionic Order. There are also sarcophagi of the usual Roman 'chest' form.

49. Lycian tombs, 3 types: a) Antiphellus; b) Tlos; c) Xanthus.

50. Lycian tombs: a) Telmessus; b) Cadyanda; c) Xanthus; d) Sidyma;
e) Cadyanda; f) Sidyma; g) Calynda; h) Telmessus; i) Araxa.

The comfort of a khan was now a thing of the past, as were the fine Derebbe castles. For the next few weeks, the party were going to have to make do with their tent. That night, they would pitch it for the first time, near the little village of BEENAJAH-COOE [Jenice]. Their oilcloth hammocks were furnished with

51. Beenajah-Cooe,
Fellows's camp.

mattresses and 'Levinge' sheets of calico and muslin, giving them mosquito-free nights. A great fire was built outside, round which the Turks bivouacked, their horses picketed nearby. The blaze was kept going all night to provide warmth and to scare away prowling jackals and wolves.

A peasant conducted the Englishmen up a steep path into the mountains and there, on the summit, remote and awesome, they discovered the tremendous walls and elegant tombs of a very ancient city indeed. The walls are of enormous blocks [pl. 52d],

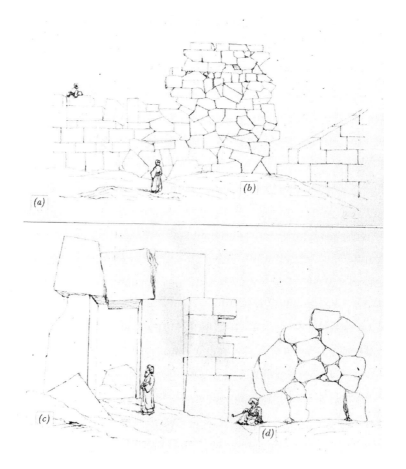

52. *Cyclopean and polygonal walls: a) Cadyanda; b) and c) Pinara; d) Calynda.*

112

piled up in the rough, irregular manner known as 'Cyclopean', supposedly the type of construction of the Cyclopean people of legend, who, according to Strabo, originally came from Lycia.

Most of the tombs are cut into the rocks and many have beautifully carved panelled doorways. Some have plain pediments, others, hollowed out of protruding peaks, have 'Gothic' lids added. "Applying this architectural test," Fellows determined it to be a city "within the confines of Lycia, and as such could be none else but the ancient CALYNDA, which, according to Herodotus, was beyond the boundaries of Caria." Spratt was later to declare this site to be Daedala [Inlice]. The remains, now called Kozpınar date back to the 5th century BC; the suffix '-inda' indicates great antiquity.

The following day, the travellers descended to the coast at MACRY [Fethiye], the name taken from the large island of Macra [Greek, *makros*, long], which blocks the entrance to the Bay. At the farther end was the hamlet of Mey, the name which had caused Fellows so much confusion on his earlier journey. Macry was a town of only some fifty houses, mainly Greek. There was, however, a large mosque, with its complex of buildings, including a theological school [*medrese*], baths and soup-kitchen [*imaret*], and

53. Macry Bay, seen from the theatre.

the odoor, or guest-house. In the late 1950s, the town was completely destroyed by earthquakes. It was rebuilt and renamed 'for Fethi', a pilot who crashed here.

The party remained four days, to examine the well-known ruins of TELMESSUS, called after the son of the Lycian God Apollo. The city was about 5 miles along the coast from Macry, its famous theatre "very perfect, [with] a good specimen of the proscenium". A decade or so later, the stone was used to build barracks at Scutari [Üsküdar] and it was finally destroyed by earthquakes. Most of the other antiquities were used in the construction of the new town.

Hundreds of tombs are cut into the cliff-face. Some resemble the mullioned windows of the English Tudor period; others, with Ionic pillars like the first rock-tomb the companions had seen near the Lycian border, resemble the fronts of Greek temples. The best known is 'Amyntas's Tomb' [4th century BC], its appearance unchanged over the centuries.

"They show distinctly the imitation of wooden structures, [giving] a perfect insight into the knowledge of the construction of ancient Greek buildings. The panelled doors, with bossed nails on the styles [stiles], knockers suspended from lions' mouths, and other ornaments in the panels, also show much taste and accuracy of execution." The building methods, which had given rise to the temple architecture of antiquity, had been carried on into modern

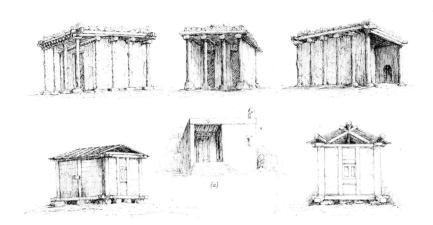

54. Huts and storehouses of the Turks; a) a Greek house.

114

55. Telmessus, Amyntas's Tomb.

times and could be seen in the construction of peasants' barns and huts.

At Telmessus, Fellows's assistants were able to see a perfect example of a Lycian 'Gothic' tomb. Half-submerged, some thirty yards from the shore, stood the 'Tomb-in-the-Sea'. Fellows hired a rowing-boat so that Scharf could sketch the details from close to.

56. Telmessus,
Tomb-in-the-Sea.

Along the base of the lid and the length of the 'hog-mane', there are scenes of combat, men engaged in some test of strength, with shields but no swords; some are nude, in the 'heroic' manner of the Greeks. Below high-water level, there are more figures, dressed in long mantles and dresses.

This lovely Tomb had attracted the attention of the Dublin surgeon, Dr William Wilde[4], when he was touring the area two years before. He felt sure that it could easily have been dismantled and taken on board a man-of-war, to be brought to England for the British Museum. He reckoned this could have been done for no more than £20 - and been well worth the expense. In recent times,

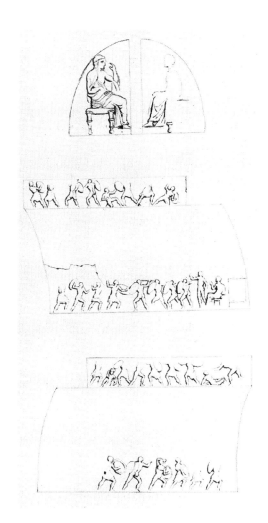

*57. Telmessus, Tomb-in-
the-Sea, details.*

the sea-level has dropped and the Tomb stands again on dry land,
a curiosity next to the Town Hall [*belediye*], in the centre of Fethiye,
which has spread along the coast to Telmessus.

The beach was then littered with dozens of such sarcophagi,
those of the Roman period being squatter, with more rounded lids.
They had inscriptions in Greek, the rock-tombs having words in
Lycian. The companions tried to copy and impress in paper a few
of them and, in so doing, noticed that the coarse conglomerate
stone had been plastered over to give a smooth surface, before the

117

letters were cut. They looked in vain for a bilingual inscription; they were, however, to be successful on their next visit in December 1843. The site dates back to the 5th century BC.

The fine weather, unhappily, deserted them, cold winds and rain forcing the party to leave sooner than they might otherwise have done. Fellows now hired a Greek guide to take them down the valley of the Xanthus. He paid him 20 piastres a day [4s.], a large sum, but this guide had considerable responsibilities since the Menzil-khanner, having taken advantage of the liquor sold in the Greek shops of Macry, was now so drunk that he had to be left behind. He was to catch up with the party later, sheepish and contrite. He had, of late, become increasingly difficult, unreliable and quarrelsome, yet it was impossible to dispense with his services. In the event, he would remain with the party until they had almost got back to Smyrna.

TUESDAY, 7 APRIL - Their line first took them back into the mountains, to a high plain over 2,000 feet above the sea. By evening, they had entered a well-cultivated valley, where, unexpectedly, they came upon a large town of some 2,000 Turks, but just one solitary Greek. His job was to keep the water-courses and fountains functioning. This prosperous place was HOOZUMLEE [Üzümlü].

The Aga was a friendly, courteous man, who still dressed in the traditional way. His turban was white, his mantle green, over a red and white striped robe, encircled by the folds of a broad orange and white striped shawl. He took great interest in the travellers' investigations and was most attentive to their welfare. Every evening, twenty to thirty men would assemble in the large khan [pl. 25] to entertain the strangers by singing and dancing to a lute accompaniment. Scarcely a man had ever left the town and everything about the Englishmen was a surprise to them. "*Allah!*" they exclaimed, asking: "*ne mene şeydir o?*" (whatever is it?) as they fingered Scharf's pencil, his glasses, the cutlery, the magnifying-lens. When they returned four years later, Fellows and Scharf were to receive the same hospitality and interest.

After breakfast, the guide took them to examine some ruins perched a thousand feet farther up the mountain, at 3,000 feet. Here, they made the wonderful discovery of the very ancient city

118

58. Hoozumlee, the Aga smoking his chibouk.

119

of CADYANDA, in Lycian, Kadawañti, which dates back to the 5th century BC. In 1842, Spratt, mistaking the name in abbreviated form, called this the site of Calynda. Fellows was absolutely delighted, as were the others, by the wonderful examples of pure Lycian sculpture, a mixture of Greek and Persian styles in the Lycian manner.

The first tomb they studied had been severely damaged by an earthquake. It remained at a very precarious angle, as if about to slide down the mountainside, but it has maintained this position to the present time. They called it the 'Thrown-down Tomb'. It is, in fact, Hector's Tomb. On the north side, he is shown as a warrior on horseback, semi-nude and beardless in the heroic manner of the Greeks, but he rides a Persian horse. It is a slender animal with long legs. A tuft of hair is caught up in a 'topknot' between his ears. Other horses show their tails tied up in the Persian way.

59. Cadyanda, the Thrown-down Tomb (Hector's Tomb).

120

60. Cadyanda, Hector's Tomb, details, north side.

On the south side, Hector is shown with long hair and a beard in the Persian (Lycian) fashion, reclining on a couch,

61. Cadyanda, Hector's Tomb, details, south side.

holding up a bunch of grapes. His dog sits by his side. There are three figures (one much damaged) at his feet. "The whole is of the purest age of art," wrote Scharf in raptures, declaring: "I thought them at the time equal to the Elgin metopes." The figures are about life-size, and seem to have been carved by Greek craftsmen.

On the end panel of a similar tomb, the figure of the owner, Salas, Lycian Zzala, a man, five foot, six inches tall, is carved in side-view in the style of an archaic Greek grave-*stele* (pillar). He grasps an elegant *oenochoë,* wine jug, in one hand, the other he holds up in the Persian way. His name is incised in both Greek and Lycian letters by his head. There are friezes along both sides of the tomb.

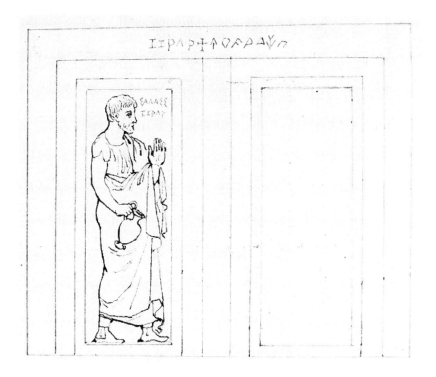

62. *Cadyanda, Salas's Tomb, Salas carrying a wine jug.*

122

On the north side, there is the 'death banquet', a very ancient funerary motif. Salas and his family recline on low couches, attended by their faithful hounds. A dancing figure at one end provides entertainment. Food is served on *paterae* (flat dishes).

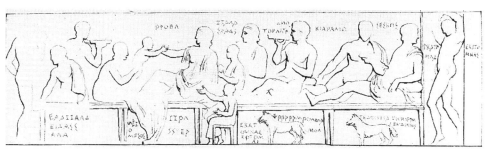

63. Cadyanda, Salas's Tomb, details, north side.

The south side shows a domestic scene with Salas's wife, Mesos, and her children. Fellows used a detail [pl. 136] of this group for the frontispiece of his *Account* of this journey. On the right of this group, people are about to sacrifice an ox. Each figure is named in Lycian, sometimes in Greek as well, in the way seen on Etruscan vases.

Fellows painstakingly copied out all the names. "This, I trust will materially assist in throwing light upon our ignorance as to the Lycian language." He also had casts of both Tombs made in 1844. Salas's Tomb [pl. 135] must have been quite as ornate as the Horse Tomb at Xanthus, but an earthquake had broken it and time had weathered the surfaces. Nearby, there was also a fallen, broken,

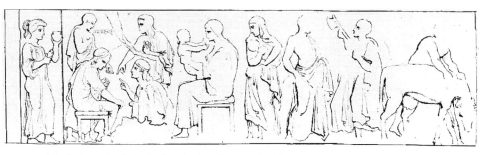

64. Cadyanda, Salas's Tomb, details, south side.

123

pillar-tomb. This damage was a grim object lesson as to the possible fate awaiting the Xanthian monuments, unless the promised Government expedition could soon remove the best into safety. Today, the tombs at Cadyanda are in a sorry condition, their lovely sculptures almost unrecognizable.

On the very summit, 500 feet higher still, was an area of level ground with yet more ruins. The Turks called this place YEDDY CAPPEE [*Yedi Kapi*], the Greeks, *Epta Portai*, both meaning Seven Gates. This 'magic' name came from the echoing subterranean vaults with their great arches, remains of Roman baths, which fascinated, but also terrified, the villagers.

Beyond a fine stadium, there is a lovely little theatre, the seats still perfect. On trying them out, the Englishmen found them most comfortable, owing to a curve in the back to accommodate the sitting posture. There is also a wall of partly polygonal, partly Greek [pl. 52a] construction. The market-place, demolished by an earthquake, appeared "like a mason's yard" and was thickly strewn with the elements of an arched colonnade. They could find no capitals, however, to give a clue as to its date.

Down the mountain on the other side, there are some Greek tombs of an entirely different character from the Lycian ones. They are built of large blocks of stone, forming an arch, stopped up with smaller stones. On either side of the entrance, there are pedestals and seats hollowed out of the rock, some fronted in marble.

Climbing back up the mountain again, the three men paused to savour the magnificent view. They could see Macry and the island of Rhodes (about 100 miles away) to the south-west, and Fellows pointed out the Xanthus river to the south-east. Its shimmering waters were visible for a stretch of some seventy miles, with Patara, its ancient port, almost due south from where they stood. For several minutes, they remained transported in imagination back two thousand years, and they peopled the landscape with the warriors of old. Their minds vanquished the distance and took them straight to Xanthus itself, but, in reality, two more weeks would pass before the Englishmen actually arrived at their goal.

VII Lycia, the valley of the river Xanthus, 1840

A five-hour ride during the afternoon of THURSDAY, 9 APRIL 1840, brought the explorers to HOORAHN [Ören, Ruins], at the head of the river XANTHUS, marked on some maps as the river ETSCHEN [Eşen][1]. About a mile from the village, the cliff-face is cut in all directions with rock tombs, their façades imitating the fronts of wooden houses. Elsewhere, hundreds of sarcophagi were half-buried in the ground or excavated into it. They were covered by lids of peculiar 'gable' form, with heavy *acroteria* at the corners [pl. 50, no. *i*]. On the sides, a stone tablet, "raised like an attic window", bears the inscription. The city is partly enclosed by a Cyclopean wall, the large stones chiselled to form the cushion-like fronts typical of early Greek buildings, such as the travellers had noticed at Alabanda and Alinda. There is also a Cyclopean tower of massive construction.

The villagers were very friendly and helpful, taking the strangers into a courtyard to see some well-preserved mosaic pavements and Ionic columns, the remains of the Roman baths. Fellows identified these ancient ruins as MASSICYTUS, but in 1842, the archaeologist, the Rev. E.T. Daniell, who was travelling with Lieutenant Spratt, discovered the correct name - ARAXA. The Massicytus Range lies to the east of the Xanthus valley, with Ak Dağ, White Mountain, rising to nearly 10,000 feet. The site of the city of Massicytus has yet to be discovered.

The party then rode north for about 6 miles, towards the head of the river. Spratt claimed that the actual source was near Araxa, the water bubbling out of the ground "a full grown river", which soon became "an impossible torrent"[1], very rapid and yellow from the stirred-up mud. *Xanthos* means yellow in Greek; the Lycian name 'Sirbis' or 'Sirmis' also means yellow.

Fellows wanted to make quite sure that there was no other ancient city hidden in the foothills, but, except for more Cyclopean walls, they saw nothing of significance. They retraced their steps to Hoorahn, where the Menzil-khanner, shame-faced and humble, suddenly made his reappearance.

About a mile below the village of SATALA-COOE, and some 7 miles below Hoorahn, the cavalcade was able to cross the Xanthus, now grown considerably wider, by a fine 5-arched bridge [Kemer, Arch]. It was the best they had seen in Asia Minor. Scharf noted that the architect, a Turk, had died on the day of its completion and was buried at its foot. This circumstance was recorded on an ornate gravestone. This SATALA BRIDGE was to play an important part in their peregrinations, and again, at the time of the Second Expedition.

Keeping the river to their right (west), the party proceeded south for another couple of hours. As they neared the next village, their nostrils were assailed by the unpleasant smell of sulphur. It came from a hot spring gushing out of the hillside. The water was highly prized by the local inhabitants as a cure for skin ailments.

By early evening, the guide had safely brought them to DOOVEER [Duvar, Wall], the end of his commitment. The hamlet had been allowed to fall into partial ruin and consisted of no more than some water-mills and the Aga's *konak*, now deserted. This the Englishmen took over. It had once been a very fine residence, the *hanay*, or principal room, ornately decorated in

65. *Lower Dooveer, fireplace in the Aga's konak.*

Oriental fashion, the floor strewn with fine rugs, and embroidered *minderler,* and there was a gleaming metal cowl over the hearth.

This Dooveer was at the foot of the cliff 'wall'. On the summit is ancient TLOS, the city Fellows had discovered shortly after finding Xanthus. A second Dooveer was built into its ruins. Tlos, Lycian Tlawa, is most impressive, the rock-face thickly pitted with tombs, faceless windows staring out over the valley, 2,000 feet below. The city, which dates back to the 4th century BC, had been

66. Tlos and Upper Dooveer.

a place of taste and luxurious ornament. The tombs are richly carved on their façades and within the chambers. Painted flowers and wreaths in red, green and white could be distinguished over the doors and the sculptures in the pediments above were also coloured. Many of the inscriptions are painted too, the letters alternately red and blue or green.

127

67. Tlos, reliefs on side of a rock-tomb.

One temple tomb, high up the rock-face, has some particularly interesting features. The columns outside the entrance porch are unfinished, only roughly blocked in, the Ionic capitals not yet cut. On that account, some might have passed it by, but that was not Fellows's way. Instead, they went inside, where a wonderful surprise awaited the investigators. On the left wall of the porch, they saw a representation of the mythical hero Bellerophon, on his winged horse Pegasus, seemingly in the act of trampling the monster, the Chimaera[2].

Legend tells how, with the help of Pegasus, Bellerophon accomplished various tasks, including the slaying of the fire-breathing Chimaera, which had its lair on Mount Olympus, in the east of Lycia. Only twenty miles from here, in the Cragus Mountains, there was also the deep Chimaera Ravine, where this beast lurked.

128

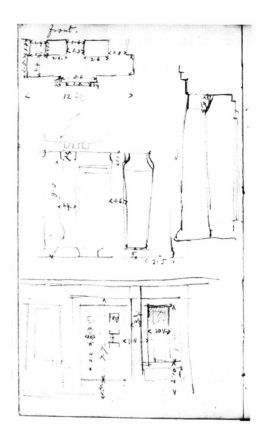

68. Tlos, Bellerophon Tomb, unfinished columns.

69. Tlos, Bellerophon Tomb, portico door.

129

70. Burgon's terracotta of Bellerophon and the Chimaera.

Scharf made a sketch of the sculpture by the light of a candle, showing a bare-headed man. On their return in 1843, Fellows had a cast made, which revealed that he was, instead, wearing the Persian *kidaris* (head-dress), his hair and beard fuller. The horse was a Persian breed too, with the characteristic topknot and square saddle-cloth-painted in red. The master craftsman had outlined the figures in black. There was, however, no indication of colour on the wings; the feathers would have been shown in paint.

This cast also proved the 'Chimaera' to have been just that - a figment of their imaginations. That part of the group was unfinished. It might have been a monster, or just as easily, as Spratt conjectured, the outlines of Mount Cragus, where it was killed. Nevertheless, the 'Bellerophon Tomb', as they dubbed it,

71. *Tlos, the Bellero-*
phon relief.

was a significant find. Fellows was to use the Chimaera on the title-page of his *Account.*

Up on the acropolis, the Englishmen continued their investigations, entering the large theatre [2nd century AD; 34 rows], which was most highly and expensively finished; the marble seats, often supported by lions' paws in the Eastern manner, had even been polished. Beyond the market-place, built of fine Greek masonry with large arches, there is a great complex of buildings, halls and arches, which had been baths. The villagers gave it the now familiar name of Yeddy Capee , with its overtones of mystery and fear.

Fellows and his friends were so enthralled by this ancient city, where the ghosts of the past crowded so thickly around them, that it was moonlight before they started their descent, each absorbed in his own reflections, leaving the horses to pick their own way down the steep, winding track.

Next day, they returned to examine the ruins afresh, every minute finding something new to admire. It was 3 o'clock before they felt ready to leave. When they got back down to Dooveer, the Menzil-khanner, now his old truculent self again, refused to go, saying he would not let his horses work in the mountains. He heatedly pointed out that the poor animals were starving. But no corn was available, even for the villagers to make bread. They said they were obliged to send it all to Macry. The Menzil-khanner had antagonized them, however, by his arrogant, overbearing manner, which may well have aggravated the situation.

MONDAY, 13 APRIL or TUESDAY, 14 APRIL - There is a difference of opinion between Fellows's and Scharf's accounts as to the date of this momentous day. Whichever it was, the former is the more likely, that was the day they discovered PINARA. They had set off in a south-westerly direction, heading towards the Cragus Mountains and, after crossing the Xanthus, arrived at the hamlet of MINARA at one o'clock.

The journey was delightful, the path winding through forests of fir, enriched by the white and lilac-coloured blooms of the cistus[3] bushes. Minara is prettily situated on a terraced hill, cultivated with olive, lemon, orange, quince and pomegranate trees, and the sprawling fig. The Englishmen pitched their tent on one of the terraces, in a bower of sweet-scented cabbage-roses, their delicate perfume filling the air. At last they were able to replenish their dwindling stores, not only with fruit, but also with eggs and fowls aplenty, though expensive, and, above all, with feed for the horses.

Fellows had made his way here, attracted by the name. In many instances, the Greek Π [*pi*,P] had become changed to M, suggesting to him that Pinara might be close at hand. *Pinara* in Lycian means something round and, like the Turkish *minare* (minaret), describes the acropolis rock [pl. 133] on which the city was built. It is an enormous truncated column, which rises suddenly from the flat plain to a height of 2,000 feet. Even so, it can be overlooked, as it blends into the mountainous background, unless viewed against the skyline.

As they rode towards Minara, from the east, this stupendous tower of rock rose up before them, its perpendicular sides speckled with black dots. On nearer approach, these resolved themselves into a mass of tomb entrances. "Choush! choush! [*çuş*] whoa!" they cried, reining in their horses to stare incredulously at this amazing sight. They tried hard to count the hundreds of cavities before

132

them, then, spurring on their mounts, fairly galloped to the foot of the acclivity and began to work their way up to the top.

In his unsuccessful search for its location two years earlier, Fellows had discovered Tlos. Now, he could write: "My search for the ancient Pinara has not been in vain, and I am amply repaid by the discovery of its most interesting ruins about a mile further up the mountain" from the village of Minara. He then dedicates several pages of his book to its antiquities. Although Fellows preferred Xanthus to all other ancient cities - perhaps because it was his first discovery in Lycia - Pinara obviously impressed and fascinated him almost as much as it did Scharf. It became *his* favourite city and, three years later, he was fortunate enough to make a second visit here.

"Walls, remains of buildings, seats and doors came thick upon us," Scharf wrote delightedly, but Fellows lamented: "How little is known even of the names of ancient Greek buildings! I find the usual vocabulary sadly deficient in supplying appellations for the many edifices crowded together in this very ancient city." It dates back to the 5th century BC.

The tops of the sarcophagi are more pointed than usual and several have the uncommon feature of inscriptions in both Greek and Lycian on them. The rock-tombs are mere oblong holes without doors, "dwelling-places for eagles". They can only have been cut by men working from hanging cradles, like the window-cleaners of modern high-rise blocks.

One rock-tomb, cut in the form of the end-on view of a Gothic tomb, had especial interest for Fellows. It confirmed the suspicion he held that the 'hog-mane' of such a tomb should have been completed by the addition of some sort of ornament or crest. Over the entrance, in that very position, are carved the ears and horns of an ox, bringing to mind the *bucranium* [ox-skull] of Classical decoration. Fellows had seen real ox-skulls placed above the doors of peasants' huts to scare away evil. This is still done today, an ancient tradition carried on into modern times. Ox-skulls are also used as scarecrows. Fellows had a cast made of the 'Ox-horn Tomb', when he came again to Pinara with the Second Xanthian Expedition.

72. *Pinara, the Ox-horn Tomb.*

Another very exciting find was the 'City Tomb', now also called the 'Royal Tomb'. Within the portico, in a position similar to the relief of Bellerophon at Tlos, there are four panels depicting

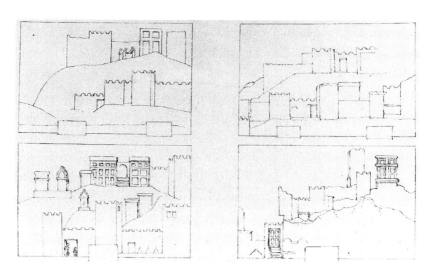

73. *Pinara, the City Tomb reliefs.*

a city with Gothic and pillar-tombs, and embattled walls - ancient Pinara itself, they liked to fancy. The travellers were to find several such walls in reality, the first the very next day, on a rocky hillside, some six hours' ride away. There is a similar scene - the so-called 'City' frieze - on the Nereid Monument, brought from Xanthus by the first Expedition.

The tomb has a very ornamental entrance. In a frieze above the doorway, there are figures apparently rejoicing and dancing, surrounding a man on horseback; in the pediment, there are women and children. The reliefs inside were much blackened by

74. *Pinara, the City Tomb, façade.*

soot from the fires lit by peasants, who used the porch as a shelter. Nonetheless, the carvings were in a good state of preservation, as were the sculptures on the façade. Alas, they are almost totally defaced today, but happily the panels are preserved in the form of casts in the British Museum.

On the east side of the acropolis, there is a little theatre (27 rows), "very perfect", with all its seats remaining. Like the *odeion* for musical performances, it faces west towards the higher ground. Farther up, there are some tremendous polygonal walls, some of them buttressed with squared blocks, the magnificent gateways formed of just three enormous, squared stones[pl. 52c], one lintel measuring 14 feet. The lower acropolis did not have any walls.

On their way back from the site, the English party were invited by some Chingenese [*çingene,* gypsy] to sit on the skins, which they had spread on the ground for their benefit, and partake of bowls of *yoğurt* with thin pieces of unleavened bread. Neither yoghurt, nor 'pitta' bread [*pide*] was known in England in those days and they tasted strange, though not unpleasant, to the unaccustomed palate. The milk was from sheep, goats or buffaloes, cattle being used as draught-animals. It was explained that the heated milk was poured onto some ferment kept from a previous batch, the mixture often drunk fresh while still warm.

The gypsies were astonished by the Englishmen's possessions, Scharf's spectacles again being the cause of much laughter. "This city is yet unknown to Europeans," Fellows observed - and vice versa - for the clothing of the gypsies was of equal novelty to the travellers. The women used the bold, silver *fibula,* the brooch of Classical antiquity to fasten their loose blouses and wore the broad, gold armlets of those ancient times. The girls had long earrings and skull-caps of gold coins, and their hair was plaited in twenty to thirty thin tails, like figures seen on archaic Greek vases. Fellows had seen this style sculptured on the Harpy Tomb at Xanthus. Several had dyed their hair red with henna and stained their hands and feet with it too.

75. *Chingenese girls wearing coin head-dresses.*

WEDNESDAY, 15 APRIL - After a terribly windy night, made the more frightening by the flapping of their flimsy tent, the day dawned bright and calm. Reluctantly leaving Pinara, the happiest and most intriguing time the Englishmen had spent so far, they returned to the Xanthus valley, riding south for a couple of hours. Then striking west again, they passed between the Anticragus and the Cragus Mountains to the north of MOUNT CRAGUS [Elmacık Dağ], which rose above them to a height of 3,300 feet.

At first, the lanes were prettily shaded by carob[4], myrtle, gum-storax, almond and orange trees. Then, as the road became steeper and higher, the scenery changed to forests of fir and the Valonia oak[5]. It took nearly four hours to ascend the difficult, rough, often precipitous, path to the summit, the horses frequently stumbling under their heavy, bulky loads, much to everyone's consternation.

At 1,750 feet up, near the village of TORTOORCAR HISSAR [Dodurga], a true archaeological 'hissar' came into view. They had discovered the very ancient city of SIDYMA - the suffix '-yma' indicating great antiquity, though the ruins are mainly Roman in date. This name was later identified as synonymous with CRAGUS.

The tombs and buildings are large and ornate, as if belonging to a much larger place, yet the market-place and theatre are quite small. The baths have fine, arched chambers with the characteristic circular ends; one room had been stuccoed and painted with borders and wreaths of flowers in red, blue, yellow, green and white, which mirrored the colours of the wild flowers. The doorway to another building, a lofty 30 feet high, is tastefully decorated with lions' heads and rosettes, like the ones they had seen at Araxa.

76. Sidyma, doorway with lions' heads and rosettes.

As at Araxa, many tombs have steep 'Carian' lids with *acroteria* at the corners. There is also a single pillar-tomb without its top. One free-standing house tomb of white marble has an elegant coffered ceiling with rosettes and women's heads, once painted in red, in each panel. The ceiling of the imposing Roman Tomb at Mylasa also had a painted ceiling, as did the Nereid Monument [pl. 108] of Xanthus. This showed traces of painted details on the friezes too.

77. Sidyma, the house tomb.

The inscriptions are mostly illegible due to weathering. There are no Cyclopean walls. Since Fellows's time, the village has much increased in size, regrettably destroying much of what he saw. Excavations are now, however, in progress at this highly interesting site.

138

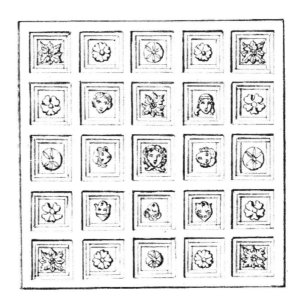

78. *Sidyma, the house tomb, details of the ceiling.*

This city, forgotten above the rocky mountain pathway, had been missed by any previous traveller through those remote regions. They would, in any case, have been more on the look-out for wild animals "of the fiercest kind", which infested these fastnesses. Fellows's party, after their encounter with the legend at Tlos, indeed felt that the Chimaera itself might suddenly burst from its lair and leap down on their straggling cavalcade.

All the local men carried guns for defence against bears, wolves, leopards and lions. "The people told us," Scharf reported, "that upon an average, they took five lions a year, which are presented to the Aga, and ultimately find their way to Constantinople, where they fetch a high price." Lions formed a very usual motif of decoration in that part of Lycia. "The lion is seen everywhere throughout the valley of the Xanthus; every bas-relief, tomb, seat or coin, shows the figure or limbs of this animal."

While at the meeting of the BAAS at Plymouth in July 1841, Fellows was to discuss with the naturalist Hugh Strickland[6], the possibility that lions really did live in these isolated mountains. Although somewhat sceptical, Strickland conceded that it was an "exceedingly interesting question", and agreed: "Its bearings on geology, zoology, and ancient history are very important." Spratt

139

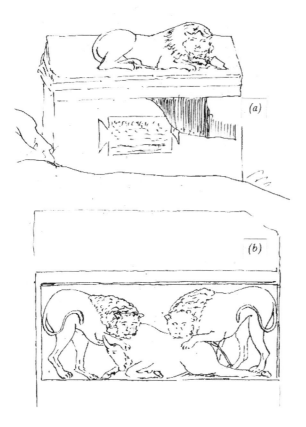

79. *Xanthus, lion sculptures: a) tomb lid; b) base of a pillar tomb.*

also looked into the matter when he was in this vicinity, but got conflicting information. The lions were alleged to be a small breed, timid, unless surprised or attacked. The Turkish word for lion is *aslan.* Significantly, the name of the next hamlet was Uslann, perhaps a derivation of the word.

USLANN was on the coast and served as a *"scala"* [Italian, stairs; Turkish, *iskele*[7], landing-stage] for shipping firewood and salted fish to Rhodes. The latter commodity was very useful, as fresh fish was difficult to obtain, the seas around Rhodes being too deep and dangerous for small fishing craft. The rivers and coastal swamps of the Xanthus valley, however, were well stocked with fish and eels. Uslann, itself, was composed of no more than three sheds - the entire population being two Greeks, who carried on this trade.

140

On a nearby hilltop, Fellows discovered the perfectly preserved ruins of an ancient fort. It has polygonal walls, 30 feet high, similar to those they had seen carved on the panels in the City Tomb at Pinara, with crenellations and eleven towers for defence, like an English castle. There is a walkway for the guards along the top, but the towers have only outer walls, the inner left open to the central ward. There only seemed to have been one building, at the lower end of the wall. It was a large square room with a circular end and smaller saloons leading out of it. Fellows reasoned that the place had been a stronghold for Xanthian soldiers, who had lived in wicker huts or tents.

The existence of the site had been indicated by Captain Beaufort, while charting the coast in 1811. "Colonel Leake had also directed me hither", Fellows explained, "as the possible site of the ancient CYDNA, or PYDNA, but of this discovery I am not satisfied." There have, however, been no recent discoveries to contradict the name. Inscriptions showed the fort to have been subject to Xanthus, some twelve miles to the east. It is now called Gâvur Ağlı, Infidel's Fold. It was the first of several forts the travellers were to find along this coast.

80. Cydna (Pydna), the fortress.

Since leaving Macry, ten days earlier, the party had journeyed seventy to eighty miles and discovered five ancient cities, lost to the modern world, their description adding greatly to the history of Lycia.

The next day was GOOD FRIDAY, 17 APRIL. No doubt the date was not lost on Fellows, for he was finally bringing his little party to Xanthus, the ancient city they had been discussing ever since the start of their travels. They would be celebrating the joyful festival of Easter in *his* "favourite city". Leaving Uslann at 10 o'clock, the long string of horses wound its way in an easterly direction along the coastal plains of the river delta.

At half past twelve, they came to the banks of the flooded Xanthus. Luckily, they were just able to ford it, though the baggage received a considerable wetting. Turning up stream, they could see a small hill to their left (west), cut off like an island at that season. It was too swampy, though, for them to get across to investigate the ruins they could see on it. Fellows correctly identified them as the remains of the LETOUM [Letoön], a shrine to Leto [Roman, Latona], mother of Apollo and Artemis [Diana]. He would be able to explore the ruins a year later, when he found himself here for the third time, with the First Expedition to Xanthus.

In spite of their mounting excitement, it took another hour to get as far as KOONIK [Kınık], near the ruins of Xanthus, ancient capital of Lycia. Alas, their arrival was marred by the unwarranted behaviour of the Menzil-khanner, who began to strike out at the peasants, who had assembled to welcome Fellows back to their village. Fellows strongly disapproved of the way he was galloping about keeping the friendly people at bay. Nevertheless, Fellows rejoiced to be back at XANTHUS again. After seven weeks of travel, passing through every variety of terrain, here he was at last, almost two years to the day since he first set foot in this fascinating place.

"I am once more at my favourite city," he wrote, full of emotion, "the first in which I became acquainted with the remains of art of the ancient Lycians, and in which I hope to find still more, embodying their language, history, and poetic sculpture. How might the classic enthusiast revel in the charms of this city and its neighbourhood! With Mount Cragus before him, he might conjure up all the chimaeras of its fabulous history."

The three men commenced their antiquarian investigations with the Lion Tomb [pl. 129]; then the Horse Tomb [pl. 17], Fellows's favourite; and the massive Box Tomb [cover], a Gothic

142

81. Xanthus, north of the acropolis rock (the Heights).

tomb, which had lost its lid. Side by side near the theatre, stood another, smaller, Gothic tomb, raised up on a pillar, and the Harpy Tomb. Fellows pointed out the friezes that had caused such excitement and had led to the Trustees' decision to acquire them for the nation. The friezes were on a pillar, 17 feet high, which Fellows noticed with anxiety had been shifted on its base by an earthquake. Two corner-stones had dropped to the ground, a fact Fellows had already marked on his original sketches of these sculptures [pl. 16].

With the aid of a telescope, they could be made out. Each side shows a series of figures in side-view, some seated as on thrones, in the Persian manner, some standing, holding up objects in their hands. Most interestingly, at four corners (on the north and south sides), there are monsters - half woman, half bird - flying off with babies clutched to them. These 'bird-women' were taken to be Harpies, as described in legend. Particles of paint adhered to the frieze, the drapery showing red, the background typically blue, but the clothes of the Harpies had disappeared, leaving only naked egg-shaped bodies.

143

82. Xanthus, the Harpy Tomb frieze at the British Museum, 1842.

83. Xanthus, the Harpy Tomb frieze, north side with Harpies.

The next three days passed happily away, as the friends explored the ruins, climbing over fallen stones and scrambling through the undergrowth. They made drawings of the tombs, mapped their positions, measured them, and endeavoured to make out inscriptions. Scharf made meticulous drawings of the Harpy Tomb frieze and the reliefs on the lower chamber of the Horse Tomb. The end walls show Lycian warriors and a naked youth. The west side shows a Satrap (Persian ruler) seated on his throne[8], and the east side a battle between Lycian horsemen and Greek

144

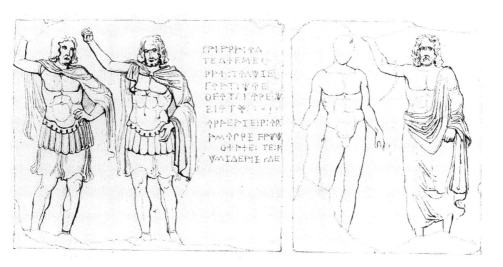

84. *Xanthus, the Horse (Payava) Tomb, end panels.*

85. *Xanthus, the Horse Tomb, west side with Satrap.*

86. Xanthus, the Horse Tomb, east side, battle scene.

foot-soldiers. The horseman wearing a leg-guard may be Payava, the owner of the Tomb. Fellows, meantime, concentrated on making another copy of the letters on the Inscribed Stele [pl. 112]. This was very tedious work, but in so doing, he discovered a curious fact.

"The characters cut upon the upper portion are larger and wider apart than those of the lower," he observed, "thus counteracting the effect of diminution by distance as seen from the ground." The stone-carvers of antiquity clearly understood the problems of perspective. The inscription runs to over 250 lines. On one side, there are 12 lines in Greek, the letters less well cut than the Lycian and more difficult to read. Nevertheless, they reveal the subject matter to be funereal, relating to Kherei [pl. 148], a ruler of Lycia, and the exploits of the Lycians in the Peloponnesian War (430-412 BC). The Monument itself speaks, using the first person.

"This monument will be esteemed a second Rosetta Stone[9]," Fellows prophesied. This prediction has, alas, not been fulfilled. In 1842, he was to make yet another copy, and in 1844, actual casts were made of this valuable relic of antiquity.

146

On the domestic front, things were going less well. The only water came from the river and was full of yellow silt. The weather had now turned oppressively hot, making drinking-water all the more necessary. The officious Menzil-khanner was preventing the peasants from offering gifts and kindnesses, demanding, instead, produce from them at too low a price. This was very distressing for Fellows, who had received much hospitality on his former visit. He also heard that their 'suspicious' activities had been reported to the local Aga, in the common belief that they must be stealing gold from the 'old castles', by deciphering the clues given in the mysterious words carved upon them. Luckily, no unpleasantness resulted from this misconception.

EASTER SUNDAY, 19 APRIL - Mania "like all Greeks, is very anxious to have a lamb for this day. Among them, whatever their circumstances, every family must kill their lamb at the threshold, a curious preservation of the Hebrew passover," Scharf observed. Mania must have got confused with the date, however, as the Greek Easter did not occur until two weeks later. On the other hand, he may have wanted the lamb for his English masters, so they could celebrate their Easter Day in the best style. In any event, they encountered considerable difficulty in obtaining an animal and had to send several miles away before one could be found. Nevertheless, the English party were able to have lamb, roasted with herbs, pilaf of rice, followed by fresh fruit and cheese, for their special Easter dinner.

TUESDAY, 21 APRIL - "This is my fourth day among the ruins of Xanthus," Fellows wrote, "and how little do I know of this ancient city! its date still puzzles me. It certainly possesses some of the earliest Archaic sculpture in Asia Minor, and this connected with the most beautiful of its monuments, and illustrated by the language of Lycia. These sculptures to which I refer must be the work of the sixth or seventh centuries before the Christian aera."

These closing remarks on the city of Xanthus reflect the affection Fellows felt for this place and suggest his resolution to make it the focus for the study of the culture and art of the Lycian people. He was to publish a chronological scheme, in which he places the Lion and Harpy Tombs in the time of Croesus, mid-6th century BC; the Horse Tomb and the Chimaera Tomb (found in

1843) he ascribes to the time of the Persian conquest, about 500 BC; the Inscribed Stele to the period when Herodotus was writing his *Histories*, mid-5th century BC. The Ionic Trophy Monument, now called the Nereid Monument, the scattered pieces of which he gathered up in 1842, so that the structure could be reassembled in the Museum, he dates to about 450 BC. Modern scholarship dates all these tombs a half century or more later than Fellows's estimations.

So, with heavy heart, and believing that he would never see Xanthus again, he struck camp, turned his back on this unique city and headed south once more. Had he known it, Fellows was to come here again twice more, each time taking up residence for several months of search and study.

VIII   Lycia, the southern coast

Leaving the course of the Xanthus, their line took them to its former outlet at PATARA, in Lycian, Pttara, the port now isolated from the sea by sand-dunes and marshes. In Scharf's eyes, its conspicuous, unadorned, triple-arched Roman Gate [c. 100 AD] was "far from agreeable", but the theatre [2nd century AD], though filled with sand, was still "very perfect". Behind it, the hillside is covered with temple tombs, cut into the rock.

87. Patara, the Roman Gate.

In the centre of the city, there is a small Corinthian temple [2nd century AD] and, nearer the former harbour, an enormous Roman granary, an indication of the great importance this port had in former ages. Fellows, of course, looked for Lycian inscriptions, but could only find Greek. There is a Latin inscription on the granary.

Scharf remarked: "We have been told that the Greeks are constantly finding statues, which they ship off to Castelorizo. Rings, coins and gems, which are found in ploughing, they said were eagerly purchased by the Consul at that Island." Fellows was, at least, able to buy some coins himself, to add to his ever-growing collection. Coins[1] of the Xanthus valley show Apollo's lyre [t-p], Bellerophon, Pegasus, lions and the *triquetra*, a three- to four-bladed figure like a swastika, the symbol of the race-course [Greek, *dromos*] - even the Satrap Kherei - but not Greek or Roman Gods.

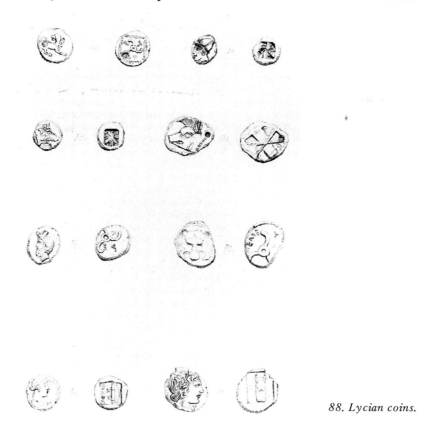

88. *Lycian coins.*

It was now early summer along the southern coast, the Mediterranean vegetation in full leaf. Citrus trees, olive groves, vines, even aloes and palm trees clothed the lower slopes and the

150

gardens were a mass of luxuriant growth. The BAY OF KALAMAKI [Greek, *Calamus sp.*, reed; now Kalkan] was called by the ancients, PHOENICUS from its date-palms [*Phoenix dactilifera*]. The route the English party took, however, returned inland, to the north-east, over a mountain pass at nearly 2,500 feet and back into winter again.

"The ground at the top was covered with hailstones, as thickly as snow," and the travellers were soon peppered with more as the storm recommenced its fury. "The awfully grand effect of these storms can scarcely be imagined," Fellows declared. "The crackling thunder was echoed instantly by the surrounding crags, and then rolled into distant ranges with almost a continuous murmur; the lightning played upon the clouds, which appeared to hover capriciously over fated islands in the expanse of ocean before us, while the sun shone brilliantly on others." Such a truly 'Gothick' landscape with theatrical sound and lighting effects heightened the feeling of mystery in this ancient land, untravelled for aeons.

THURSDAY, 23 APRIL 1840 - "Many happy returns of my Father's birthday[2]," wrote young Scharf, with a pang of homesickness. Birthdays and anniversaries were red-letter days in the Scharf household, and he sorely missed being at home on such a day.

The road continued to rise steeply, but their efforts were constantly rewarded by spectacular views over the indented coastline. At one point, the explorers came across a group of rock-tombs [4th century BC], which Fellows thought might have marked the site of ancient PHELLUS - meaning 'stony ground' - but two hours of diligent searching disclosed no inscription giving the name. When Spratt visited the site, he voiced the opinion that this was the PYRRHA of Pliny, and the Phellus was located some way away, about seven miles north of Antiphellus.

Four more hours of this 'stony ground' and the party regained the coast at ANTIPHELLUS [Andıflı; now Kaş]. It was a tiny place, a mere *scala* for the island of Castellorizo. There were, however, over a hundred tombs. In modern times, the reverse is the case, Kaş becoming a popular resort, but most of the tombs have, in consequence, disappeared.

The party stayed in the odoor, a stone house jutting out over the sea. Taking advantage of this, the Englishmen took a welcome bathe. They never seem to have sampled the Turkish *hamam*, a public steam-bath, which most European travellers tried - and wrote about at length. Across the bay, was the modern PHELLUS, a few houses at the foot of precipitous cliffs, amongst which two Gothic tombs stood out conspicuously.

FRIDAY, 24 APRIL - Fellows had brought his party here, not especially for archaeological reasons, but for the more mundane one of replenishing their diminishing stores at the important trading-place, CASTELLORIZO, the ancient MEGISTE [Greek, largest; now Meis] - Fellows's mistaken 'Macry' of his first journey. It was an entirely Greek town of some 600 houses of typical cube-like form, "all built upon one model," as Fellows so aptly observed. They spread up the hill to form a white pyramid, unrelieved by any trees. At the apex were the ruins of a castle, built by the Knights of St John. It was of reddish sandstone, the 'Castello Rosso' of the name and landmark for the Genoese trading vessels along the coast.

The Greek character of the town was immediately apparent on landing. It was as if visiting another country altogether. Cafés were selling wine and spirits, pigs wandered about the streets. Greek women did not, of course, wear the veil. The Englishmen were much taken by the Classical appearance of their costume. They were decked with gold and silver ornaments, chains and

89. Castellorizo, a Greek woman.

bracelets, many of which were family heirlooms. New ones were copied from traditional designs, thus perpetuating the styles of the ancients. In particular, their blouses were fastened by a row of large *fibulae*, like those of the Chingenese women at Pinara. The brooches were of chased silver, three inches across. Scharf bought two, to give as presents to his mother and aunt.

The travellers were offered the use of somebody's house for Mania to make bread and candles. Fellows purchased rice, sugar and much-needed boots. He also obtained a lamb for Mania to kill two days later on his, Greek, Easter Day. Late in the afternoon, the group returned to Antiphellus and the Menzil-khanner, waiting there with the horses.

Fellows had hired a sailing-boat for the voyage of 5-6 miles. The outward trip had taken an hour and a half. The return took only one hour, due to a following wind, but that had made the sea choppy, and Fellows, a bad sailor, arrived back feeling distinctly queasy. A bowl of arrowroot from their medical supplies, however, soon revived him and they could enjoy a quiet evening in the house-over-the-sea.

Before leaving next morning, the companions strolled along the beach looking at the tombs, searching for a bilingual inscription. In this they were successful, and a cast was made in 1844. They sketched a particularly lovely, slender Gothic tomb [pl. 13], which years earlier, had taken Captain Beaufort's eye. It escaped destruction when the modern town was built and now stands, a curiosity, in Postane Sokağı, Post Office Street.

They climbed up to the theatre, from where a quite sublime view is to be had of the whole bay. The theatre is almost perfect, though lacking the proscenium. Unusually, they found the stage devoid of scrub, and could count the 28 rows of seats with ease. There are now only 26, but the theatre is in use again, a majestic setting for traditional wrestling-matches.

Reprovisioned, the party could bypass the coastal towns and go back into the mountains. It took two hours to get only as far as AVVELAH [Avullu], 7 or 8 miles inland, but nearly 5,000 feet up. The trees here had all the appearance of winter, and the weather was to match. Frequent rain and hail made the going extremely hazardous, especially while descending a cutting through the limestone hills, all distorted into fantastic forms by "volcanic heavings". Spratt thought ancient PHELLUS must be near here, Avvelah being a corruption of that name.

Late in the day, the cavalcade plodded into a surprisingly large and bustling town. This was CASSABAR [Kasaba, Small Town], the seat of a Pasha and capital of the district of KAASH [Kaş]. The Greeks called it PHELLUS, adding to the confusion surrounding this appellation.

Cassabar was the largest town the travellers had been in since leaving Moolah, in Caria, a month before. As well as a splendid bazaar, there were nearly a hundred good houses and a large, domed mosque. It had a single minaret, the only one they had seen in Lycia. The Aga lived in a fine *konak*, probably an erstwhile Derebbe castle. He was an imposing-looking man, who still wore a full beard and turban, and was wrapped in a rich fur-lined mantle against the bitterly cold wind, blowing down from the mountains.

Fellows's party lodged in a more modest abode, a square house under a grass-topped flat roof. The porch, supported by tree-trunks, gave it an ancient 'Greek temple' appearance. Here, they rested for a couple of days, to let their good servant, Mania, celebrate his Easter SUNDAY, 26 APRIL, in traditional Greek style.

It was then time to be on the move again, up the river valley to a point where the DEMRE [ancient MYRUS] takes a south-easterly course, to flow through a narrow but magnificent gorge, seventeen miles long, cut between perpendicular cliffs of limestone, luxuriantly clothed in trees and shrubs. It reminded Fellows of Cheddar Gorge in Somerset.

On the summit of an isolated rocky mountain, near the head of the ravine, they found a Greek wall flanked by square towers, like the forts they had found in the Cragus Mountains. This fortress commanded the entrance to a pass. Some Lycian tombs were cut into the rock-face and there was one arched building. From its position, Fellows identified the place as the remains of the city of TRABALA.

They followed the course of this "stupendous pass", the sound of rushing waters reverberating all around them. The water was up to four feet in depth, and, during their descent, they had to wade across it some forty times. For the Englishmen, the excite-

154

ment and the singularity of the scenery overcame their tiredness; as for the horses, they had hardly strength enough to complete the journey. The 25 miles had taken a wearisome seven hours. Then, quite suddenly, the valley opened into a plain and they saw before them the astonishing view of the rock-tombs of ancient MYRA [Kocademre, Old Demre], a marvellous sight in the deep glow of the evening sun.

90. *Myra, rock-tombs, the western group.*

Myra, in Lycian, Méré, was one of the oldest and most important of the cities of the Lycian League, though little of it now remains. The large Roman theatre [2nd century AD; 29 rows] has a fine proscenium and indicates the size of the population. Unusually, it is built up in the plain, not excavated out of a hillside. To support the seating, there are two arched corridors running round behind, reminiscent of the Colosseum, which is, of course, also

155

free-standing. The Granary of Hadrian [2nd century AD] and some other remains in the plain were, however, inaccessible to the travellers, being either, appropriately, standing in a field of corn, or surrounded by uncultivated swamps, the home of the much-feared malarial mosquito.

The most important remains of Myra are, indubitably, the rock-tombs, which cover cliffs in two separate groups[3]. They are mainly of the 'window' type [4th century BC], many seemingly constructed for whole families. Some have impressive rows of elegant figures (more than life-size), family portraits, carved "in the chaste manner of the Lycians" into the rock around the tomb entrances.

91. Myra, rock-tombs
with figures.

156

One such, the English party dubbed the 'Painted Tomb'[3], because traces of colour could be discerned on the sculptures. The flesh was tinted a natural colour, the drapery purple or yellow, the backgrounds red or blue. This confirmed a theory propounded by the German archaeologist, Carl Otfried Müller, who maintained that the Greeks tinted their statues, but painted their bas-reliefs and backgrounds, the colour applied over plaster, if the material were too coarse. This Fellows had already seen used in inscriptions and on several ceilings.

There was another question of debate: did the Lycians use a kind of wax to preserve and polish the surface? This certainly seemed to be the case. The party was to meet Professor Müller in Athens, on the way home, when these speculations were discussed at length. Fellows published a coloured plate of these figures in his *Account* and, in 1844, casts were taken and coloured in facsimile of the originals.

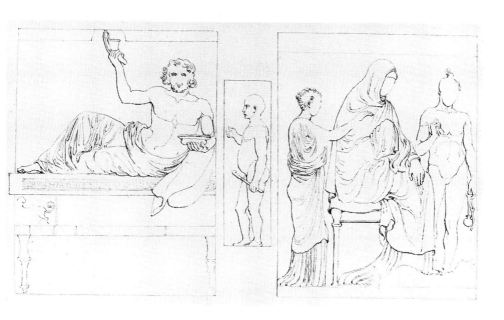

92. *Myra, Painted Tomb, figures in the portico.*

157

The Englishmen stayed in the Aga's *konak* out in the plain. It had been a Derebbe castle of some magnificence. The open, airy loggia on the first floor, commanded views to three sides. The arches were finely carved and painted, and texts from the *Kuran* formed a frieze round the walls. The most important building at Myra was, however, the very famous eleventh century church of Saint Nicholas, *Baba Noël* (Santa Claus).

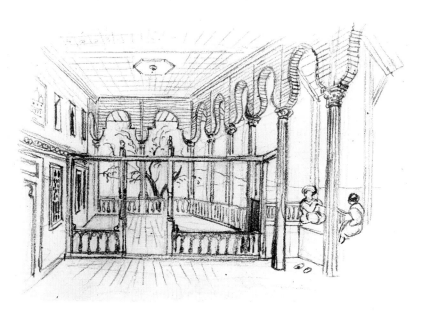

93. Demre, inside the Aga's konak.

Services were conducted by a solitary Greek priest [pl. 140], who was left all by himself in summer, when the rest of the villagers went up into the mountains, to get away from the unhealthy climate of the coast. On their next visit, in the spring of 1844, Fellows and Scharf would have the privilege of staying in his little house.

"The peasants here are very attentive in keeping back their fierce dogs." Fellows's remark is actually of more significance than might at first be supposed. When Spratt was in this neighbourhood studying the ruins, his cavalcade was ferociously attacked by a pack of these brutes, which are still kept to guard the flocks from wild animals. One day, one of Spratt's horses was killed and eaten by a dozen of them. Travellers all told fearful tales of being savaged by these great dogs, which could terrorize even a large group of horsemen. The animals are highly prized by their owners and could cost seven or eight times more than a boy slave.

They are a sort of mastiff, descendants of the fighting-dogs of antiquity. They are called *karabaş*, black head. They have prick ears, long bushy tails and a ruff of thick, coarse hair round the neck, generally reinforced by a spiked collar, which serves to protect them from the bites of wolves. Examples can been seen in ancient art and sculpture, such as the bronze in the Uffizi Gallery, Florence, of the Dog of Alcibiades, a Greek general who campaigned in Asia Minor, and the *Cave canem* mosaic of Pompeii, now in the Museo Archeologico of Naples.

WEDNESDAY, 29 APRIL - Leaving these lovely rock-tombs behind, the intrepid party once more struggled up the mountains to the east, the animals led by the bridle the whole way. The ascent was precipitous with hardly a level area to stand on. It was a path totally unfit for horses, let alone baggage-animals, but there was no alternative.

On a ridge about 5,000 feet up, they were rewarded for their effort, by discovering another of those fortresses, guarding yet another pass. They seemed to be a feature of this part of Lycia. The walls had the now familiar square towers, where the sentries of this remote outpost had kept watch. There were also a few sarcophagi.

Always cautious unless positive of his facts, Fellows thought this was probably the ancient ISIUM. His enthusiasm, however, never faltered. "What a wonderful people the ancient Greeks were!" he exclaimed. "This mountain country was literally strewed with cities and stately towers, which stand uninjured and unoccupied two thousand years after their builders are removed!"

Descending the other side of the pass, nine hours of exertion brought the party to the river ARYCANDUS [Yaşgöz Çay], and finally to PHINEKA [Finike], ancient PHOENICUS. It is situated about two miles from the coast, up the only navigable river in Lycia. The village had the usual custom-house and Aga's *konak*, and just a few other houses. There was also a Greek café, which supplied the Sultan's ships plying between the Capital and Alexandria, then under Turkish rule. The area is reputed to have the mildest climate in Turkey and Finike is now a popular holiday resort.

The region is richly covered in fruit trees and flowering shrubs, such as *Cistus, Daphne*[4], and gum-storax. An exotic air is lent by handsome castor-oil plants [*Ricinus communis*] and grey aloes [*Agave americana*], their flowering stems standing straight as guardsmen. Magnificent spreading carob, walnut, mulberry and plane trees [*Platanus orientalis*] cast welcome shade, in contrast to the long cascading pinnate-leaved date palms, which gave rise to its ancient name. Confusingly, this port is situated in the east of the Bay of Phoenicus, almost symmetrical with that of Kalamaki (Phoenicus) in the west. Fellows took the opportunity to add fifteen more genera to his plant collection, but the specimens suffered badly in the moist heat.

The party stayed here two days, during which time they managed to get their horses reshod. Turks would not do this job; it was done by the Chingenese tinkers. The shoes, quite unlike English ones, are thin plates of iron with a hole in the middle to allow the escape of moisture. The nails project to take the wear. This type of horseshoe is still in use in Turkey and in modern Greece. The horses of the ancient Greeks remained unshod, their hooves strengthened by ointments and exercise.

The Englishmen set out to walk to LIMYRA, Zemtiya in Lycian, only about 3 miles away by direct route, but they were obliged to skirt round the large marsh of the delta, doubling the distance. Hundreds of tombs, many more than at Myra, stretched along the road for several miles. Beyond the tombs lies the ancient city, marked by a long wall with towers. There is a small theatre and, farther on again, more rock-tombs. All are in a fine state of preservation. Many still bore traces of paint. Like the ones at Tlos, the letters of the inscriptions were in alternating colours. Fellows noticed with interest that the Lycian characters were always better and more deeply incised than the Greek, a fact he had remarked on before. In Asia Minor, over the centuries, the Greek language declined in favour of the various provincial tongues.

160

Standing a little apart on the approach to the site is a 'house' tomb, which held special significance for Fellows. It is raised on three deep steps. The upper chamber has an ornamental doorway under a pitched roof; the lower has a long inscription beside the entrance. This inscription is bilingual. Years before, Fellows had seen a drawing of it in one of his books[5], with a description and a copy of the inscription made by the young architect Charles Cockerell. He had found this tomb, while voyaging along this coast in 1812. His account was the first to attract the attention of scholars to the language of Lycia.

94. *The Lycian Tomb with Lycian inscription.*

Fellows had long entertained a wish to see this tomb for himself, and now, here it was before him. Needless to say, he set himself the task of making a faithful copy, though the letters had become badly eroded by time. Spratt had found the task almost impossible. He and his friends had tried every way they could think of, "such as wetting the surface, casting strong lights on it in various directions, and even shutting our eyes and trusting to touch. Often at a distance the letters appeared very distinct, but seemed to vanish as we approached, reminding us of the writings on the rocks concealing treasures - so often mentioned in Eastern stories - seen by all men from afar, by the chosen only when near."

Limyra epitomized a Lycian city, having all the essential features: rock-tombs; coloured inscriptions; Gothic tombs; a theatre;

161

a city wall. All that wanted were pillar-tombs, but they are less of a feature of eastern Lycia. One Gothic tomb had a *quadriga* on its lid, like the Horse Tomb at Xanthus, and death banquet scenes on its

95. Limyra, reliefs showing 'death-banquets'.

sides, as on the tombs at Cadyanda. Another tomb had a lively battle scene and a long Lycian inscription, the letters coloured

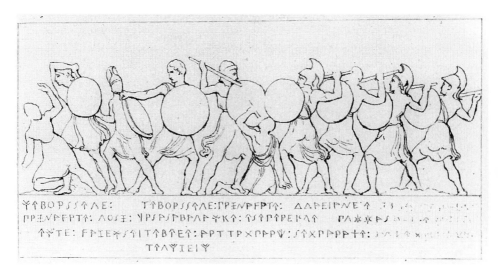

96. Limyra, reliefs showing battle scene with Lycian inscription.

alternately red and blue. Some of the rock-tombs even had figures carved on either side, similar to those at Myra, and all in a fine Graeco-Persian style. This was a truly wonderful place, and Fellows and his friends enjoyed themselves hugely in the bright sunshine.

97. Limyra, rock-tomb figures.

The site was excavated in 1969 and 1973, and work has now started again. Archaeological work has also been done at Myra.

Back at Phineka, the Englishmen were thankful to sit down to a delicious meal of roast kid and fresh fruit. Meat was plentiful here, so they ate well, making up for the meagre rations of the Xanthus valley.

FRIDAY, 1 MAY 1840 - "Another month has commenced and how little do I know of Lycia!" was Fellows's despairing cry. "The

163

province of Lycia, which has never been corrupted by the Roman or Christian styles, and retains the simple beauty of the early Greek, has for me the greatest attraction." Initially, he had thought to continue his investigations into the province of Pamphylia, at one time joined with Lycia, but with so many discoveries and with so much more of Lycia to explore, Fellows decided to limit his range and turn his attention to the hinterland.

First they continued past Limyra along the fertile coastal strip. "What would be the produce of this plain of Phineka under the management of an active and industrious people!" Fellows exclaimed[6]. Today, its full potential is exploited in the cultivation of oranges, grapes and tomatoes.

About 2 miles beyond Limyra, they came across a group of highly decorated rock-tombs. All the inscriptions were in Lycian, except for one in red, which was in Greek, and another in blue, in an unknown language, possibly Phoenician. This coastal area was very marshy, added to by the river ALLAGHEER [Alâkır Çay], which they crossed by an almost perfect Greek bridge. The large, square stones of its causeway, nearly a quarter of a mile in length, were supported by 25 low arches, composed of a double row of narrow bricks.

Five hours farther on, the travellers came to HAGGEVALLEH [Hacıvelier], near to which they discovered some walls of very inferior workmanship, due, no doubt, to the hardness of the volcanic stone. There was also a well-preserved theatre and a single rock-tomb. "The ruins, I fancy, must be those of GAGAE," Fellows decided, in agreement with Leake and Beaufort. Spratt, however, was later to identify them as CORYDALLA. Fellows believed Corydalla to be situated more to the north. Gagae [ga in Rhodian Doric signifies 'land'; modern Greek, ge] is, actually, farther along the coast. Very little of either site remains today, the stones having been used for building.

The following day, the weather began to deteriorate at an alarming speed and, before long, they were soaked to the skin. This was a great pity, as their route took them south-east, across a mountain pass at the head of the PROMONTARIUM SACRUM [CAPE CHELIDONIA, Greek, Swallow; Gelidonya Burun]. The panorama from this high pass appears like a topographical model of the coast and islands: to the west, Finike Bay with the island of Kekova in the far distance; to the east, nothing but the wide, open sea. To the north, the peaks of Mounts Phoenicus, Olympus, Solima and Climax rise one after the other, in a chain of barriers. "The scenery was very grand and would, if seen under more favourable circumstances, have been excessively splendid," they all agreed.

Many swallows skimmed across their path to catch the insects that were biting and molesting the horses. When Beaufort was sailing these waters, hundreds of them perched on the yards and rigging of the *Fredericksteen*, to rest during their migration northwards to England. Fellows and Hesketh shot a few birds for their skins and gave Scharf a bee-eater [*Meriops apiaster*] and a roller [*Coracias garrulus*] to send as presents to his father. John Gould, the bird-artist and taxidermist, stuffed them for him and mounted them in a glass case.

The travellers journeyed on through forests of beautiful great oaks and immense myrtles. In the villages, every hut was completely concealed in an orchard of pomegranate and pistachio trees. That night they lodged in a smoky wicker hut, congratulating themselves that the rain had ceased, to give them at least a dry night.

SUNDAY, 3 MAY - A day of disappointment and frustration for Fellows. "Started early for CHERALEE [Çıralı]." In high hopes that the 'old castle' reported to be the ruins of Corydalla, Fellows was bitterly disappointed to find that Cheralee was just another name for DELIKTASH [Deliktaş, Pierced Rock], or PORTO GENOVESE, near the city of OLYMPUS. He had been here before, in 1838, and had not been particularly impressed by the Hellenistic port, or the Roman remains.

More curious and exciting was a fascinating bright light, high up on the hillside. This was the YANAH DAH [*yanar dağ*] or 'Burning Mountain'. It was supposed to be the den of the fire-breathing Chimaera, whom they had already encountered at Tlos. The 'volcano' is a mephitic flame, which "has issued continually, and unvaryingly, from time beyond the reach of history." It gives a brilliant light and a very hot, smokeless flame.

It is the source of many legends, including that of the Phoenix, which rises uninjured from the fire. In science, *Phoenicopteris* (Greek, crimson wing) is the flamingo. As it flies up, the 'glow' of the 'flames' can been seen under its wings, the tips 'burnt' black by the mythical fire. More practically, the real fire was used by peasants for cooking - though it would not function on stolen meat! The soot was a valued cure for sore eyelids. In the bottom of the hole was a deep pool of sulphurous water, a sovereign remedy for all skin diseases.

The flame is visible quite far out to sea. Captain Beaufort had been so intrigued by the bright light, seen unwavering all night from his ship, that the next day he took to horse and rode up the mountain to investigate the source of this phenomenon. He was most gratified to find that he had discovered Pliny's Chimaera. He made a sketch of it in his notebook and added a passage about it from a French translation of Pliny's text, which he had on board amongst his extensive library of over two hundred books, including many in French, a language he enjoyed reading.

Mount Olympus marked the extent of the peregrinations of Fellows's band of explorers and now it was a case of his taking them all the way back again, to get to Macry in a week's time, in order to be there for his appointment with Captain Graves. Macry was on the west coast, well over 100 miles away, and there was no road to follow and no map marking the route. So, having wasted valuable time coming here, Fellows unhesitatingly turned back into the mountains again, to join their former path at Haggevalleh. It was annoying to have to forego exploring Pamphilia, but to find a way across the vast hinterland of Lycia would bring him ample compensation.

166

IX Lycia, the interior; Rhodes

Turning inland to pass behind MOUNT PHOENICUS, at their *menzil*, CHICOOE (River Village), at first the travellers were unable to obtain provisions, the villagers having mistaken the strangers for Turkish officials, agents of the hated Pasha of Idin, come to seize their produce. In fear, they had denied having any, but when they realized their mistake, and that they would also be paid for their foodstuffs, plentiful supplies were forthcoming, with firewood as well. By the time the party were back in Smyrna, the wicked Tahir Pasha had been apprehended and brought to justice.

MONDAY, 4 MAY 1840 - The Englishmen recrossed the long Greek bridge and passed the tombs of Limyra for the third time. It was intensely hot, but there was ample shade from the dark myrtles and the oleanders, their delicate pink blossoms a poignant reminder of the English dog-rose, in flower at home at this same time. "Under every spreading tree...a platform is erected, which, with a fountain, is the never failing companion of the Turk roadside." Pitchers of water would be left for the use of travellers, and for the ablutions of the Faithful.

About 6 miles north of Limyra, up what Fellows assumed to be the Arycandus river, the explorers discovered a marvellous group of about twenty rock-tombs, "all as if fresh from the chisel", their good preservation due to channels cut into the rock above them, which drained off the rainwater. With wooden doors fixed across the entrances, they had been put to practical use as granaries[1]. Real granaries [pl. 54] were constructed in a similar way, once more showing how the architecture of domestic buildings, which had been the models for temples and tombs in antiquity, had remained unchanged over the centuries.

That night, their tent was pitched on a knoll, in a very pretty, but apparently uninhabited, place, until they saw an overshot mill in the valley below. Its kindly owner provided the party with eggs and milk for their evening meal. The day's ride had been so peaceful in the lovely sunshine that Fellows, whose emotions were always easily aroused, was greatly moved.

"I had heard others speak of a melancholy being caused by an overwhelming effect of the sublime," he mused; "but it is not melancholy when better analysed; it is a thoughtfulness and feeling of gratified pleasure which affects me, and I long to express what perhaps is better indicated by the prostration of the Oriental worshipper than by any verbal description; I feel as if I had come into the world and seen the perfection of its loveliness, and was satisfied. I know no scenery equal in sublimity and beauty to this part of Lycia."

WEDNESDAY, 6 MAY - This was to be another glorious day of picturesque scenery, with the excitement of a discovery. Climbing slowly up the ravine, the group left the colourful fruit trees and softer landscape of the river valley to enter the "wilder grandeur" of the mountains. Their rugged outcrops were covered in the deep green of walnut trees and pines; different trees, and they could have been riding through the Peak District of Derbyshire.

About 35 miles from the sea, the Englishmen had the joy of finding the extensive remains of a forgotten city. With great zest and enthusiasm, they set about the search for an inscription giving the name. This was no easy task. Among the broken walls and fallen columns concealed in the thick scrub, it would not have been surprising had one of them tripped and sprained his ankle, even broken his leg. In the sunshine too, many a snake found the warm stones an inviting place to bask and a convenient location for a search of its own - for a tasty rat or lizard, whose scurryings often startled the Englishmen, absorbed in their - antiquarian - hunt.

They, at any rate, were successful. This was ARYCANDA, confirming Fellows's hope that they had, indeed, been travelling up the ARYCANDUS river. The termination '-anda', of course, indicates great antiquity, though the remains are mostly of the late Greek or Roman period. The city had been abandoned in the 6th century AD. Excavations began in 1978 and many more ruins have been uncovered.

One large Roman tomb has a particularly ornately carved doorway, with winged figures flying on either side of a bust over the lintel. Benches, like the Turkish *peyke*, supported on lions' paws, ring the inside walls; the back wall is of polygonal masonry. The chamber itself is over 20 feet square, the benches 5 feet wide. The ceiling had been plastered over and painted.

168

*98. Arycanda, tomb
entrance.*

There are several similar buildings, arranged in terraces, one above the other, the roof of one forming the 'patio' entrance to the building above it. Higher up the mountain, there is a theatre. Some of the Cyclopean walls are buttressed, but they had all been much damaged by falling rocks. The baths are extensive, with two tiers of windows and large halls with the characteristic circular ends.

The Englishmen spent two hours here, the first major discovery they had made for some time. It renewed their zeal and enthusiasm for the archaeology of this lovely country and brought the history of its people closer. "There is great excitement and pleasure in discovering these cities, once so splendid," Fellows averred, "whose sites even have been for twenty centuries unknown."

Leaving behind the forest and entering a flat, barren, plain, the explorers pressed on for another two-and-a-half hours, and by nightfall had reached AVELAN [Avlan], a tiny place with only three "miserable" houses. They had journeyed about 25 miles, an unusually long distance, but they were crossing flat terrain, the going much easier than mountain tracks.

Still heading north by compass bearings towards the great Taurus Mountains, the following day, they came upon an enormous lake, AVELAN GOULOU [Avlan Gölü], three to four miles wide and ten miles long, much the same size as the Lake of Ascania and nearly four times that of Lake Windermere in England, but where their maps showed nothing at all. It took the cavalcade two hours to pass along its shores and they were all gladdened by the sight of such an abundance of waterfowl, ducks and swans.

The plain, at an elevation of about 3,000 feet, stretched away in all directions as far as the eye could see. It was terribly bleak and bitterly cold, even their thick felt capotes failed to keep out the icy wind. The land was given over to the cultivation of wheat. Fellows observed that only the bearded variety was known in Turkey. This plain is still the largest tract of arable land in the country. The lake was drained in 1953, but the plain is frequently under flood.

The river they had been following all the morning, a noble stream some thirty feet wide, quite suddenly disappeared with a tremendous roar into a large cave. The Englishmen were told an interesting story concerning this cave. *Vaktiyle* (in the past), at a time of drought, the Pasha of the district had rewarded some men, who, greatly daring - and well armed with guns and talismans against all eventualities - had entered the cave. Much to everyone's relief, Allah be praised! the men were not assailed by any wild beast, murderous brigand, or evil genie and, after walking for about three hours, along a level, sandy plain inside the mountain, had returned unscathed, heroes of the hour.

But their fears were real enough, and, likewise, the courage of Fellows and his companions in crossing this unexplored, unmapped territory should not be underrated. "This district is entirely unknown to Europeans...no maps of course exist. The disadvantages of this are very great, as we know not where to steer or what places to ask for." Few Turks would ever have left their villages and, in any case, villages were a rarity in this wilderness. Apart from getting hopelessly lost, there was always the anxiety of finding provisions for seven people and ten or eleven horses. Unexpected illness or accident could spell total disaster.

Nothing daunted, and dismissing these fears of the faint-hearted, Fellows was equal to the task. The map he laid down of the interior of Lycia, if not completely accurate, was to be of inestimable value to Lieutenant Spratt and his companions in 1842, as well as to many other travellers, who would explore Lycia during the next decade as a result of this journey.

About an hour farther on, in the middle of this hinterland and much to their surprise, they arrived at a large, bustling town, ALMALEE [Elmalı], the modern capital of Lycia. It was far larger than Idin, and Fellows reckoned there were as many as 25,000 inhabitants. Spratt proposed the more modest figure of only 8,000, much the same as today's population. Only a few were Turks, however, the majority being Armenians or Greeks.

The tanning and dyeing trades flourished here, as well as commerce in grain, leeches and the skins of hares, which coursed abundantly over these high grasslands, their fur much prized for the linings of the traditional long robes of the wealthy. Cereals, sugar-beet, fruit and vines are the produce of today. Two khans bore witness to the importance of this place, the bazaars were busy, and fountains spouted in the streets. Despite the small number of Turks here, several mosques were a reminder to the travellers that they were in a Moslem land. In Fellows's view, the oldest, built in the fifteenth century, even rivalled the mosques of Constantinople for elegance and beauty of decoration. It had the full complement of four minarets. The air was perfumed by the cedar-wood fires. The cries of the *müezzin*, the sound of the camel-bells, and the rattling of stork-bills, all added to the Eastern magic of the place.

So, for the first time since they were in Hoozumlee, a month earlier, the Englishmen put up in a khan. It was large with two storeys, under a flat, grassy roof, but the building was rather broken down, the loose slats in the walkways and stairs making them a hazard. Fellows remarks on a curious practice: here, and at every other town where the population was not predominantly Turk, the Governor sent a Kezann to stand outside the door of their room. The reason given was that they and their property were under his protection and he could not answer for the honesty of people, other than his own.

The friends took their breakfast on the roof-top, a splendid vantage point from which to look down on the town and into the courtyards of the houses, hidden at street level. The panorama of the distant Taurus Range to the north and east was a spectacle of grand proportions, and the everlasting plains all around them, so different from the mountains and the coastline that they had travelled through so far, invoked sensations of awe and wonderment at the diversity of creation.

The Englishmen spent their leisure taking a 'lounge' through the bazaars, but they were troubled by boys pointing at them and shouting the insults "Frango" or "Ghiaour", on account of their strange appearance and Frank clothes, their pale faces, blue eyes and fair hair perturbing, even menacing, to those unaccustomed to such complexions. Mania was not with the friends to shoo the lads away, having remained in the khan to mend their torn clothes and worn saddle-bags. The Menzil-khanner, meanwhile, lay back smoking his chibouk, complaining loudly that, in spite of the large non-Moslem population, he was unable to obtain his arrack, the newly-elected Governor having imposed severe penalties on anyone found disobeying the Prophet's Law.

SATURDAY, 9 MAY - With the cavalcade reassembled, the party set off once more, initially in a northerly direction, but they soon turned westwards, keeping the Taurus on their right. Shortly after leaving Almahlee, they came to a mountain [Elmalı Dağı], which they skirted on the west side, to arrive at a village encouragingly called ESKY HISSAR. It was reported to be full of ruins, as its name suggested, conjuring up visions of a wonderful city like Stratoniceia, that other Esky Hissar. Disappointment followed, when, after much searching and questioning of the peasants, nothing more than two or three rock-tombs could be found, and a portion of Cyclopean wall. None the less, this was an interesting discovery: it was the site of PODALIA.

Its importance was reinforced later in the day, when the travellers came across a curious rock sculpture, a tablet on which were clearly carved a wild boar, and above it, in a pediment, an eagle. There was also an inscription, some other figures and a swag of leaves. Fellows fancied it might have been placed there to mark the boundary between two districts of this area, known in antiquity as MILYAS.

99. *Carved tablet near Podalia.*

Ascending ever higher into the foothills of the TAURUS MOUNTAINS, the air became extremely crisp and cold. For the next three days, they would be travelling through the Yeeilassies [*yayla*, high summer pasture]. Villages in these cool uplands corresponded to others nearer the coast, or in river valleys. The entire population and their animals migrated from one to the other according to season. Twenty or thirty groups a day, with their entire stock, were trekking up from their winter quarters to this vast fertile tableland, 4,000 feet above sea-level.

The gatherings looked like scenes from an illustrated Bible. In the early morning [*sabah*], the Englishmen might see as many as one hundred head of cattle, sheep and donkeys, with several camels piled high with agricultural implements, household utensils and the tents [*çadır*] and awnings [*tente*], carpets and cushions of a family home. They would be led by the father [*baba*], staff in hand. By his side, a young man [*adam*] would stride along, his gun

173

slung over his shoulder, carrying their precious decoy partridge [pl. 134] in a wicker cage. A slender, classic gazehound followed at their heels. The mother [*anne*, or *ana*] with the rest of the family and their pets and servants came next, some walking, others riding donkeys. At the rear were the shepherd boys, guiding the animals and looking after the young calves and lambs, carried by donkeys in panniers.

The tranquil rhythm of this life, though hard, was apparently a very healthy one; there were many centenarians among the family groups, lovingly cared for by the younger generations. Scharf sketched these caravans, his artistic eye relishing the gay colours and picturesque groupings. At home, he worked them up into a large oil painting which was bought by his friend John Kenyon, for the generous sum of 25 guineas. The picture - *A Lycian migration from the valley of the Xanthus* - was hung at the Royal Academy exhibition of 1845.

On their first day of travel across these pastures, they completed a seven-and-a-half hours' ride. That night, they rested very contented with their progress, revelling in the immensity of the plains under a clear, frosty, night sky, in which the moon and the stars shone with a crystal brilliance. Three fires were needed to give any semblance of warmth, the wood coming from the sweetly-scented cedars and the *arbor vitae* trees [*Thuya orientalis*].

"They are very large [over forty feet high], of distorted and wild shaped branches, spreading like a fir." Earlier in the day, while sketching one, a young lad, curious to see what Scharf was doing, had unwrapped his turban to bring out his treasure of snuff, which he politely offered to the artist, a gesture typical of the delicacy of manners, which so appealed to the Englishmen.

The next day - had they known it - marked the centre of this huge plateau, SATALA-YEEILASSY, the *yayla* of Satala, being the summer quarters corresponding with Satala-Cooe, Satala village, in the Xanthus valley. Many archaeological remains lay scattered about, and they saw several more tablets, corroborating Fellows's theory that they were boundary markers. From here on, the path gradually descended and they had the guidance of a westerly flowing river, which would join the river Xanthus.

After trudging through the soft, marshy uplands for nine hours, the party came to their first "green spot", where they could, thankfully, pitch the tent. It was typical of Fellows to remark: "No place is without its interest." His attention had been caught by two springs of icy water, spouting out from some rocks, and the ruins of a Turkish khan, composed of pieces of old sarcophagi, including a portion of a Greek inscription, which, of course, he instantly copied down.

MONDAY, 11 MAY - The day began as before, but after three-and-a-half hours, the travellers came to the SATALA BRIDGE over the Xanthus, which they had crossed five weeks earlier. It gave them that cosy feeling of pleasure as of unexpectedly meeting an old friend. Fellows could now be positive that he had been travelling in the right direction and that his party would arrive in Macry on time. They could even allow themselves the luxury of resting up to let the heat of the day pass, before commencing the final descent, down the valley of the GLAUCUS[2] to the coast, by the route Fellows had discovered on his 1838 journey. The river flows almost due west for about twenty miles to debouch into the Bay of Macry.

Late in the day, the cavalcade wended its weary way into MACRY, the Englishmen's excited anticipation tempered by a dread foreboding - from the heights above the town, they had not seen the *Beacon* riding at anchor as expected. They had been travelling for three months, over hundreds of miles of unmapped country, yet Fellows had managed to bring his party to Macry exactly as planned, in accordance with the Instructions from the Admiralty. His dismay and disbelief can only be imagined, when, on enquiry, no news of Captain Graves, or of his ship, was to be had.

Perhaps his orders had been countermanded; perhaps he would yet sail into the bay. Only one person was likely to be able to shed light on the matter - the Vice-Consul at Rhodes. Fellows resolved to go there forthwith, in spite of the lateness of the hour. The companions took a hasty meal, while Mania was dispatched to hire a boat to take them across the fifty miles of water to the island. Then, leaving their baggage in the questionable care of the Menzil-khanner, with the temptations of this Greek town to try him, the three Englishmen and Mania embarked. With Fellows's habitual bad luck at sea, the wind immediately dropped.

TUESDAY, 12 MAY - "Lay tossing in a scorching sun with scarcely a breeze to move us. Our capotes alike sheltering us from the night air and noon-day heat."

WEDNESDAY, 13 MAY - "At two o'clock, Mr. Fellows awoke me saying the light-house was in sight. On looking out, I found we were just entering the harbour. Windmills and palm trees lined the coast. The moon, large and red, was nearly sinking to the horizon and the deep blue sky was thickly studded with stars, each reflected in the sea. The strong turreted walls and massive towers impressed me with the grandeur of the chivalric ages, and the domes with slender minarets peeping between cloven battlements, told a tale of the victorious Moslem over the Templar, the call of the Guards round the walls, breaking the silence of the night."

Scharf woke up to think himself back in Covent Garden Theatre, RHODES looking exactly like a stage-set for Shakespeare's *Hamlet*, with the Ghost walking the battlements, his disembodied voice echoing in the stillness. "The morning soon began to dawn 'in russet mantel clad'," he quoted, "bringing with it a series of magnificent effects."

They landed, the thirty-six hours' endurance at an end, spread their carpet on the quay, and indulged in the luxury of tea and toast by a charcoal fire. "Truth-telling daylight", however, brought Scharf sharply back to reality, showing that the romantic walls and towers were nothing but empty ruins. When the Gate was opened, they found the town in an uproar, due to the murder of a Greek youth in the Jewish quarter. The population at that time was about 33,000, mainly Greeks, with some 7,000 Turks, 3,000 Jews and, according to Spratt, a dissipated, reckless collection of Frank leech-merchants and some "mongrel" Europeans.

The British Vice-Consul, Mr G. Wilkinson, entertained the party very agreeably, but was, alas, unable to throw any light on the whereabouts of the naval Captain. He was, however, able to hand Fellows a letter dated 7 March, from Lord Ponsonby, the British Ambassador at Constantinople, which explained that in February he had applied to the Sublime Porte for a Firman for the excavations at Xanthus. This had been refused, owing to the "generality" of the demand. He wrote of other difficulties too, but added the assurance that he would continue to do all he could to resolve the problem.

It was a severe blow, as Fellows had been hoping to see an expedition mounted that autumn. This was now clearly out of the question and, in spite of the success other countries seemed to have in obtaining Greek sculptures for their museums[3], he feared the Marbles from Xanthus might now be lost to England. He would, of course, find out more once back in London, but for the present, there was nothing else he could do. After buying some much needed provisions for their return journey, the group set sail again for Macry.

Was ever a man so unfortunate at sea? The boat scudded over the water at a good pace in a strong breeze and in only three-and-a-half hours they were already halfway across. Then catastrophe. First of all the foremast snapped off, leaving only one sail and causing the boat to roll horribly; then the wind turned about, the breeze from the Turkish shore sending the craft back again towards Rhodes.

"For nearly twenty hours we made scarcely any way, suffering much from the broiling sun, and paddling along with the feeble oars of the idle Greek sailors." At last, at one o'clock in the afternoon of the second day, they landed, returned to their lodgings and partook of some restorative arrowroot. This whole sorry episode had cost Fellows three-and-a-half days, and nearly £2 for the dreadful voyage out and another guinea for the equally appalling return.

For relaxation, the next day the Englishmen rode southwards, up a steep zigzag path, then down through a highly cultivated valley of vines and mulberries, to the Greek town of LEVISSE, called by the Turks, TUSHLEE [Taşlı, Stony; now Kaya, Rock], built on what Fellows believed had been the site of CISSIDAE. Levisse was considerably larger than Macry, but its 300 stone-built, square, Greek houses were deserted for the summer, as were the few Turkish houses clustered round the Aga's residence and mosque. Except in a metropolis like Smyrna, the two nationalities lived separately. All official business was done here, Macry forming a port for this place.

During the afternoon, the Englishmen sat contentedly in the shade, but ruefully deliberated on the failure to obtain the necessary documents from the Turkish Government and its dismal consequences to the long anticipated expedition. In more positive vein, Fellows discussed the book he would write of this journey, of the many discoveries they had made, and how, with Scharf's illustrations, the wonders of Lycian sculpture and monumental art would be laid before the public, encouraging others with more specialized knowledge than he, to take up the study of the Lycian people.

X The return to Smyrna; Ephesus

"From its geographical situation, Macry is very unhealthy: the winds from the sea eddying and the clouds driven back from the mountains" keep the air stagnant and oppressive. Dr Wilde spoke of an early morning "fen-damp" and of the dangers inherent in the pools of lying water. "Plague generally lurks within it [Macry], or its neighbourhood, and it suffers periodically from intermittent fever, which generally breaks out in the month of May." It was high time to leave Lycia and head back towards Smyrna, before the journey became exhaustingly hot.

Though sad at having to depart, and thinking that he would never see this intriguing land again, Fellows had the gratification of having made a number of important discoveries - and with friends to share his joy and enthusiasm. They had travelled through a most enchanting landscape and had got to know and appreciate its charming, courteous people. Personally, he had gained much knowledge from this excursion and had taken great delight in its archaeological treasures. His dream to see some of these glorious works of art preserved in the British Museum was stronger than ever, having found out how the weather, earthquakes and the ignorance of the Turks, all combined to destroy the ancient cities, and that the museums of France, Germany and Austria were clamouring to get antiquities for their collections.

Scharf was sad too, but the immediate cause for his sorrow was the disappearance of the little dog, which had attached itself to the party at Mellassa and had accompanied them ever since. Mania had named her Canilla (Greek, cinnamon, her colour) and taught her to perform tumbling tricks and to beg for her meals. Her favourite food had been toast. Now she was gone - but not so their drunken Menzil-khanner, who was to remain with the party for another week yet.

The long journey back to Smyrna, roughly 300 miles, began on SATURDAY, 16 MAY 1840. It was to take them ten days of hard riding. To avoid the heat, they would start before dawn, covering a distance of a nine-hour ride, only stopping if there were ruins to examine. At the hottest part of the day, they would rest for a couple of hours. By this system, they hoped to advance 30-35 miles each day. They had first to cross the Taurus Mountains; then, although he had no map or chart to refer to, Fellows aimed to steer his party in a northerly direction, across a hundred miles of unknown territory, to strike the river Lycus near Laodiceia. Here, he would be in country he had travelled before. A westerly course, veering slightly to the north, should then bring the explorers safely back to Smyrna, and civilization.

Fellows wrote: "I have long wished for this excursion, but could gain no information as to its practicability: having however, when on the Yeeilassies, noticed the direction of several ranges of mountains, I resolved to explore the country further, and expect to lay down a map for future travellers." He was to accomplish both tasks - superb achievements by any individual, by any standard - but for neither of which has he received proper credit.

They completed the first 30 miles without stopping, except to rest. "In this sultry weather, Yar-hoort [*yoğurt*] with sugar and rice is very cooling and refreshing. Arrowroot is now our chief support with Greek bread [pitta] and cold fowls, which we have always ready. Our Rhodian tea will just take us to Smyrna."

In the Yeeilassies, they continued to see fragments of temples and tombs, but nothing worthy of close investigation. Climbing to a height of over 4,000 feet, the lonely cavalcade crossed the Taurus and entered a well-populated area of corn production. The only trees were the *arbor vitae* and the cedar. The higher slopes were quite bare and the tops of the mountains snow-covered. Their *menzil* that night was idyllically located on the hypothetical junction of Lycia to the south, Caria to the west and PHRYGIA to the east.

MONDAY, 18 MAY - The explorers had now entered another high tableland, the plains of GULE HISSA OVASSY [Gölhisar Ovası, Rose-Castle Plain], which stretched away for ever. In the distance, sixty miles to the north-west, the majestic peak of Mount Cadmus [8,000 ft] assured the English party that they were truly on their way back, for had they not spent several days at its foot examining the ruins of Aphrodisias, two months earlier?

180

As on the plateau of Almahlee, they were not altogether surprised to discover a vast lake, but this one was three or four times the size of the other. This lake [Gölhisar Gölü] has since been partially drained. It was then the home of enormous fish, the barbel [*Barbus barbus*], 2-3 feet in length and weighing up to 20 pounds. Like its relative, the carp, it is very good eating. The whole tableland was highly cultivated and spotted with villages. The Englishmen found a number of archaeological stones in the Turkish burial-grounds, but none of 'pure style'. Needless to say, this large area was a total blank on Fellows's inadequate maps.

Next day brought the party a gruelling trek across a feature-less sandy plain with gravelly hills, the poor soil reflecting back the hot sun and no shade given by the dwarf furze bushes that were scattered here and there. In that barren land, the travellers crossed the DOLLOMON-CHI, fifty miles above the place where they had forded it so long ago, to take them into Lycia. Here, appropriately, they at last lost sight of the mountains heading the Xanthus valley, "the richest country in the most beautiful specimens in nature and art."

WEDNESDAY, 20 MAY - A day of incident to break the monotony of the journey. Mid-morning, the travellers came unex-pectedly on the bustle of a great bazaar held in two large sheds at the small town of CARREEUKE [Karahuyuk]. Fellows and Scharf

100. Carreeuke bazaar.

181

took the opportunity to sit under a tree by a fountain, paying the 'owner' for the shade! From there, they watched the scene of people coming and going, their animals waiting patiently to be loaded with their purchases.

Fellows estimated that there were some two thousand beasts of burden - donkeys, horses and camels. "The women had purchased shoes and spinning-wheels and the men were driving home cows, oxen, mares with foals, and asses laden with bags and pots of all kinds. The men and children are equally laden with apparel, carpets and new jars." He recorded that the useful ploughing oxen [pl. 35] were sold for as little as 80-100 piastres, less than £1, a cow and calf cost 150k.[1], but the horses as much as 2½ *Türk lirası*[1]. He also found out that in Turkish auctions, the final bidder buys the 'lot' at the price offered by the preceding bidder.

The market came to an end at noon precisely, proclaimed by the town-crier, who then locked the gates. Hesketh now joined the other two, his hand injured and bleeding. He had been off on his own, shooting, and the barrels of his gun had exploded from his doubly charging them by mistake. Mania soon had the hand bound up, and fortunately, that was the only accident the party suffered on the whole of their travels.

They were surprised to find that their clothes were not remarkable in this town. The Englishmen had, in fact, been mistaken for the Frank leech-dealers, who were expected to arrive any day. The leeches [*Planaria fusca* and *Hirudo medicinalis*] came from the great lake and the surrounding swamps. They were plentiful in these Yeeilassies, where they were collected in the summer months, and all the year round from the coastal marshes and river valleys. Some Agas actually farmed them.

Medicinal leeches were bought by licensed dealers, generally Italians, who took them to the Capital to be exported to Europe and America. There was a considerable black-market trade too. In Spratt's view, all leech dealers were "unprincipled fellows, fertile in plans for defrauding the revenue." Almahlee, with its important leech-bazaar, was the centre for the trade.

Leeches are collected by simply wading into the water with bare legs, allowing the blood-suckers to stick to the skin. They drop off when gorged, and are carried in linen bags, which can easily be soaked in streams on the way to market. Any that die, float to the top and can be discarded. There was a considerable mortality rate, but at 120k. the oke [*okka*] (£1:5:0 for 2¾ lbs), the merchants made a great profit and, like Demetrius Scufi, Fellows's former dragoman, could live well and even travel the world.

THURSDAY, 21 MAY - The line of their route still took them northwards, over a pass on MOUNT HONAZ [nearly 8,500 ft]. "A perfectly new and splendid view then burst upon us, and showed me at once that I had completed a circuit in my travels, as I now recognized before me the peculiar features of the hills of Hierapolis and the valleys of the Lycus and Maeander." What a triumph for Fellows, whose experience and skill in direction-finding had brought his party to his intended destination.

The limestone plain was bleak in the extreme, flanked by barren sand-hills. Some twenty miles away, they could make out "the bright, white spots" of Pambook-kallasy [Pamukkale] on the slopes of Çal Dağı, where they would be in two days' time. As they rode on, the ground grew wetter, cut up by the irrigation channels of DENIZLEE [Denizli, having a sea]. "My horse", wrote young Scharf, "is at times very obstinate...but he is strong and admirably suited to the Turkish roads, and at clearing mud and ditches was an excellent leaper." He clearly appreciated its skills in this type of going. The Zoorigees called the animal '*deli beygir*', crazy horse, but Scharf had a better name - 'Old Scratch', the Devil.

Although one of the largest towns in Asia Minor, Denizlee was unaccountably quiet, the shops and bazaars closed, the streets empty. It transpired that the Governor had abused his powers and imposed extra taxes, contrary to his Firman from the Capital. The inhabitants had risen up in arms and he had just escaped as the travellers arrived. The Englishmen had, indeed, remarked on the stud of fine horses that had passed them, which apparently belonged to the fleeing Aga. An armed deputation of a thousand men was even now on its way to Constantinople, to put their case before the Sultan. The few people left behind had locked the gates of the bazaar and shut themselves up in their houses.

This had fortunate consequences for the English travellers, who could, for once, stay in the khan, undisturbed by the usual crowd of watching Turks, and they were more than glad to remain quietly indoors after the long, arduous ride of these past few days. The Menzil-khanner, however, thinking to take advantage of the situation, insisted on remaining longer than a day, but here Fellows could at last dismiss him and rid the party of this ill-tempered, drunken individual, who had caused them so much embarrassment and distress by his disgraceful behaviour. He was now free to return to his home, about fifty miles away. He had been with them for two-and-a-half months.

A Turkish merchant was now engaged to take them to Smyrna in five days for a fixed sum - about 9 guineas. He was, in any case, going there himself, to pick up some merchandise, so it was an excellent arrangement for him. The new cavalcade consisted of this fat Turk; an immense Zoorigee; four riding horses for Fellows's party; two pack-mules; and another, loaded with extra pack-saddles for the merchant's return journey; and two donkeys.

On the way to Smyrna, Fellows wanted to show his friends several sites well-known for their archaeological and biblical associations. The first of these was LAODICEIA, once famous for its fine-quality black fleeces. It was one of the Seven Churches of the Apocalypse, which had been Fellows's chief interest at the start of his first tour, but had become eclipsed by the excitement and overwhelming importance of the discoveries he had made later.

When Fellows was here before, the ruins had presented a melancholy sight, deserted but for a flock of bustards[2] standing in the fields, looking like four-foot tall, bewhiskered, tawny turkeys, and several sinister vultures wheeling about overhead. Now, it was alive with hundreds of sheep and goats, as of old, and cattle, horses, camels and donkeys pastured in the once open market-places of antiquity. The Yoorooks [yürük; nomad, from the verb yürümek, to walk] had set up their black goat-skin tents on the site, but they would soon be moving on, leaving the ancient city to its habitual gloom. Nearby, there was a little village, a truly-named ESKY HISSAR.

The investigators could find nothing to suggest a Christian church, but could identify a Roman gymnasium, an *odeum*, and a very long stadium [AD 79], all close together. On the other side of the city, there is a small theatre and a second, larger one with 43

184

rows of seats of fine marble, supported by lions' paws, many having letters on them, like a modern seating system. "The style of architecture spoke of a late age," Scharf wrote disparagingly. The site was excavated in 1961-63.

Looking up the valley of the LYCUS [Çürüksu Çay], they could see a strangely pointed hill, about two miles away. At its foot stood the ancient city of COLOSSAE, to whose Christians Saint Paul had addressed one of his Epistles. The party did not pause, however, pressing on instead to the ancient city of HIERAPOLIS[3]. The remains are extensive and on the immense scale of the Romans. The earlier Greek city had been destroyed by an earthquake in AD 17.

The baths (now a museum) are a complex of buildings, covering quite a large area. In the centre, there is a vestibule with a colonnade of 8 square pillars. Three of these had somehow become warped, giving them a curiously artificial appearance, which indeed they are, being made of chips of marble set in a matrix. Leading out of this vestibule, there are several massive, high, vaulted chambers [52 ft high] and another great hall. The theatre is also on the grand scale of the Romans. It could hold 15,000 spectators, the frontage measuring 300 feet. It has recently been restored and is used again for productions of the Classics, and for folklore.

Beyond these buildings, there is the 'Sacred Pool' - medicinal baths and shrine of the Romans. It is quite deep, but the mosaic pavements and pieces of broken columns can easily be seen through the warm, crystal-clear water. Bubbles of carbonic acid gas continually broke the surface, giving off an unpleasant smell from the admixture of sulphur. The water tasted strongly of soda. Nevertheless, the Englishmen put it to its use and enjoyed the luxury of a hot bath in this Roman pool. The town has now reverted to its former rôle of spa and holiday resort, the medicinal bath used as a swimming-pool.

To the north of the city, there is a vast necropolis, as many as 2,000 tombs have been counted. They are mostly of the temple or house types, and contain seats for mourners, who, it is thought, may have lived above the grave-chamber. While resting here themselves, some kindly villagers brought them newly-made, hot yoghurt, deliciously refreshing in the sultry heat.

The English tourists then started to inspect the cause of the 'bright, white spots' they had seen from the distance. Strange calcified deposits from the saturated waters, which gush out of the limestone hill, 330 feet high, have spread over the land for an area of some 300 yards. Fellows aptly describes the material as resembling cuttlebone. Scharf gives a good idea of the scene by comparing it with waterfalls, which appear motionless, when seen from afar. Some petrified cascades are piled up like the dripping basins of a tiered fountain. "The whole of the mountain foot is covered with long, high ridges, which are the self-made channels of the rushing water, the original bed having been long washed away."

This phenomenon dates back to time immemorial - over 14,000 years has been estimated. The material sparkles in the noonday sun and at dawn and dusk takes on a pinkish hue, giving the place an air of enchantment. The nearby village is called PAMBOOK-KALLASY [Pamukkale; Cotton Fortress]. It is now a noted tourist resort.

SUNDAY, 24 MAY - "Rose before 4 and before ½ past 5 were on our journey." Travelling north-west, they crossed into the province of LYDIA by a bridge over the MAEANDER. About thirty miles down stream were the ruins of Antiocheia, the first of the antiquities they had gone expressly to examine. That was nearly twelve weeks ago; within a few days, they would be back again in Smyrna and this incredible journey just a memory.

They paused briefly to look at ancient TRIPOLIS [Buldan], the city where the Apostle, Saint Bartholomew, had once taught, and where Saint Philip suffered martyrdom in AD 80. There was little to see, the city having been destroyed in the Middle Ages.

The following day, the travellers got up at two in the morning and were on their way by a quarter past three. They were making for PHILADELPHIA, another of the Seven Churches. Nothing remained of the ancient city, beyond some fragments of walls and four immense brick piers, from which arches would have sprung. This had been a Roman temple, "dedicated to nominal Christianity, but showing...traces of heathen superstition." In the modern town of ALLAH-SHEHR [Alaşehir; City of Allah], there was still a flourishing Christian community.

The plain was made beautiful by fields of the opium poppy [*Papaver somniferum*] in full bloom. Though the white, lilac or purple flowers are less showy than the red English field poppy [*P. rhoeas*], they are a spectacular six inches across and make a foil to the bright clothes of the women, who were collecting the sap. The great globular seed-pods are scratched, causing the milky sap to exude; it dries and is scraped off. "The entire produce is monopolized by the Government at a fixed price, and the sale of opium is not allowed in any part of the country," Fellows was informed. The town of Afyon - meaning 'opium' in Turkish - is the modern centre for its production, under strict licence.

By TUESDAY, 26 MAY, the party had arrived at one of the most important places of historical and Christian interest - SARDIS [Sart, near the modern town of Salihli]. Under King Croesus [6th century BC], it had been the richest city in the world. Sardis was rebuilt in AD 17, after an earthquake, but since the Middle Ages, it had been allowed to decline.

Fellows and his friends found only some Yoorooks and a Greek miller, who gave them hospitality. His mill was turned by the waters of the PACTOLUS [Sart Çayı], a tributary of the ancient HERMUS [Gediz Çayı], in which King Midas was supposed to have washed away his curse of gold. There is still a mill at Sardis, and the river does, in fact, contain gold[4], washed down from the mountains.

Fellows's party went first to examine the well-known Temple of Cybele[5] [c. 300 BC], only slightly smaller than the great Temple of Diana at Ephesus. It exhibits the oldest known example of the Ionic Order, though the columns remain unfluted and the lovely swirling capitals are also unfinished. When Chandler visited the site in 1765, 5 columns were standing; Cockerell in 1812 saw only 3; and by 1824 only 2 remained, "melancholy proof" of the ravages "not of time," wrote Strickland in 1836, "but of wanton barbarians, who, from the absence of limestone in the vicinity, resort hither as to a quarry, and consign these marble columns and capitals to the lime-kiln." The site has been excavated several times, and many buildings have been unearthed. In 1958, 13 columns of the Temple were re-erected.

Tons of earth, thirty feet deep in places, had buried much of the city, obliterating the huge theatre [3rd century AD], with seating for 20,000. "Tho' numerous, [the remains] fail in carrying the mind back to the Lydian Kings," Scharf averred; "the Romans have intervened." A series of strange mounds, like tumuli, not far away, were, however, believed to be the tombs of the Lydian kings.

WEDNESDAY, 27 MAY - The Englishmen took leave of the kindly Greek before dawn. They were now travelling along the regular caravan route from the interior of the country to Smyrna, almost directly west from here. After a six-hour ride [28 miles], the party stopped at the opulent town of CASSABAR [Turgutlu]. On this excellent road, by evening they were more than halfway to Smyrna, now less than 50 miles away.

That night, they set up their little encampment for the very last time, the ultimate *menzil* of their journey. It was with real sorrow that they reflected that their carefree, nomadic existence was drawing to its close. But all good things come to an end, or as the Turks have it: *hangi gün vardır akşam olmadık?* - has there ever been a day without an evening?

THURSDAY, 28 MAY - The last day of their great trek through untrodden Asia Minor, or, as Fellows euphemistically called it, their "excursion". During these last days, the unimpressive scenery had been much enlivened by the many camel-trains, ten to fifteen animals linked together by a rope. Their heads were decked with some dozen bells; fifty more were festooned along their backs, making a brave show - and an appalling din. Charms and tassels hung from their necks, and a tassel extended the length of the tail. The camel-muzzles were adorned with beads and shells. The *kervanbaşı* rode in front on a little donkey looking ridiculously small, over-burdened by its large, gaily-coloured pack-saddle. Its braying and the raucous cries of the Bashee added solo parts to a ground-bass of low, gargling complaints from the camels and a counterpoint of merry jangling bells.

"By a quarter after 4, we were all moving along the road." Four hours later, from the top of a mountain, the English travellers caught their first sight of the Bay of Smyrna [pl. 19] and the roofs of the town. Scharf was entranced. "The descent into the valley, thro' a narrow pass in the rocks, was magnificent. The pale blue distant mountains contrasted with the deep azure blue of the bay (on which the white sails of many vessels glittered as stars at the commencement of evening, before the moon, with her curious beams, has assumed nocturnal sway) is indescribable. It is impossible, without seeing it, to conceive the undulating form and delicate tints of the mountains, contrasting with the high, round, yellow hill, topped with a Castle, and surrounded by Cypress groves. Between the trees, the red roofs of many houses peeped, but the minarets were not yet visible."

Two hours outside Smyrna, at BOURNABAT [Bornova], "a busy little colony of Franks", they rested at an inn kept by an Italian. "The re-occurrence of familiar European luxuries: table, chairs, napkins, etc., only rendered the distinction of European and Turk customs more palpable and to the latter of which we had become perfectly reconciled," Scharf reflected. They breakfasted in 'pure English style' and took the opportunity to catch up on world news and local gossip, learning that the hated and feared Tahir Pasha of Idin had been taken into custody by the Sultan.

When they at last arrived in SMYRNA, their passage through the crowded town on their way to Salvo's Navy Hotel was a very public one. Scharf recounts: "I was recognized by many of my Turkish friends and, in the Greek quarter, no door or lattice was unoccupied by some gazer, many bowing to acknowledge us as a brother Frank in a Frank town." It was an affecting 'homecoming'. That evening, the 'celebrated' Englishmen joined the *passeggiata*, sauntering along 'Bond Street' to receive the congratulations of their acquaintances and to experience again the charms of this cosmopolitan city.

Fellows found great satisfaction in the successful outcome of his endeavours. "I was rejoiced at the termination of a journey so pleasurable in itself, and promising to afford me subjects of high interest for research and reflection to the end of my life." He contemplated quiet study and discussions amongst his scholarly friends at home. But Fate held a different future for him. When, later that evening, Mania came to take his leave of the gentlemen he had served so well for the past three months, he spoke the Turkish proverb: *dağ dağa kavuşmaz, insan insana kavuşur* - mountains never meet, but men do! - a truer saying than any of them could have believed.

Finding that they had a couple of days to wait before a steamer left for Athens, Scharf and Hesketh decided to make a quick trip to Ephesus. Fellows had, of course been there on his previous journey, so he stayed behind to arrange their passage to Greece. They hired horses and a French guide for the 50-mile ride south to this famous ancient city.

They set off at 10 o'clock. The day was oppressively hot, but the good road brought them to their destination by 8 pm, reducing the scheduled posting-time of fourteen hours by a good four hours. They had, of course, been unencumbered by baggage-animals. They entered the cafinet and were offered only pilaf of plain rice, yoghurt, pitta bread and water for their supper. There was no sleeping accommodation at all, the *peyke* already occupied by some Greek farmers. Nothing daunted, the young men dossed down on the ground outside, wrapped up in rugs.

SATURDAY, 30 MAY - Not surprisingly, they rose before dawn, eating up the reheated left-over pilaf and, by daybreak, they were among the ruins of EPHESUS. In antiquity, it had been one of the principal ports of the Mediterranean, but by late Roman times, the harbour was completely silted up and the city abandoned to the ever-enveloping sand. In its day, Ephesus had had a population of 300,000; now it was just the haunt of wolves and jackals, the usual denizens of ruins.

The first building to claim their attention was the vast complex of the Roman gymnasium [2nd century AD]. The huge arched chambers, with recesses and alcoves much excited their imaginations. The massive columns measured 4 feet, 6 inches in diameter and 40 feet high. "We did not feel surprised at visitors carrying off chips of this costly marble," Scharf declared, "as [coming] from the great Temple of Diana, tho' more deliberate authority places the vestiges of its foundations much nearer to the sea and without the walls of the city." This was, indeed, the truth. Its imposing dimensions can only be imagined - it had 127 Ionic columns, 60 feet high, 36 of them sculptured, and was considerably larger than the Parthenon at Athens.

The tourists now began to walk round the base of MOUNT PION [Panayır Dağ; 510 ft], keeping it on their right. They found the small *odeum* [2nd century AD] and, farther on, the shattered columns of the forum and the famous theatre [2nd century AD], more than a semicircle in the Asiatic manner. From the 66th row, nearly 100 feet up, they reflected on the grandeur of this structure, which could hold 25,000 spectators. No seats remained, and the proscenium was only a mound of rubble, yet the giddy drop to the stage below was indeed awe-inspiring. In their imaginations, they could visualize the scene when the silversmith, Demetrius, rushed in with a mob, while Saint Paul was preaching[6]. The accoustics of this theatre are superb, and it is again in use for pop concerts and the like.

Near here, the young men remarked on a "vast pile of ruins...thrown together in one heap," all that was left of the Library of Celsus (now reconstructed), and beyond it, the ruins of the Temple of Serapis. Broken, monolithic, granite columns and blocks of costly marble all spoke of the former magnificence of Ephesus, but, with so little visible, let alone still standing, the tourists were bound to agree with Fellows's sentiments. "Ephesus, a place so familiar to the mind that one cannot but feel disappointed at not seeing realized all the ideas associated with it...whilst contemplating the few silent walls which remain." The ancient city presents a very different picture today, with streets and buildings reconstructed and filled once more with throngs of holiday-makers.

Continuing round the mountain, the young men came first to the large Coressus Gate, constructed out of assorted elements from former buildings, then to the stadium [1st century AD], "tolerably entire", and some buildings that might have been prisons. Beyond these again, was the Grotto of the Severn Sleepers[7], which they could not examine, being without lights. Finally, they arrived back at their starting-place, the Magnesia Gate [1st century AD].

The tourists then turned their attention to the "extinct" town of AIASALOOK [Ayasoluk]. It was built on a hill, about 1½ miles north of Ephesus. There, "the most costly marble and stones of the Ephesians were destined to sparkle in a second, but ephemeral existence." The city had been built almost entirely with stone pillaged from the ancient site. The hill was crowned with a Byzantine Castle, now in total ruin. This town had, in its turn, been destroyed in the fifteenth century.

At its entrance stands the Gate of Persecution [7th century AD]. Over the arch, some pieces of broken sarcophagus had been set to form a frieze. They showed a scene from the *Iliad*. This frieze had been the subject of comment ever since the end of the seventeenth century[8]. When John Cam Hobhouse, friend and executor of Byron, went there with him in 1810, he noticed that parts were so damaged that they were in danger of falling down, prompting him to remark: "It is to be lamented that this fine piece of sculpture has not been secured in the cabinet of some European antiquary." The chief portions were, in fact, soon to be acquired by Sir Gregory Page Turner, of Battleston Park, Bedfordshire. In 1824, they were sold to the 6th Duke of Bedford for Woburn Abbey.

Lower down the hill stands the Basilica, or Mosque of St John, built in the sixth century on the site of the Saint's grave. It had been a huge building [400 ft x 130 ft], and had contained columns taken from ancient Ephesus. In 1330, it was converted into a mosque, sacked seventy years later, and finally destroyed by an earthquake. In the Mosque of Isa Bey [1375], Scharf remarked on the pretty arabesque and net-work ornamentations and the alterations made to Roman capitals to create Turkish designs. The village of Aiasalook has now disappeared. At the foot of the mountain, there is now Selçuk, a town of 200,000 inhabitants.

Back at the cafinet, the young men joined the Greek farmers for a cup of coffee, and learned that they had come over from Kirkadazi [Kuşadası; now a holiday resort], to harvest the already ripe corn, growing in the fields all around the ruins. By 9 o'clock, they were on their way back to Smyrna. This time, the ride took them nearly twelve hours, having taken a 'short cut' near Caravan Bridge, which, by the very nature of such things, had taken them well out of their way.

Back in the Navy Hotel, Scharf was overjoyed to find some letters waiting for him, telling him that all was well at home. Thus ended a most satisfying and delightful excursion, a fitting finale to the magical weeks spent in this enchanting antique land. A veritable dream come true.

XI The voyage to Athens

Fellows was now taking his young assistants to Athens. Scharf and Hesketh would then be able to contrast the Asiatic-Greek tombs and temples of Asia Minor, and the distinctive Persian-Greek style of Lycia, with the 'real' Greek art and architecture of the Acropolis ruins.

It was not yet ten years since Greece had gained its independence from Turkish rule and the country still remained relatively isolated from the rest of Europe, and was seldom included in the Grand Tour. It was too far away, too wild and too dangerous, so lately the scene of bloody battles and lawlessness. Were there not perfectly preserved Greek temples in Italy, which a tourist might visit without risk, while enjoying the pleasures of polite society in Rome or Naples? Of that, there was nothing in Athens, a small town under construction, the home of 'exiled' Bavarian officials and some dubious foreign merchants.

SUNDAY, 31 MAY 1840 - The English party were up at dawn as usual, and, after a light breakfast, they went on board the French steamship *Dante*, bound for Syra [Siros], an island of the Cyclades group. The Captain greeted them warmly, remembering having taken their baggage from Livorno to Civita Vecchia on their way out in November. What a long time ago, that now seemed! True to form, during the night a gale sprang up, tearing the sails to shreds and making the voyage extremely unpleasant.

MONDAY, 1 JUNE - The ship steamed into SYRA at 7 o'clock. After breakfast, the passengers were taken to the New Quarantine Establishment (Lazaretto) across the bay from the town. It was still unfinished, the foundation stone having been laid by King Otho just over a year before[1]. Disinfection was insisted upon by all European nations for people, merchandise and letters coming from the Levant, as a necessary precaution to stop the spread of plague and other contagious diseases endemic in the East.

There were quarantine stations at all ports in every country, varying from miserable old hulks moored off shore, to large complexes affording every possible comfort. The best Lazarettos were almost like hotels, except for the restrictions imposed on contact between people. Others were filthy, run-down hovels that could cause more illness than they were trying to prevent. Confinement was from one week, if no epidemic were raging at the time and the traveller arrived in good health, to about forty days, as implied by the word 'quarantine', from the Italian, *quarantina*.

The New Lazaretto at Syra was to become one of the best of such establishments. Fellows had seen to it that his companions should pass their period of detention here, instead of at Piraeus, the port for Athens, where Strickland had spent a truly dreadful time in 1835, obliged to begin each day with an exhaustive "bug-hunt". Although they are now derelict, the buildings of the Syra Lazaretto remain. It is just like a khan, being a series of rooms off an arcaded walk, where the occupants could take the air, protected from the hot sun. There is a two-storey block in the centre, where the Governor lived. An imposing double flight of marble steps leads up to his quarters on the first floor. Below, is the accommodation for his staff. There are also the ruins of the fumigation rooms, hospital and barracks.

Every group of inmates was under the care of a shabbily clad *Guardiano*, whose duty it was to keep the groups apart by brandishing a long wand. But for this restraint, 'guests' were free to spend the time how they liked. Food was purchased from an adjacent restaurant and delivered to them by the Guardian.

Quarantine was, inevitably, tedious, but to people such as Fellows, it could present an enjoyable period of repose, a time in which to recover from the rigours of a journey, and in which to adjust the mind to the changes they were about to experience on re-entering a European country. "Quarantine and the existence of a regular post, marks the verge of our European world," Fellows reflected. "I have been so perfectly withdrawn from the moving world, that I know nothing of England, since Feby last, when the Queen [Victoria] was about to be married."

Part of a letter was published in *The Athenaeum*, and gave a list of the places he had discovered, so announcing to the world of art

Quarantine guardian, Syra, June 11th 1840

101. *Syra, Guardiano of the Lazaretto.*

and letters the existence of the ancient cities of Lycia, the rivers
and the plains, all new to the antiquarian and the geographer. "The
letter was rendered so very indistinct by the process of fumigation," the Editor complained, "that we are not certain that the

names are all correctly copied," which, in fact, they were not. The information was valuable, nevertheless, and scholars could look forward to learning more precise details, when Fellows's account was published in book form in 1841.

Reviewing the achievements of his journey - "threshing out the corn of our late abundant harvest" - as he put it, Fellows could congratulate himself on the discovery of 7 more Lycian cities, to add to Xanthus and Tlos, found on his first journey. He listed them as "Pinara, Arycanda, Cadyanda, Sidymeus, Massicitus, Calynda, and Gagae", their names ascertained by inscriptions and coins. He had amassed a sizeable collection of unique coins, to be described in a supplement to the book, and his plant collection would become the basis for a Flora[2], another supplement.

Scharf meantime, busied himself inking-in his drawings and painting some of his larger sketches. He would supply 30 plates of the archaeological remains - their appearance as a whole and details of their sculptures - to illustrate Fellows's *Account*. Hesketh, on the other hand, passed his time in the congenial company of a group of Englishmen and some German musicians, who were also immured. He was able to roam the barren island with his gun, looking for game, or row out to sea in a boat provided by the British Consul, Richard Wilkinson, brother of the Vice-Consul at Rhodes.

SUNDAY, 14 JUNE - Each day passed in much the same way until that morning, when the *Guardiano* announced loudly that they had received their *Pratique*, or Certificate of Health, and were free to go. Needless to say, the Englishmen did not delay their departure, but repaired at once to the Hôtel Pension de l'Europe, which had been recommended to them. Later, their erstwhile Guardian, now clean and neatly attired in Greek dress, called to receive his payment of 3 drachmas a day, about 26 shillings each.

The companions spent the day in the town, which had greatly expanded since Fellows was here on his way home from his earlier journey. The island is composed of two conical hills, the slopes covered with square, white houses, like those of Castellorizo. The people of Syra were mostly Catholics, whilst those of Ermoupolis, the town on the second hill, were Greek Orthodox.

The *Aphrodite* was supposed to sail for Athens the following Tuesday, but two more days went by in constant anxiety as to whether she would sail or not. The Englishmen went on board to sleep, but had to go ashore for meals, returning at intervals for news of the sailing. The Captain, having successfully augmented his passenger list and his cargo, weighed at dawn on THURSDAY, 18 JUNE. The whole of the next day, his ship lay becalmed under a hot sun. As ever, Fellows was to have an aggravating and uncomfortable voyage.

SATURDAY, 20 JUNE - At 10 o'clock, they landed at PIRAEUS. This new town had 300 houses, its busy streets and waterfront giving the impression that it would soon outstrip ATHENS in importance. Fellows hired a hackney carriage to carry the friends the 5 miles between the two places. It was a monotonously straight road, but the Acropolis hill stood out magnificently before them the whole way, unspoilt by any sight of the modern town below, hidden from view behind a high wall.

They took rooms for a week's stay at the Hôtel des Etrangers and dined early. The afternoon was spent pleasantly enough in a 'lounge' through the town, having decided to leave the excitement of the ancient ruins until the following day. Morritt had declared it very agreeable to walk here. "Over almost every door is an antique statue or basso-rilievo, more or less good though all much broken, so that you are in a perfect gallery of marbles in these lands."

Scharf said: "My first impression was the ample fulfilment of every idea I had entertained of the remains of the most glorious city." Of the actual antiquities, it was their colour, as much as anything, which gladdened his heart. "The singularly beautiful colour of the marble (white, stained with yellow and orange) varied by the reflected light of the deep blue sky and glittering in the intensely bright sunshine produced an effect dear to me."

When, regardless of the Athenian sun, he climbed up onto the Acropolis to make sketches, he found that his efforts were frustrated. The heat caused his water-colours to dry too quickly and a high wind made the paper move about, so that he could not draw the straight lines the buildings demanded. Notwithstanding, he declared: "The mind was additionally gratified by a tremendous roaring of the wind amongst these mighty columns, which materially heightened the effect produced by their visible magnitude."

Fellows, meanwhile, was making social calls. He went first to present himself to the British Minister, Admiral Sir Edmund Lyons. He had escorted Otho, the second son of Ludwig I of Bavaria, to Greece in 1833, as King of the new nation. Fellows then went to see the historian and friend of Lord Byron, George Finlay, who had made his home in Greece. Finlay accompanied them to the Acropolis, where excavations and restoration work were going on, so that they might be given access to the store, where the latest "discovered marbles" were being kept.

One sculpture[3], called 'Venus stepping into her car' (now known as 'A charioteer mounting'), formed the subject of a foot-

102. Athens, 'Venus stepping into her car'.

note by Fellows in his *Account.* He was "much struck by the similarity" of this figure to those on the Harpy Tomb at Xanthus [pl. 82]. At that time the Athenian sculpture was attributed to the 7th century BC (now dated to c. 500 BC) and suggested an equally early date for the Xanthian Tomb.

"The spirit of Restoration is strongly working and at present chiefly devoted to the Erectium [Erechtheion]." Scharf's eye was caught by some slabs from the Temple of Wingless Victory [Apteros Nike; c. 410 BC]. "One figure of Victory[3] is especially beautiful. The perfection and symmetry of the visible form, through the exquisitely sharp-cut drapery, is inconceivable," he wrote, 'inconceivable' being his highest term of praise. "Besides this are two other pieces of the same subject: Victories leading a Bull to sacrifice[3]. This Victory is the identical one mentioned by ancient authors as considered by the Greeks as the beau ideal of art and the subject of wonder to all the connoisseurs in the great Periclean age" [5th century BC]. He was thrilled.

Finlay introduced them to Kyriakos Pittakys, another of Byron's friends and now Superintendent of the excavations. "He is a talkative little man and expressed much interest in our researches of Asia Minor," Scharf was pleased to say. Pittakys took them to the Temple of Theseus [now called the Hephaisteion, the Temple of Vulcan], which had also been made into a storehouse for newly-unearthed sculptures.

Here, they saw an unusually large (more than life-size) upright bas-relief of a man in armour "cut in the Eastern style", the pose reminiscent of the figure of Salas at Cadyanda [pl. 62]. This was a *stele* or grave-marker [c. 510 BC][4]. The ornamental parts of the armour, the short pleated skirt, the background, and the letters at the bottom giving the names of the deceased, Aristion, and the sculptor, Aristokles, all had remains of a red colour on them. There were also traces of blue on the body-armour. Pittakys gave Scharf permission to sketch these 'new' sculptures, otherwise kept from public view. Many years later, he was to incorporate these drawings into a comprehensive history of Greek art[5]. These 'discovered marbles' were immensely exciting to see, at a time when the Elgin Marbles were almost the only Greek art known outside Greece itself.

THURSDAY, 25 JUNE - "On returning home to breakfast, I found Professor Müller with Mr. Fellows. He breakfasted with us and expressed great interest and curiosity in our drawings and inscriptions, which he read with great facility. He gave us much valuable information and his deep learning illustrated many curious points." This distinguished German archaeologist died only two months later, at the early age of 43. Fellows, expressing his deep personal sorrow, wrote of the immense loss which Europe had sustained by the death of "one of her greatest scholars in all the vigour of life". Carl Otfried Müller is buried in the Ancient Academy of Plato.

They all met again at Finlay's house, at a dinner party arranged for the tourists to meet Professor Ludwig Ross[6], the German architect and archaeologist, who had been Conservator of Antiquities in Athens from 1833 to 1836, and was now engaged on reconstructing the Temple of Wingless Victory, which had been destroyed by the Turks in 1688. Ross was to visit Xanthus in 1844. One of the many interesting subjects they discussed at length was the question of the use of polychromy by the ancients[7].

Müller's thesis was that every building and all statuary had been coloured to some degree - the buildings and temples actually painted, the statues only tinted. To corroborate this, he quoted Plutarch, who stated that it needed the skills of a tinter, a gilder, and a varnisher, to finish the work of a sculptor, as is known to have been the case in ancient Egypt, from whence the Greeks gained much of their knowledge.

With regard to statues, Müller said that flesh was left uncoloured, except for wounds, blood and lips, which were tinged red. Eyes were painted or, in the case of a Deity, they were made to sparkle by the insertion of coloured glass or gems. The whole figure was then lightly waxed or varnished over, which rendered the flesh a creamy ivory and muted the colours.

After dinner, the men retired to the library, where their discussions continued, turning now to modern Greece, its politics and the unpopularity of the young King, only 17 years of age, when he ascended the throne. Finlay, an authority on Greek affairs, asserted that the people completely ignored the policies and regulations of the Bavarian Government, never considering obeying the edicts of the Monarch, since he had no power to

200

enforce them. He told his listeners that the King's position had recently deteriorated on account of the proposed return of the Islands to Turkey, which would engender a loss in revenue and a crippling increase in taxation.

"The King, since his accession, instead of devoting himself to improving the country agriculturally and facilitating commerce by roads, had amused himself by building an enormous palace." It had a frontage of 300 feet, and had already cost the colossal sum of £150,000. [It is now the Parliament Building.] Scharf went on to report that King Otho had just laid out a garden [National or 'Royal' Garden], monopolizing the greater part of the city's water supply. "It is expected that some act like this, some deprivation felt by everyone, will cost him more dear, than any diplomatic actions." Quite true, for there was a bloodless revolution in 1843, bringing a new constitution, lessening the King's power. He retired to Bavaria in 1862 and was deposed a year later.

Scharf had, as usual, been taking an interest in the Greek people. "The costume of the lower Athenian women is very striking," he declared. "Their dark hair is brought, in a plaited band, over a white fillet, which half covers the fez. The hair is also let hang down the back in many close plaits, resembling the ancient Carians. Their jacket is long and braided (but coarsely), the under-vest is a loose white dress, the girdle of which reaches over the loins, and the breast is left very much exposed. Few women are without their distaffs, or the little boys without their kites.

"The costume of the men is particularly elegant, but, when worn with affectation, as we have seen lately, it becomes disgusting," using the word in its original meaning - 'tasteless'. Unlike the Greeks of Turkey, the Athenians wore bright colours over a white shift. Finlay's servant was attired in "purple and crimson velvet, covered profusely with gold, and a white petticoat, with crimson leggings. [It] made me regret that the imposing effect of this livery is not more generally known."

SATURDAY, 27 JUNE - "Ascended for the last time the Parthenon steps...I never believed myself so fully sensible to the beauties of the Parthenon and Erechtheum and Propylaea as they, one behind the other, vanished from my sight as I, from time to time, turned back on descending the Acropolis steps." Although he would never return here, the joy of these days and the splendour

103. Athens, George Finlay's servant.

of the ruins would be remembered, and the knowledge acquired used again and again during his future career.

That afternoon, the tourists returned to Piraeus and boarded the *Giovanni, Archiduca d'Austria*, a steamer of the Austrian Line, established in 1837, running between Greece and Trieste, then part of the Austrian Empire. Once again, the much-travelled Fellows knew the Captain from taking this Line on his way home in 1838. Amongst the other passengers, they struck up a friendship with Sir Charles Bannerman of Aberdeen, who was travelling with his son, Alexander (of much the same age as Scharf) and his tutor, before Alexander went up to Cambridge. They were all to meet frequently in Venice and go sight-seeing together.

XII Homeward bound

The passage through the Greek islands to CORFU and then up the Adriatic coast to Ancona took a week, but, for once, the weather was good, and the ever-changing views made this a voyage of real enjoyment. By FRIDAY, 3 JULY 1840, they had reached halfway, the vessel putting in at ANCONA, where there was a very good Lazaretto. Many passengers disembarked here, to continue their journeys overland, after a period of quarantine.

At this point, Fellows's architect, Robert Hesketh, chose to leave and return to England independently. During the latter part of their time in Turkey, a rift seems to have developed between him and the other two. Scharf mentions his name less and less, but finally makes the comment: "We felt his parting less on account of the gradual manner in which he had weaned himself from us. He had never attached himself to us by a single act of assistance during the whole of our travels. Selfishness has been his main principle, his sketches he kept to himself[1]and he seldom spoke except to argue, contradict, or find fault. On entering a town, he invariably separated himself from us and preferred exploring the antiquities alone. Few persons with equal talent and opportunity have made less profit by them. We parted coldly and always on good terms, without a single expression of Gratitude from him to Fellows."

It must have been a severe disappointment to all concerned that Hesketh's personality was so incompatible with the others. In an obituary, Robert Hesketh is described as a "genial, happy companion". In 1842, he became District Surveyor for Bermondsey; other, similar, appointments followed. He was the architect of several schools and churches in the City. In collaboration with F.P. Cockerell, Charles Cockerell's son, he lengthened the nave and made extensions to the Church of St John-at-Hampstead, giving the interior a look of St Peter's in Rome. In 1849, he was elected a Fellow of the RIBA. In 1868, he became Surveyor to the Worshipful Company of Goldsmiths, a position he held until his death in 1880, aged 63.

One more night on board brought Fellows and Scharf to TRIESTE, where they disembarked directly into the New Lazaretto for a second period of quarantine, necessary as Greece was still regarded as an Eastern country in this respect. The establishment had accommodation for 200 persons and the quarantine harbour anchorage for 60 ships. It was one of the most famous, set up in 1720 and rebuilt in 1769 to an excellent design, making a stay here a pleasurable experience. The travellers only had to remain one week this time, but vowed they would not have minded had it been for longer.

Before leaving for Venice, Scharf joined young Bannerman and his tutor on a two-day trip to see the stalactite caves at ADELSBURG [Postajna, in Slovenia]. The 28-mile journey took ten hours, so it was late evening before they arrived. Nevertheless, guides took them to explore the huge halls and passages of this subterranean labyrinth, hung with all manner of fantastically-shaped, petrified 'icicles'. The caves extended for nearly three miles, the river Poik running through them. In its waters lives the primitive amphibian, *Proteus anguinus*, which has both gills and lungs.

These shadowy vastnesses, lit by the moving torches of the guides, of course encouraged Scharf into all sorts of imagery, transporting him into Hades one minute and onto Prospero's Island the next. The party spent three hours underground. When they returned to their hotel, they found a good supper waiting for them, though it was long after midnight. Back at Trieste, Scharf assured Fellows that he had never enjoyed "so great a treat".

WEDNESDAY, 15 JULY - The vessel from Trieste steamed into VENICE and moored at the entrance to the Grand Canal. "By the form of every distinct building and object, I knew I was in Venice," Scharf wrote, "but having entered at the widest part, I missed the compactness and effects of the canals conveyed to us by paintings and descriptions." As at Rome, he felt he already knew the place, yet somehow it was subtly different. Scharf was not prepared for the extreme ornateness of the architecture.

"The minds of these ancient Venetians appear to be too full of quaint devices and ideas to permit a row of 5 columns or railings [to be] of the same pattern, or one window or capital to be like the

204

other." As for their art, he confessed: "The grand works of the Venetian School present a new style to me, but as yet the severer Roman and Bolognese Schools claim my preference." Except for paintings by Canaletto, there were very few examples of the Venetian School to be seen in London at that time - there were only some 200 paintings in the National Gallery all told - so Scharf's mind was not accustomed to their style of painting. "Here glorious colour appears connected with unrelated vulgar forms and coarse action. The silks and satins are almost as offending as Rubens's costume and, with P. Veronese's architecture, is always obtruding."

He held the works of Tintoretto in the highest esteem, but had to deplore his "want of expression and sootiness of colour." He could not credit that so great a Master should have used them so opaquely. The poor quality of the paintings was, however, due to dampness and layer upon layer of grease and soot from the thousands of altar candles burnt over the centuries. Modern cleaning has revealed his bright palette. Scharf made copious notes and sketches, amongst which was one of the famous painting, *St Peter, Martyr*, by Titian, in the Church of SS. Giovanni e Paolo. In 1866, it was destroyed by fire, so, like others of his sketches, this is a valuable reminder of a vanished work of art.

Fellows had taken rooms at the expensive Europa Hotel [now Europa-Britannica], while the Bannermans had gone to Danieli's Hotel Royal [Royal Danieli Excelsior], then, as now, considered the best. They met frequently to go sight-seeing together. Fellows and Scharf were also to encounter several of their artist friends from Rome, escaping from the heat and pestilence of summer there.

On the night of SATURDAY, 18 JULY, they crossed with a small party of friends to the island of Giudecca, to the Church of SS. Renditore (the Redeemer), built in thanksgiving for the deliverance of Venice from the plague of 1575/76. There was an all-night festival to celebrate that salvation. "The concourse of people was very great and illuminations, paper lanterns, music, singing, and eating seemed equally attended to everywhere."

THURSDAY, 23 JULY - The long journey back now began in earnest. They made brief stops at PADUA, VICENZA and VERONA, before taking the mail-coach through the TYROL to

INNSBRUCK, where they rested for a day, after this stage of four days without a break. Another full twenty-four hours, sitting with their feet up in a coach with a pool of water sloshing round in the bottom of the carriage, brought them, at last to MUNICH, capital of Bavaria.

This town was still under construction, building having started less than twenty years earlier, on the accession of King Ludwig I in 1825. Edifices had been commenced at many different points at once, leaving great empty spaces in between. As the buildings stood isolated from each other and could not be seen together at one glance, they failed to make any grand effect. "The new streets are very wide, the houses are high and empty and grass still grows in the midst of the roads...In the best streets, the most superb palaces are occupied by bakers and cheesemongers, for want of better tenants."

Two conflicting styles of modern architecture were in evidence here. The chief municipal buildings, museums and theatre were designed in flamboyant Neoclassical style by Leo von Klenze, who had been employed by King Otho in the restoration and rebuilding of Athens. Unlike English Neoclassical architects, von Klenze followed the concept of polychromy in ancient Greek buildings and had painted the backgrounds of the pediments, the spaces between the gilded leaves of the capitals, every cornice and every moulding, either an overpowering red, or a harsh, bright blue. Allegorical statues were gaily coloured and a lavish use of gold, glittered in the sunshine.

It was an extraordinary experience for Fellows and Scharf to see the actual effect of painted sculpture and architecture, the recent subject of discussion at Athens and just faintly glimpsed on the ancient buildings and carvings in Lycia. The impression given was altogether startling, but it was all so freshly done, no weathering having as yet softened the impact.

In marked contrast was the restrained Neo-Gothic style of the domestic buildings and University, designed by Professor Friedrich von Gaertner, Director of the Bavarian Royal Academy. He had also worked in Athens and was the architect of the Royal Palace. The façades of his houses were elaborately ornamented, but they were all of the same proportions, presenting streets of long perspective lines, unvaried by the slightest projection, Gothic arch after Gothic arch, receding into the distance. Any carved decoration was so flat that it looked more like painting, the converse of *trompe-l'oeil* architecture, as it were. The roof of the Ludwigskirche really was painted.

The Professor's own home was squeezed in between the church and the University Library. Gaertner was an old friend of Scharf senior, and young George took this happy opportunity to bring him his father's greetings. In 1846, on a visit to his native land, Scharf senior was able to see Gaertner for himself, just before the Professor's untimely death at the age of 55.

George Scharf senior was born in Mainburg, forty miles from here, and had studied art in Munich from 1804 to 1810. Then he wandered through Germany to the Low Countries, joining the British Army fighting Napoleon, serving as Lieutenant-of-Baggage. He was present at the Battle of Waterloo. Lieutenant Scharf went with the army to Paris, where he had the unique experience of seeing the greatest works of art from all over Italy collected together in the Musée Napoléon (Louvre), before they were returned to their owners, or dispersed. He came to London on 6 January 1816, celebrating that anniversary every year thereafter.

George Scharf senior seems to have been a good linguist, though towards the end of his life, his spelling betrays an increasingly heavy German accent. George junior, when young, must have been influenced by his father's speech, judging by his style of writing. Father Scharf taught his sons both French as well as German, which they understood and spoke well. This was, of course, of great benefit to young George in his travels. It enabled him to enjoy the delights of theatrical productions, and to converse with the various influential people in the art world, whom he met through Fellows's wide circle of friends.

One such was Professor Friedrich Thiersch, a philologist and philhellene, whose opinions on Greek art and culture Fellows greatly valued, and with whom they had a lively debate concerning the emergence of Munich as a major cultural city. With Professor Thiersch as cicerone, two-and-a-half days went rapidly by, visiting the King's art collections in their new buildings. Many of the best pieces had been purchased by Ludwig whilst Crown Prince, when Napoleon's loot was sold off in Paris in 1815. The paintings in the Pintothek were arranged in historical sequence, the sculptures in the Glyptothek, chronologically.

Of especial interest were the Aegina Marbles [c. 500 BC]. These are figures fallen from the pediments of the Temple of Aphaea[2], on the Greek island of Aegina. They had been found in 1811 by the architects, Charles Cockerell and Baron Haller von Hallerstein. Cockerell intended them to go to the Prince Regent, but a muddle and delay in negotiations allowed them to be snapped up for Prince Ludwig's budding collection.

In the spirit of the time, the Danish sculptor, Bertel Thorvaldsen, had restored them, making them 'as new'. The Townley Marbles in London had also been restored and 'improved', but when the Italian sculptor, Antonio Canova, was asked to do the same for the Elgin Marbles, he refused to touch such wonderful works of art. Though damaged, they are, today, considered more valuable than the 'perfect' Aegina Marbles, 'spoilt' by restoration.

The two tourists continued their homeward way through Germany by coach, newly-opened rail services and Rhine steamer, as far as COLOGNE, where they arrived, late in the evening of THURSDAY, 4 AUGUST 1840, after three days of travel. The ruined Cathedral was being rebuilt, only the medieval choir and the apse then existing[3]. Scharf was enchanted by the ancient building. "I never conceived so chaste and perfect a piece of Gothic architecture," he wrote in admiration. "They were chaunting the service and the organ struck me as being very fine."

He was less enthusiastic, however, about Rubens's *Martyrdom*, in St Peter's Church, which he described as a quite "unpleasant" composition. It was hung on a pivot-system, like a swing-mirror, with a "wretched" copy on the back. The original was turned to view only on Sundays and festivals. On the other days, the sacristan turned it round on the payment of 16 *groschen* [1s. 8d.]. Scharf admired the strikingly clear colours and found the head and expression of the Saint admirable, but censured the attitude of the limbs as "very disgusting".

Their travels now took them into Belgium, a newly-created nation, having gained its independence from the Netherlands in

1830, just ten years before. A railway, established in 1835 between Liége and BRUSSELS, brought them to the capital at the alarming speed of 20-25 miles an hour. The shops were all delightfully showy and lit by gas, which meant they could stay open until a late hour. At the Royal Gallery of Arts [Palais des Academies], Scharf saw more of Rubens's works, but he still could not get a taste for them - they were "too bloodily painted and vulgar". At 6.30 the next morning, the two travellers were on their way to the port of Antwerp, the train taking an hour-and-a-quarter to go the short distance of some 27 miles to the coast.

SUNDAY, 9 AUGUST - The last day of their great journey. Fellows and Scharf had now been away for almost ten months, with thousands of miles of travel behind them, in every conceivable conveyance: steamers, gondolas and ferry-boats; mail-coaches, diligences and light, one-horse carriages; trains and omnibuses; on horseback and on foot. So many changes of country; language; climate; currency - all now drawing to a close.

The day began by stowing their luggage on board the *Soho*, a vessel of the General Steam Navigation Company, which plied out of Antwerp every Wednesday, Friday and Sunday to St Katherine's Dock, hard by Tower Bridge. The crossing would take twenty to twenty-four hours, but they would tie up in the heart of London, enabling the travellers to go straight home from there. That settled, there was still the whole morning to devote to this city, the home of Scharf's least favourite artist, Peter Paul Rubens.

ANTWERP was more old-fashioned than Brussels, and completely Flemish. The women still wore the costumes to be seen in his paintings. The place was full of bustle and excitement at the forthcoming bicentenary festival of the artist's death on 30 May 1640. From 15 August to the end of the month, there would be celebrations of all kinds: fireworks; pageants; exhibitions; ships launched; the fountains were even to run with wine. The great Master's chair, with his name on the back and preserved under a glass case, had a garland of flowers on it in honour of the occasion.

Dutifully, Scharf entered the Cathedral to view Rubens's *Descent from the Cross*, which, in the event, pleased him better than the Cologne painting. The colours were less vivid, though that might have been due to the poor condition of the painting. "We

209

have a good copy in our Academy," he commented with satisfaction. By the time he left, all the covers had been closed over the pictures. In the Academy of Painting [Museum voor Schone Kunsten], he studied more works of the Flemish School and another crucifixion by Rubens, again "glaringly coloured, streaming with blood and very butcher-like in every department" - in a word: "disgusting".

A little before one o'clock, they went on board the *Soho*, Fellows finding, as always, several acquaintances with whom to while away the voyage. By 9 o'clock the following morning, they were in London - only to incur an irritating delay of three hours in the custom-house. Their main baggage had been sent from Trieste and arrived in mid-October[4].

At last, they were free to return home. Scharf thanked his generous friend and mentor for this marvellous and happy excursion and was assured that they would be meeting again quite soon to discuss the illustrations Scharf would do for Fellows's book. When young George finally arrived back at 14 Francis Street, he was happy to record: "I found home and friends as I left them, unaltered and the whole of my ten months' absence like one vast dream."

Two days after his son's return home, father Scharf called on Fellows to congratulate him on the success of his tour through Asia Minor and to thank him for all he had done for young George. He was delighted to hear Fellows praise George's work and express the high opinion he held of his behaviour and his admirable curiosity in the objects of their journey. Scharf junior, meantime, "ran" round calling on his artist and musical friends. He renewed his acquaintance with Charles Macready, who was now able to tell him personally how pleased he had been with the little book of theatrical scenes, George's first publication.

Scharf senior took a portfolio of his son's work to show Hullmandel, the Hawkins family, and all his learned acquaintances. He introduced his talented son to the Marquis of Northampton, a Museum Trustee, who had already taken a great interest in Fellows's discoveries of 1838, and who was to play an important part in the negotiations to acquire the antiquities from Xanthus.

Father Scharf soon set about helping his son to prepare his Lycian drawings for publication. He spent long hours shading and drawing on stone the figures from Cadyanda, which form the frontispiece to Fellows's second book of travels; the colour-plate of the figures of the Painted Tomb at Myra; the reliefs on the Horse Tomb and the Harpy Tomb at Xanthus; and many others, while George prepared wood-engravings and etchings of the smaller reliefs and scenes. By NOVEMBER 1840, all the plates were ready for the book Fellows had set himself to write, in order to publicize the existence of so many ancient cities and promote the study of the Lycian language, its culture and the natural history of that whole area of southern Asia Minor.

By the end of the following year, parts of the book had been published in German scientific periodicals, translated by Georg Friedrich Grotefend, the German philologist, who had deciphered the Assyrian cuneiform alphabet in 1802. As a result, many eminent scholars, especially from Germany, did, indeed, travel to

Lycia to explore that land and also made the journey to London, to examine the newly-acquired Xanthian Marbles.

George Scharf junior's skill as a draughtsman was beginning to be recognized and, in early DECEMBER 1840, he was offered a new opportunity to travel abroad, this time as artist to the geographer and naturalist, Sir Robert Schomburgk, who was being sent by the Government to survey the boundaries of British Guiana [Guyana] in South America. This tract of land, some eighty-eight square miles in extent, had been acquired in 1803. Schomburgk's name is remembered by the Schomburgk Line, which he established, and by the introduction into England of the giant water-lily, the *Victoria regia*, now called *Victoria amazonica*.

Scharf rejected the offer, however, and this time it was to be William Walton, Hullmandel's artist, who considered the appointment. He was to receive the standard salary of £100 a year with keep, for a three-year period. It would seem that George had had enough of foreign travel for, the following October (1841), he turned down the chance of becoming government artist to the South Seas Expedition.

Perhaps he just wanted to concentrate on ancient Greek art. Even so, shortly before, he had declined to return to Xanthus with Fellows on the first Xanthian Expedition. But that was a very rushed affair, and he would not have wanted to cancel his commitments at such short notice. Instead, Scharf continued with his art studies, making a little money by giving drawing lessons and fulfilling a few private commissions for portraits and Turkish scenes. One day, his father saw a fine young negro with a broom in Oxford Street and, knowing that his son wanted a model of that sort for a picture of Smyrna, took him home for young George to paint. Scharf also worked with his father on the architectural drawings for a course of lectures given by Charles Cockerell, Professor of Architecture, at the Royal Academy.

Fellows had been instrumental in obtaining some commissions for both the son and the father. George had been asked to make drawings of the Elgin Marbles for the British Museum, and Fellows had introduced Scharf senior to the Trustees as a lithographer of distinction[1]. He had also recommended him to a firm of booksellers to make a series of lithographic views of Fellows's home town of Nottingham, for which Scharf senior was to ask £3 each print.

By the SPRING of 1841, Fellows's second book, *Account of Discoveries in Lycia*, with illustrations by George Scharf junior, was published. But only the first half of the book is about his journey. In his enthusiasm for Lycia, especially its unknown language, Fellows devotes the whole of the second half - well over two hundred pages - to these subjects. He quotes dozens of Lycian inscriptions, with translations as far as possible and an essay by his friend Daniel Sharpe. There is also a long section on Greek inscriptions found in Lycia, the translations by Hermann Wiener. Fellows prints his own drawings, with explanations, of many Lycian coins [pl. 88], and there is the Lycian Flora by David Don.

Fellows settled back into his routine of attending the lectures and meetings of various Societies, including the BAAS meeting at Plymouth in JULY 1841. Soon, a whole year had passed by since his return to England, with no news of an expedition to Xanthus. Was that too to be nothing more than "one vast dream"?

PART THREE

I Preliminaries, 1841

Early in OCTOBER 1841, Charles Fellows unexpectedly received
a letter from the Trustees of the British Museum informing him
that a Firman had at last been received. They requested him to
send details regarding the exact locations of the various 'Marbles',
which he had recommended should be collected for safe keeping in
the Museum. With hope renewed, he replied at once, sending a
sketch of the site with the principal objects numbered in order of
importance.

*104. Xanthus, Fellows's sketch of the positions of the principle Marbles
to be collected.*

Then, fearing that the undertaking might fail through want of
local knowledge, Fellows offered to accompany the Expedition at
his own expense, so that he could point out the actual objects to be
removed. Three days later, on 15 OCTOBER, he had their answer
accepting his proposal and, with incredible speed, thirty-six hours

214

later found him at Southampton, on board the steam-packet *Tagus*, complete with tent, bed and bedding, canteen and stores. All at once, after the disappointment of Macry, the long-anticipated Xanthian Expedition had become a reality.

Fellows arrived at VALETTA, Malta, on the 30th, and there transferred to the naval steamship *Vesuvius* (6)[1], which was carrying stores to the survey-vessel *Beacon* (6), under the command of Captain Thomas Graves. The ship was lying off the island of PAROS in the Cyclades. Here, a week's delay occurred before she could sail for Turkey. This set-back was the first of many serious impediments to this Expedition; bad luck and mismanagement were to hamper the undertaking right from the start.

Captain Graves's Instructions were to sail first to Smyrna to pick up the Firman, and thence to the mouth of the Xanthus river, to put on board the objects indicated by Fellows. No funds had been allocated for the work, however, nor for the maintenance of the workforce. Fellows offered to provide this himself - money for tools, pickaxes, shovels, etc.; for food bought locally; for tips and presents to the Governors and helpful peasants; and lastly for the hire of camels and draught-oxen to pull the heavy cases of stones from the site to the sea. The financial problem solved, the *Beacon* sailed for SMYRNA, arriving there on 15 NOVEMBER. But a month had already gone by.

"A heavier cloud here hung over the expedition." The so-called 'Firman' turned out to be only letters dated as long ago as June, proposing no more than an inquiry on behalf of the Sublime Porte into what exactly the British Government intended. Fellows had not had any hand in the wording of the request and, unknown to him, an extra demand had been made to remove some stones from the Sultan's Palace at Bodrum, the site of ancient Halicarnassus. Xanthus was referred to only vaguely, as a village in the dependency of Macry.

Thus, the Expedition must have failed at the very outset, since Captain Graves would have first to return to Malta to report to the Admiral, before any new request could be sent to the Sultan. In the slowness of diplomatic proceedings, Fellows feared that months, even years, might go by before work could start at Xanthus. The only solution would be for him to set out for CONSTANTINOPLE himself, to sort the matter out.

Fellows took Captain Graves, resplendent in his naval uniform, with him, to give himself, a mere civilian, an appearance of authority. "I was gratified in finding that I had judged rightly," he commented with great relief. Xanthus was identified as being near the village of Koonik [Kınik] and the stones at Bodrum[2] were withdrawn from the request. The Firman was granted. Nevertheless, Fellows still had to wait for the official paper. A little over a week later, the Permit was handed to him. As an expression of sincere friendship between the two nations, it gave authority to the British Government to remove antiquities from Xanthus for the purpose of putting them in the Museum. The Captain, meanwhile, returned to his ship. His presence at the Capital had cost Fellows a further £50.

In modern times, allegations have been made against Fellows, accusing him of being personally responsible for the unlawful removal of the Xanthian antiquities. Apart from this action to save the Expedition, he had no rôle in this Government enterprise. On the contrary, his laudable attitude towards saving these unique sculptures from probable destruction, is deserving of the highest praise.

Fellows quickly bought a suitable present for the Pasha of Rhodes, to whom the Firman was addressed, and sailed for SMYRNA on an Austrian steamer. The passage should have taken only thirty hours, instead, it took an agonizing sixteen days. More precious time wasted. It was now mid-December. He then organized the purchase of the tools, and the *Beacon* at last sailed for RHODES. Six days later, on 21 DECEMBER 1841, she steamed into harbour.

A seventeen-gun salute was fired and Fellows and Captain Graves disembarked to present the Firman to the Pasha, Governor of this region of Asia Minor. The Firman, "a prodigious document", written on very thick paper and signed with the ornamental *turré* [*tugra*], the Sultan's official monogram, was read out aloud with great style and dignity. Yet another obstacle to the enterprise was here revealed. The river Xanthus belonged to the Pashalic of Rhodes, but the archaeological site belonged to the Pashalic of Adalia [Antalya], over a hundred miles away to the east, at the opposite end of the province.

Hadgi Ali Pasha himself resolved this difficulty. He explained that the Permit would be the same to whomsoever it was addressed, advising the Englishmen to begin their excavations, whilst sending a messenger to Adalia for confirmation. This was received, several weeks later, the Pasha of Adalia proclaiming that "the Queen of England was good, the Sultan was good, and that we were all brothers, and that we might take what we liked," Fellows recorded.

The Expedition had, therefore, full authority to take whichever stones were considered the most valuable as works of art, in the spirit of a gift from the Sultan to the Queen, to be kept in the British Museum for the pleasure and erudition of the public and antiquarian scholars. The presence of two Cavasses [*kavas*], official guards, protected the interests of the Sultan and his people. Two years later, the Firman was renewed without question for excavations to resume, proving that the Turkish authorities were quite satisfied. During the course of that Expedition, a representative of the Pasha of Adalia came over to verify the nature of the work.

Once more, the voyage proved painfully slow, taking five days to cross the 50-mile distance between Rhodes and the Lycian coast. It was after Christmas, when the ship finally anchored off KALAMAKI [Kalkan], two months since Fellows had arrived in Malta. Any relief he may have felt to have got this far at last was, however, to be short-lived. "My surprise was great," he wrote in careful understatement, when, just before disembarking, he found out that the Captain had no intention of taking command of the shore party and would, instead, sail away as soon as he had landed the men. A young Lieutenant, John Freeland, who had only joined the *Beacon* in April, was to be left in charge.

The whole Expeditionary force was to amount to no more than fifteen men and a boy, the Lieutenant, a Gunner, and a youth, the son of Consul Wilkinson. The assistant surgeon of the *Beacon*, Frederick Harvey, was to join them later. With almost unbelievable indifference as to the management and purpose of the enterprise, Graves refused them any engineering help and consigned the whole operation to Fellows, who was, after all, there only in a voluntary capacity, through his own initiative.

Leaving Fellows and the Lieutenant to search for the river
Xanthus, which was not marked on the charts, the *Beacon* sailed,
not to return until March. The castaways contemplated their
predicament with foreboding. There was no sign of human life, but
the dunes all around showed the ominous tracks of wild animals
and the men had the uneasy feeling that ravening eyes were upon
them, the fear reinforced by the circling vultures overhead. Large
fires were the answer, and at least there was no shortage of
driftwood.

As a measure of the difficulties they encountered without
proper equipment, it was found necessary to employ all hands to
haul one boat at a time - they had a cutter, a galley and dinghy - up
the river in full spate, to a temporary camp below the ruins. It then
took four more days of heavy toil to bring up their tools and tents
to the final camp on the acropolis of XANTHUS, only 9-10 miles
distant.

It was New Year, 1842, before a permanent camp was established. It consisted of a peasant's barn, twelve feet square, used by

105. Xanthus, the camp.

218

Fellows, the Lieutenant and young Wilkinson, but often sleeping more when visitors arrived; another, roofed over by sailcloths, was for the men. One of their five tents was used by the Gunner, another as a store for the tools. The Cavasses commandeered a hut from the villagers for themselves. Fresh milk and vegetables were bought from the inhabitants and game was shot in the country round about.

During those days at the end of DECEMBER 1841, the weather was remarkably fine and mild (up to 64°F), so Fellows was able to explore the walls and ruins to the south of Xanthus, which had been inaccessible, both when he first discovered them in 1838, and when he was here again in 1840. The beautiful little theatre [27 rows] had a series of grotesque masks over the door, but no proscenium. "I was again induced to believe that this part of the ancient theatre might have been sometimes constructed of wood and destroyed by time," he conjectured. This is, in fact, the case.

The remains of a temple, which had been ornamented with columns, confirmed his earlier assertion that this was the site of the LETOUM [Letoön], or shrine of the Goddess Leto [Roman, Latona], mother of the twins, Apollo and Artemis [Diana]. Excavations began in 1962, but they are constantly hampered by flooding, due to the high water-table.

II The work of the Expedition, 1842

During the first week of JANUARY 1842, Fellows walked about
the site looking for pieces of sculpture or worked stone, that might
have been hidden under bushes or concealed among the piles of
rocks and fallen debris, at the same time, keeping a watchful eye
for any snakes or scorpions, which might also be sheltering there.
He began to track the paths taken by elements of a large edifice -
maybe a tomb; maybe a temple - which an earthquake had sent
crashing down the hillside and into the plain below.

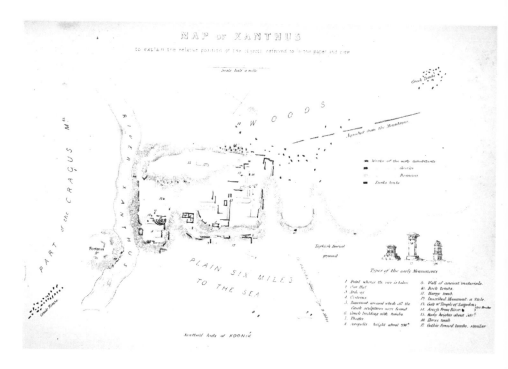

106. Xanthus, Fellows's map of the archaeological site.

This building had once stood near the side of the acropolis, a pile of rubble marking the spot. There were blocks of marble of four different sizes, carved with city walls and figures; pieces of fluted columns, cornices, and Ionic capitals; even statues of young women and lions. "We found, I think, between thirty and forty pieces of sculptured frieze, making about 220 feet of frieze and eleven statues [of two sizes] from the site of the basement." They discovered over one hundred fragments, all of which were painstakingly mapped and numbered.

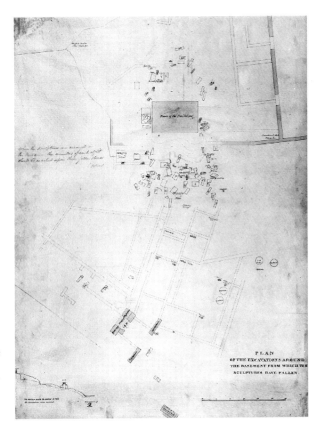

107. Xanthus, the Ionic Monument. Richard Hoskyn's plan of the elements.

Although modern archaeological technique, which may be termed the 'inch-by-inch' method, was yet to evolve, Fellows employed a scientific system in an approach to the subject, very different from the antiquarian investigators of previous centuries.

221

He insisted that nothing be moved until the position had been charted, signs of damage assessed to determine its place relative to other pieces, a number allocated, and the description recorded.

He also believed buildings should be considered as a whole structure, not just viewed as providing individual pieces of sculpture, whatever their beauty. To this end, he had collected the plain slabs, as well as the sculptured frieze blocks and the statues. This was to be of great significance, when it came to reconstructing the edifice, a mammoth task, to form a fascinating study for him and for scholars and architects, both now as then.

Fellows is to be congratulated, since he found the greater part of what turned out to be a unique structure - an Ionic Tomb - the

108. Xanthus, the Ionic Monument. Fellows's reconstruction.

plain blocks proving that there had been no steps and, for this reason, the building could not have been a temple, which the columns initially suggested. Missing stones have been recovered during modern excavations. The French, under Professor Demargne[1] in the 1950s, found two more slabs[2] and casts were sent to the British Museum. Another cast was added in 1976, from a slab now in the Archaeological Museum in Istanbul. The rebuilt façade[3] is one of the finest treasures of the British Museum. It provides an elegant background to the official functions, sometimes held in that Gallery.

At first glance, the structure appears to be a temple, but the absence of steps, to give access for worship, confirms that, in fact, it is a magnificent house-tomb in 'temple' style, externally somewhat reminiscent of the Roman Tomb at Mylasa [pl. 37]. It also lacks an architrave (the plain course between capitals and frieze), usual in a temple, but not a feature of Lycian tombs.

The *cella* [central chamber; 9 ft x 15 ft] was surrounded by a peristyle (colonnade) of 14 columns, the statues [pl. 111] placed between the columns at either end, the crouching lions perhaps guarding the door. Portions of the coffered ceiling were found, which disclosed that it had been decorated, like the one at Sidyma, in vermilion paint with an *anthemion* [Greek, *anthos*, flower], honeysuckle design, in the panels and a *trompe-l'oeil*-effect border.

Fellows had blocks of wood cut to scale to represent the four friezes and the plain courses. Applying his scientific mind to the problem, he moved them about until he arrived at an arrangement that satisfied both structural and aesthetic requirements. From their forms, he established that there must have been three external friezes - two below the columns and one above - the fourth would have been round the outside of the *cella*. From the ratio of two plain to one carved slab, he concluded that there had been two plain courses below each of the lower friezes. The whole structure had stood high on a solid base, the columns displaying slight *entasis* (swelling), a device used in Classical architecture, to create the illusion of straight sides when viewed from below.

In this regard, Fellows points out another fact, evidence of the great skill and high art of the architects of antiquity. The sculpture of the lowest frieze is in low relief, the figures all highly finished with solidity of form, spaced out, only two or three per slab. The

109. Xanthus, the Ionic Monument. Amazon slab.

upper frieze, on the other hand, is carved in high relief to overcome the effect of distance, the figures massed together in groups
of six or more, their arms and legs crossing, to form an airy tracery

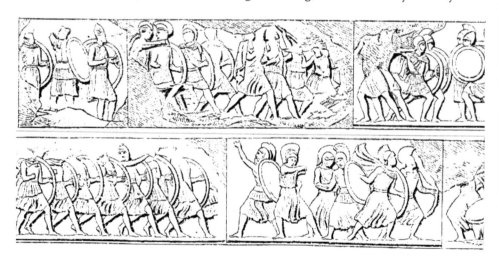

110. Xanthus, the Ionic Monument. Upper frieze.

224

on looking up. This effect is lost in the present reconstruction (1969), after the design (1921) of the Austrian architect, George Niemann[1], with the two friezes placed directly one on top of the other.

Back in England, Fellows had a scale model made, which he presented to the Museum. Unfortunately, this has not survived. Fellows called the building the 'Ionic Trophy Monument'[4]. This was changed to the 'Nereid Monument', after the statues of the young women[3] - Nereids are Nymphs of the Sea. Later scholarship has inclined to the view that they are Aurae - Nymphs of the Breezes. Benjamin Gibson[5], brother of the sculptor, argued that they represent the cities of Ionia and Aeolia, having their symbols beneath their feet.

111. Xanthus, the Ionic Monument. Nereids.

Fellows waited eagerly for MONDAY, 10 JANUARY to come round, so work could begin. The Captain visited the site and Fellows enthusiastically told him of his discoveries and began to discuss their removal. Then another blow fell. Graves declined to sanction the construction of the flat-bottomed boats, essential for bringing the crates of Marbles down river, which Fellows had requested and which had been authorized by the Admiral.

Thus, whatever was collected, there would be no means by which to transport it to the coast; there was even insufficient wood to make the crates - and no help forthcoming from the Captain, who, notwithstanding his Dispatches, was now refusing to take anything whatsoever back to Malta. He was anxious to continue his surveying elsewhere and would only return to Xanthus, to take the workforce off. Fellows was utterly dumbfounded. His dream, so near to becoming a reality, had turned into a nightmare.

"Before me lay a mine of treasure just opened, and all, whatever the extent, at our disposal; I had an excellent set of willing working men, the best season in the year, ample authority from our own as well as the government of the Sultan, and no difficulties or wants but to communicate with Malta for the simple boats and machinery required. This was refused." Worse still, "whatever we found must be left behind until other ships were sent; and, by the delay...the expedition would probably be too late for this season." Alas, his warnings against working in summer in this climate were also disregarded - with literally fatal results.

"A year might pass over before the treasures would be safe in English custody; ignorance of the peasantry, the curiosity or wantonness of travellers, might do them injury, or political changes might check the expedition," Fellows agonized. *Ne hayal sukutu!* - what collapse of imagining, as a disappointment was poetically described in the archaic Turkish language of those days. Or, as Turks might say today: *ne düş kırıklığı* - what broken dreams!

"I took a walk of some hours." Fellows was, justifiably, furious with the attitude adopted by Graves. He needed time to cool his temper, before considering what could be done to save the situation. If Graves was prepared to abandon the enterprise, Fellows certainly was not. He felt his responsibility to the Government too keenly.

After searching his mind for a practical solution, he decided the only way was to employ the two carpenters solely in making crates to protect any sculptures collected. Half the men would bring in timber, and the few remaining hands would continue to search for hidden Marbles and participate in the excavations. A day's work was from 9 till 4.30, dusk, with an hour's dinner-break.

Before long, two water-cisterns had been uncovered, filled with miscellaneous pieces of sculpture, portions of friezes, columns and cornices, even some heads, but none of the Nereids. Not one has ever been found. Fellows's spirits began to rise. "The pleasure and excitement of these discoveries were entered into even by the sailors, who often forgot the dinner-hour, or worked after dusk to finish the getting out of a statue." Great care was necessary in doing this, since pieces can easily be broken off when handling soft, saturated stone, which remains very fragile until it dries out.

In spite of all the difficulties, the work went so well that in just two weeks - by the 21st - it had come to a halt for want of tackle and boats. Fellows wrote to Graves at Macry, reiterating their problems and asking that he at least send a proper supply of nails. The niggardly quantity of three hundred sent over were not sufficient for even one day's labour; he needed thousands to be sure of casing all the Marbles. Fellows himself, ceased to seek out more objects - that was too tantalizing. He confined his activities instead, to recopying, collating and taking impress casts on paper

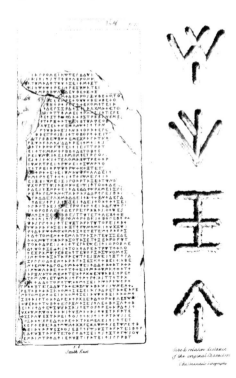

112. Xanthus, the Inscribed Stele, south-east side.

of the long Lycian inscription on the fascinating Inscribed Stele, the top of which he had had turned over. On it, there was a short passage in Greek.

Of the Marbles collected, those elements which composed the Ionic Monument formed the major part. Miscellaneous inscriptions and sculptures of men and animals [pl. 146] were eased out of the city walls[6], where they had been used haphazardly in its

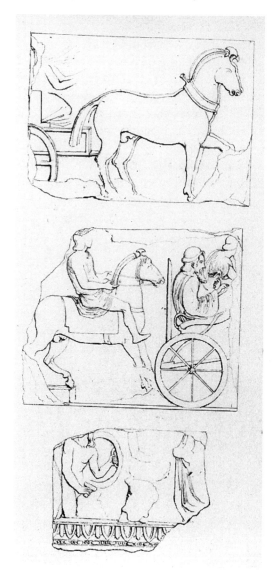

113. *Xanthus, sculptured wall slabs.*

construction. The Lion Tomb [pl. 129] was too deeply buried to be excavated. The other pillar-tomb, the Harpy 'Tomb[6], was in a very unstable condition, two angle-stones having already fallen. Fellows determined to rescue the frieze. As best they could, the sailors built up the centre under the cap-stone, before removing the sculptures [pl. 124]. Thanks to his forethought, no further damage was sustained, and casts could be made from the originals, when the Tomb was reconstructed in 1957. A few years earlier, some more fragments were found, completing the frieze.

When these reliefs were first seen in the British Museum, in 1843, they caused a major sensation. Thousands of curious public came to see them, and artists and antiquarians journeyed from near and far, to examine and draw them, and so increase their knowledge of ancient art. The figures are carved in the archaic manner, stiffly posed in side-view, the drapery hanging in rigid folds, the hair in multiple plaits [pl. 82].

The only significant loss to the site today is the Horse [Payava] Tomb[7] [pl. 17]. It was very badly cracked from an earthquake and the middle section must have given way under another tremor, which would have caused the whole structure to fall and break. Before allowing the sailors to start dismantling this

114. Xanthus, the Horse Tomb being dismantled.

Tomb, Fellows again carefully mapped the cracks and holes in the sides, numbering each piece, so that it could be reconstructed in the Museum. He was a pioneer in the concept of removing entire structures under threat, to be rebuilt in safety elsewhere.

Anyone censuring his action must realize that this was the only way to ensure the preservation of such objects. Many works of beauty, admired and valued today, owe their very existence to being in a public or private collection. Scholarship would have been hindered, and the world a poorer place, had piecemeal collection, pillage and wholesale destruction been allowed to hold sway.

With these Marbles, Fellows could visualize a completely 'Xanthian Room' in the British Museum. He could see the Harpy Tomb, the Horse Tomb, and the Ionic Trophy Monument all reconstructed, to typify the differing styles of Lycian architecture. There would also be the sculptured wall slabs, and his squeezes of the Inscribed Stele to complete this demonstration of a unique culture.

Richard Hoskyn, Master of the *Beacon*, came over from time to time and mapped the site. He was engaged on a survey of the Cragus Mountains, but he took a lively interest in the work at Xanthus. Early in January, Lieutenant Thomas Spratt, assistant surveyor of the *Beacon*, and Edward Forbes, its naturalist - a great friend of Strickland's - together with an amateur archaeologist, the Rev. Edward Daniell, availed themselves of the hospitality of the camp to stay a few days. They were making a complete study of the Cragus, and later extended their field to include the whole of the province of Lycia. With them, Fellows was surprised to see Mania, who was now acting as dragoman to the naval party, they benefitting greatly from his experiences while with him. Daniell struck up a firm friendship with Fellows and repeated his visits several times.

The surveyors were there when the first of the buried stones from the Ionic Monument were dug out and brought to view. "The search for them was intensely exciting," Spratt wrote[8]. "As each block of marble was uncovered, and the earth carefully brushed away from its surface, the form of some fair amazon or stricken warrior, of an eastern king or a besieged castle became revealed, and gave rise to many a pleasant discussion...conversations which all who took part in will ever look back upon as among the most delightful in their lives." At night, they used to "sally forth, torch in hand, Charles Fellows as cicerone, to cast a midnight look of admiration on some spirited battle-scene, or headless Venus, which had been the great prize of the morning's work."

They were not the only visitors to Xanthus at this time. "Five learned Prussians" came to inspect the site, including Professor Augustus Schoenborn[9], who, with his friend Herr Loew of Posen [Poznan, in Poland], had been sent by the King of Prussia to study the natural history, geography and inscriptions of Lycia. They acknowledged making this journey as a consequence of reading Fellows's book[10].

Gratifying though this was, it again raised the fear that other nations might be seeking to acquire Marbles from here. Fellows had informed the Trustees that he had taken steps to forward their intentions to prevent, at least for a time, "the French and Austrian Governments from taking possession of the reliques." There had already been two expeditions from Prussia, "to bring away all that can easily be removed," he added.

By the end of FEBRUARY 1842, Fellows began to organize the transfer of the cases of Marbles from the site to the mouth of the river. The spades and other tools, he had bought for the excavations, he distributed amongst the kindly, helpful villagers, and he later had a grindstone sent, having found that farmers came from miles around to sharpen their ploughshares, pruning-knives and yataghans, the local limestone being a poor substitute for a revolving whetstone. "We kept admirable terms with the peasantry, and I believe our departure was a subject of regret to all."

The *Beacon* arrived on schedule on TUESDAY, 1 MARCH 1842, to take the men off. Disregarding his orders "to put on board and bring away to Malta such objects as should be pointed out by Mr. Fellows," Graves left all the cases behind. Fellows carefully numbered each, corresponding to his descriptive catalogue[11]. He also compiled two lists, one for the Aga of Fornas, the local Governor, and the other for the Pasha of Rhodes. The Aga declined responsibility for the cases, saying rightly, that should anything happen to them, he could not possibly replace the loss. Hadgi Ali Pasha, likewise, sent over two Cavasses to protect them, but declared himself answerable only for the conduct of the men.

By 3 MARCH, all were on board and, by the 5th, the *Beacon* had arrived in RHODES harbour. A few hours sufficed to complete the official business with the Pasha and Consul Wilkinson, and the ship sailed for MALTA. A speedy passage brought her safely to VALETTA on 14 MARCH.

Ironically, it was only now that Fellows's reports and requests could be handed to the Admiral, too late to be of any use. Whilst Fellows was undergoing quarantine, he received daily visits from him and from Major Yule of the Royal Engineers, who was to take charge of the recovery of the cases left at Xanthus. On MONDAY, 4 APRIL, a new Commander-in-Chief Mediterranean, Admiral Sir Edward Owen, took over. His first action was to interview Fellows and Graves. The Captain then expressed his wish to be relieved of duties with respect to the Expedition, and this was immediately granted. Captain Frederick Warden, Commander of the survey-vessel *Medea* (4)[12], was now called upon to direct operations at Xanthus with Major Yule RE. The principal personae of the Second Xanthian Expedition thus entered the scene. Had they been involved from the start, there need only have been one sortie to Xanthus, avoiding much trouble and expense - and many lives saved.

III The sequel

Misfortune continued to follow this ill-starred Expedition. Further delays prevented the *Medea* from sailing at once, in fact, she did not weigh until 28 APRIL 1842, after which she had to call in at Athens. The Admiral also ordered the much larger *Monarch* (84)[1], under the command of Captain Samuel Chambers, to go to take off the heavier cases.

The *Medea* did not anchor off the mouth of the XANTHUS until FRIDAY, 13 MAY - a date of ill-omen if ever there was one! The inhabitants had already departed to their Yeeilassies in the mountains, surrendering the valley to irrigation. As Fellows had predicted, "noxious evaporations and malaria were the consequence." He had repeatedly warned against the dangers of the summer climate and had done his best to avoid the makings of a tragedy.

A total of 160 men were now engaged in work at Xanthus. Lieutenants Frederick Hennah and Walter Need of the *Monarch* were in charge of the Lower Station, Lieutenant Charles Barker was at the site. Lieutenant Hennah later applied for promotion for his services. Both the other Lieutenants were made Commanders, in 1847 and 1845 respectively, but the unfortunate Hennah had already died, in July 1843.

On board the *Monarch*, a dozen deaths from Walcherian fever[2] were recorded, including that of three officers. Captain Chambers died in October 1843. The following year, several men suffered a recurrence of the disease. As well as these fatalities, earlier, in January 1842, two sailors had been drowned, when a boat overturned whilst unloading stores. To add further horror, when young Wilkinson had gone to give assistance, his horse had become stuck in the muddy ground. On going to collect him the next morning, he found the spot marked by a gathering of evil-looking vultures, too bloated to fly away, having feasted on the corpse of the poor animal, killed by a pack of wolves.

When the *Beacon* sailed, Spratt and his companions had remained behind, to continue their researches along the coast. On the way back, in May, they had passed through Xanthus and stayed in Fellows's hut. Illness and death then lurked in the swamps and the Rev. Daniell was struck down with fever. He seemed at first to recover, but later the malady returned and he died in Adalia, the following year. Spratt always maintained that Daniell's fatal sickness was due to the time he had spent on the coast that summer.

"A great part of those who had been members of the shore party were disabled with fever," Spratt reported. "The officers and men were beginning to suffer much from the mosquitoes, which, at sunset, rose in myriads out of the adjoining morass. It was impossible to escape these merciless tormentors, and the countenances of many of the party bore witness to their tortures." About half of the workforce went down with fever.

The heavy cases were transported down the river on pontoons, under the guidance of Seaman Daniel Burch of the *Monarch*. He was to be promoted to Boatswain, and his experience would be called on for the Second Xanthian Expedition. Other cases were placed on planks mounted on gun-carriages, and hauled along by seamen or by draught-oxen. Sa-Alik Effendi, a Turkish officer of the *Monarch*, took charge of this.

It was WEDNESDAY, 8 JUNE, before the vessels sailed for Malta. On board were sixty-nine cases containing the hundreds of pieces of the Ionic Monument, and nine more, containing the Harpy Tomb frieze and the animal slabs from the city wall. The four cases containing the Horse Tomb had, in the event, to be left where they lay. By the end of JUNE, the vessels had arrived at VALETTA, and the *Cambridge* (80)[3] brought the Marbles to England in DECEMBER.

Even then the troubles of this Expedition were not over. Edward Hawkins, Keeper of the Antiquities, reported to the Trustees that there seemed to have been "very great carelessness" during the transshipments. Cases had been broken, some had their contents rearranged without reference to Fellows's list, and others had been re-packed with their sculptured sides facing, without any protection between the surfaces.

Later, Hawkins and Fellows were to fight a losing battle with the Trustees' chosen designer, Sir Richard Westmacott, who

234

insisted on arranging the Marbles in what he deemed to be an 'artistic' way, but which was quite at variance with Fellows's wishes and which showed a fine disregard for their history, subject, or chronology.

By the middle of APRIL 1842, Fellows was back in London, and his travel expenses of £260:18:6 were repaid. At their meeting on 14 May, the Trustees acknowledged his "public spirit in voluntarily undertaking to lend to so distant an expedition the assistance of his local knowledge and personal co-operation," affirming their satisfaction in his decisive action of going to the Capital to obtain the necessary authority for the undertakings. They praised his "judicious and persevering exertions at Xanthus, by which the most desirable of the valuable Monuments of Antiquity...have been placed in Safety and as the Trustees have every reason to hope secured for the National Museum."

Fellows prepared an account of the Expedition, as a register of the incidents connected with the acquisition. He fully anticipated that the Museum would publish an official report of its own, but time passed and nothing was produced. "Finding that vague rumours, imperfect accounts and misrepresentations were appearing," Fellows finally felt obliged to publish[4] the circumstances of the enterprise himself, "notwithstanding the necessary egotistical character of the narrative". One hundred and fifty years on, and there is still no official publication, but the 'imperfect accounts and misrepresentations' persist.

At that time, the sculptures from Xanthus were generally referred to as the 'Xanthian Marbles', a convenient title in keeping with the designations: 'Townley Marbles', 'Phigaleian or Bassae Marbles', and 'Elgin Marbles'[5]. It was even suggested that they should be called the 'Fellows's Marbles' - but he would never have agreed to that: they were not his.

The word 'Marbles' was loosely used to comprise any ancient sculptures, whether of genuine marble or of stone - or even plaster casts. The Harpy Tomb and the Ionic Monument are indeed of marble, but the Horse Tomb, and the carved slabs are of local limestone. After the Second Expedition, the display also included many casts. The name was then changed to the more appropriate 'Lycian Marbles', as the casts came from many locations besides Xanthus.

When they were first put on display, the objects received the greatest attention. The graceful Nereids were much admired by artists, who considered them to rank amongst the loveliest figures from antiquity. At that time, there was nothing in the Museum of a similar date, to compare in style - figures carved in the round, clad in clinging dresses that reveal the young bodies beneath, the material fluttering away at the back. The Amazons on the Bassae frieze wear the same type of dress, but they are not free-standing; the garments of the women of the Parthenon are much heavier and do not float in the breeze. Those figures are seated, and only lightly carved at the back, since they were disposed against the fabric of the tympanum. Even the Caryatid[6] from the Erechtheion stands rigidly to her task, the folds of her dress hanging in straight vertical pleats.

It was the Harpy Tomb, however, that most captured popular imagination, and the relevance of the story to Xanthus became a favourite topic for scholastic discussion. It was conjectured that it showed Harpies snatching away the children of Pandarus, to give them as servants to the Furies. This was to punish Pandarus, a Lycian hero, for some misdeeds. There was a cult of Pandarus at Pinara, only a few miles to the north. Modern opinion now favours the theory that the 'Harpies' are, instead, Sirens, who are bearing off the Souls of the Dead, in the form of children, to the Isles of the Blessed.

"Whilst all must sincerely rejoice that Mr. Fellows's public spirit and enterprise have enabled him to secure remains of so much interest for our national museum, it is to be hoped that this harvest is not the last which we shall reap from the same country through his exertions," wrote the scholar Sir Edmund Head[7], observing that "it is only by the accumulation of monuments of this description in the museums of Europe that additional light can be thrown on the history of Greek art, and these Lycian remains could nowhere be studied more profitably than in close contact with the marbles of the Parthenon and of Phigalia."

In an era without the aids of photography and video, and when foreign travel was restricted to the very few, this was a powerful argument. As far as Fellows was concerned, however, he had played his part and did not contemplate any further excursions of that nature. But Fate would decree otherwise.

236

Two days after he got back to London, Fellows called on the Scharf family, to see how his protégé had been faring in the interim. He was to learn that George had been fully occupied teaching and painting. One of his pictures was of a Turkish dancer, another showed himself and Fellows watching such a performance. George presented this painting to Mrs Pearson, who was delighted to have this keepsake of her brother's travels.

George had also resumed his theatrical studies, drawing scenes from Macready's new production of *Acis and Galatea* at the Drury Lane Theatre, with Clarkson Stanfield's remarkable panoramic effects. Father Scharf considered these outlines very clever and took them to show his friend Charles Hullmandel. When Scharf junior presented them to Macready, he was equally impressed and gave him a season ticket (worth £4), as a token of his appreciation. The whole Scharf family went frequently to the theatre and, in November 1842, brother Henry finally resigned his position with the College of Surgeons, to take up an acting career, initially at Newcastle[8].

Fellows kept up his friendship with the family, often inviting George to dine at his home. He also took an interest in the work of Scharf senior. Through Fellows, he had been able to attend lectures at the Royal Institution, where he learnt of the new printing process, 'Electro-type'. He was already using Hullmandel's new technique of 'Lithotint' (patented in 1843), which gives lithographs the appearance of water-colour paintings. Scharf senior was making lithotints of the sculptures from Xanthus, clocking up twenty-eight hours of labour on the Harpy Tomb alone.

In all, 1842 was a good year for father Scharf, his income amounting to the large sum of £177, ten pounds more than his average, though he did complain that on 21 June, the "burdensome" Income Tax of seven pence in the pound was passed in the House of Lords. He was so busy, in fact, that regrettably, he could not finish the lithotint of the lettering on the Inscribed Stele[9], which Fellows had copied out that spring. The illustrations had to be completed, instead, by William Walton.

Then, quite unexpectedly, in MAY 1843, almost exactly a year after his return to London, Charles Fellows received a letter from the Secretary to the Trustees, to the effect that the Government had given authority for a resumption of operations at

Xanthus that autumn. Fellows was requested to lead the scientific part. "It would be very satisfactory to the Trustees, if it were consistent with your engagements and inclination," he read.

The letter continued: "The Trustees have already incurred so great a debt to you for your zealous, judicious and patriotic exertions...that [they] could not have been induced to suggest to you an undertaking calling for so great a sacrifice of time and comfort, unless knowing your love of ancient art, and your desire to increase the remains of it contained in the Museum; they had hoped that in the satisfaction of completely accomplishing under your own superintendence, all you originally designed regarding the Xanthian marbles...you might find no mean nor transient recompense for your valuable services."

Fellows replied immediately, expressing the great gratification it would give him "to continue to render any assistance in his power in forwarding the knowledge of art and enriching the National Collections." All previous frustrations and regrets could now be forgotten, as he began to make his plans.

The Expedition was to be a major undertaking, lasting from 15 September 1843 to 1 May 1844. More excavations were to be made, and a proper survey of the site carried out. More Marbles were to be collected, and casts taken of sculptures at Xanthus and at several other Lycian cities. Fellows was invited to select an architect, a draughtsman, and a foreman of carpenters and masons. They would receive £100 with victuals; he would have his expenses reimbursed.

Within a couple of weeks, Fellows had chosen his team. George Scharf junior would, of course, be the official artist, and Rohde Hawkins, third son of Edward Hawkins, would be the architect. On the advice of Thomas Cubitt[10], the builder, George Jackson was taken on as Foreman. Cast-makers would be hired in Rome and stone-masons in Valetta.

Preparations now went ahead in a flurry of correspondence - between Fellows, the Trustees, and Sidney Herbert, Secretary to the Admiralty, in London, and, in Malta, Admiral Sir Edward Owen[11], C-in-C Mediterranean, and Captain Frederick Warden[12] of HMVS *Medea* (4), who was to command the naval workforce. The Admiral sought Fellows's opinion on practical matters relating to housing at Xanthus, weather conditions to be expected, and equipment wanted. To save expense, stores and tools were to be purchased in England.

The Second Xanthian Expedition was thus initiated. In contrast to the earlier one, it was to prove a very well organized and most successful enterprise.

From the moment that his appointment was confirmed, on 27 MAY, George Scharf junior began to consider the requirements for his task. He needed pens, pencils, brushes and paper, watercolours and fixatives, a telescope and his new camera lucida [13], to enable him to sketch distant landscapes and the sculptures high up on towering monuments and rock-faces. He knew already that a thick capote, waterproof cap [14], and large green umbrella were essential items. He must revise his notes on the sculptures too and brush up his Italian, since one of his duties would be to take charge of the cast-making, in the hands of Roman *formatori*.

Fellows again invited young Scharf to accompany him on another lengthy tour through Europe beforehand, as he had done on their first journey together. He proposed leaving London in late summer, spending three weeks in Naples. Young Hawkins would join them there, and they would then visit the Vesuvian towns of Pompeii and Herculaneum, as well as the very ancient Greek temples at Paestum. This would complete Scharf's education of Classical antiquities. There would be occasion to pass a few days in Rome and Florence too, where Scharf hoped to see his friends once more. The prospect filled him with great joy.

During the whole period of the Expedition, Mrs Pearson, the Hawkins and the Scharf families, would keep up a constant exchange of correspondence, news and tracings, their letters to Xanthus sent through Hawkins, via the Admiralty.

PART FOUR

I The journey out

Their preparations completed, Fellows and Scharf crossed to BOULOGNE on the new ferry service from Dover, two steamers a day making the voyage in just three to four hours at the cost of 10s.6d. each, as opposed to the 15 shillings from London Wharf. SUNDAY, 6 AUGUST 1843, found them in PARIS. On this visit, the sculpture in the Louvre claimed priority.

Scharf was surprised to find inferior pieces mixed together with universally acknowledged fine works. The architecture of the Galleries, he thought overpowering and distracting. Many antique statues had been brought from Italy by Napoleon and had remained here after his fall. A later acquisition was the controversial statue of the Venus di Milo, given to the Museum in 1820.

More recently acquired still were the Assos Marbles, which Fellows had seen in 1838 and sketched on the spot [pl. 9], and some 250 feet of frieze from the Temple of Artemis Leukophryene at Magnesia-ad-Maeandrum in Lydia. These slabs [2nd century BC], showing the Battle of the Amazons, and the archaic Assos sculptures had been collected by the archaeologist, Charles Texier[1], as fine examples of early Greek sculpture. He personally conducted the Englishmen to view these treasures.

Scharf remarked on their poor state and the coarseness of the workmanship. "The style and proportions vary extremely; in the latter respect the inequalities are extremely remarkable. Many figures are unaccountably dwarfish," he observed, though conceding that some groupings and attitudes were admirable. In 1836, Strickland had seen them where they lay, a confused heap of ruins of the purest white marble. "Nothing appears to have been removed," he noted, "for Magnesia enjoys the advantage of not having been succeeded by any modern town, which might consume the materials of the old one." But now the frieze was in Paris.

240

Karl Humann removed more sculptures to Berlin from his excavations in 1891-93; others are in Istanbul. A road now passes directly through the centre of the site.

TUESDAY, 15 AUGUST - "At 8 o'clock in the morning, we entered one of Lafitte's Diligencies and drove to the Orleans railway station beyond the Jardin des Plantes. By cranes on sliding rests, we were hauled off the carriage wheels and let down on to a usual train waggon; judging by others, the effect of a carriage body [up in the air] with people in it was very ridiculous. There were no fewer than 7 diligencies undergoing the same operation, as all went the same road and branched off at Orleans...There our diligence was let down onto a fresh set of wheels, ready waiting for us and we proceeded on our journey briskly without even a single passenger alighting." The train had raced along at 25-30 miles an hour, giving them an exhilarating experience.

After several changes of vehicle, the tourists arrived at AVIGNON. The Pope's Palace was in use as a barracks and presented a sorry appearance of dirty neglect, the walls covered with graffiti. The *Concierge* who took them round was equally squalid in appearance, and was dubbed a 'She-Goblin' by Charles Dickens in describing his encounter with her the following year. From there they continued, by steamer and by carriage, south to MARSEILLES, arriving at 6 am, with plenty of time to take a 'lounge' through the streets before boarding the steamer for Italy.

The novelty of the shop-fronts caught Scharf's attention. They were small, but with shutters each side. "To assist the display of goods, many of these shutters are painted to continue the display, and many shops, especially those in the narrow streets with less light, are excellently done and so as to entirely deceive." The boulevards were broad, well paved and clean.

"Marseilles is a great place for the manufactory of soap, which somewhat offends the nose of a new comer, [but], as it is made exclusively of vegetable oil, it is not so unsavoury as in England." Down on the waterfront, the stench and dirt were very apparent, so the travellers were not sorry at 3 o'clock, to board the *Leonidas*, a ship of the regular service to the Levant, inaugurated in June 1837.

WEDNESDAY, 23 AUGUST - The steamer put in at LIVORNO at 8 am and would not leave until three in the afternoon. Scharf, therefore, had plenty of time to make a rapid trip to PISA, to refresh his memory of its famous buildings. Hiring an express carriage, he dashed off and was back again at the docks by one. The following day, the *Leonidas* steamed into CIVITA VECCHIA, where the tourists left the ship, to take a carriage to ROME. For this short stay, Fellows took rooms at the Caesari Hotel near St Peter's, but they regularly dined at Lepri's, as before, to meet their old friends, who all lived in the centre of the city.

Fellows's first consideration was to call on the Scottish sculptor Lawrence Macdonald at his studio, 6 the Corso. His portrait busts were extremely popular. There were row upon row of noblemen and illustrious personages, creating "a plaster galaxy of rank and fashion". He was to help Fellows choose the *formatori*, for the cast-making project in Lycia. Macdonald willingly entered into the spirit of the enterprise and two cast-makers and their assistants were selected.

On the first moonlight night, Scharf took his habitual walk in the Forum. "Never did the antiquities appear so simple and grand...The moon behind Phoca's column shed her silver points upon the Severus Arch and the Capitol tower. The church of St. Pietro in Carcere was bright light at the side and dense black in front...The rich trees in the Campo Vaccino [Forum] furnished the scene," and, in those far off days, "the chirruping of distant grasshoppers was the only sound that the attentive ear could reach."

Sculpture was still the chief purpose of this journey. Besides those in the Galleries of the Vatican, Scharf went to see the works in the Villa Albani. The collection had been made in the mid-eighteenth century by Cardinal Alessandro Albani and described by J.J. Winckelmann, his librarian. Nearly 300 of the best pieces had, however, been taken by Napoleon to Paris and then sold to Crown Prince Ludwig of Bavaria, forming the nucleus of that collection.

Fellows claimed that the only ancient Greek sculpture of a similar age and style to that of the Harpy Tomb was a sepulchral relief[2] at the Villa. It shows a mother, seated in side-view, with an infant on her lap. Another woman stands before her. The chair, the hair bound by a filet, the dresses, and the attitudes are certainly very similar to the carvings on the Harpy Tomb frieze. In 1845, Fellows obtained casts of it for the British Museum, paid for out of the funds allocated to the Xanthian Expedition. In thanking him, the Trustees affirmed that "the Casts...have been generally esteemed curious and valuable, not only on account of the illustration, which they afford to similar sculptures in the Collections from Lycia." The casts are, sadly, no longer to be seen.

SATURDAY, 2 SEPTEMBER 1843 - "Again I feel the regret of leaving Rome, my future companion only in Histories, Arts and Literature. Few periods have been more pleasing than this last 10 days in which were being realised the anticipations and labours of the past two or three years. In its Art I have gained much; of History I know more and yet thirst; and of its actual beauties become daily more and more convinced," Scharf reflected. "Now I strain for a presentiment of returning." This very lucky young man was, in fact, to come to Rome the following April, for two more happy days.

The following evening, Fellows and Scharf took their places in the coach to return to CIVITA VECCHIA, where they embarked on the *Rhamses* - her boilers now working well - bound for NAPLES. Fellows took rooms at 47 via Vittoria, a small, quiet house overlooking the sea, for a stay of three weeks. Here, they were joined by Rohde Hawkins, who had come out from England separately.

The first thing to strike the visitor to Naples was the incessant noise. Every horse and every street-hawker jingled and tinkled with many little bells. The cries of the vendors mingled with the continuous whines of entreaty from the begging children and the importunings of troublesome cabbies. There was no peace at night either, for the streets were always full of merry-making crowds celebrating some Feast or Saint's Day - any excuse for a firework display.

FRIDAY, 8 SEPTEMBER - The Feast of the Nativity of the Virgin Mary. This was observed by a great military procession, forty-eight regiments, some with supporting cannon, taking two hours to pass by. The whole way from the Royal Palace to the

Church of Sta Maria di Piedigrotta was lined with soldiers, standing three deep. Strangely, in spite of so much pomp, and in so densely crowded a city, there were scarcely any spectators. The English tourists were told it was out of fear[3].

There was also panic among the ladies, for, on several occasions, there had been reports of their dresses catching fire, either through chemicals or burning lenses, introduced by unknown hands, twenty ladies having died from the effects.

The royal carriage was proceeded by pages dressed in blue and silver, the colours of the House of Bourbon. Ferdinand II, King of the Two Sicilies, was clad in dark blue and gold. "He is stout, light reddish brown hair, florid complexion, whiskered and rather young-looking." He was 33 years old. "The Queen [Maria-Theresa-Isabella of Austria] is pale, with dark hair and pleasing countenance; her dress was principally of silver tissue, which looked well upon the rich crimson lining of the carriage...The next 6 carriages were devoted to the children, one in each; the eldest is a boy of 9 or ten years, the youngest an infant girl, not more than four months old. The separate pomp, attendants, and manner of keeping them all up to view was very amusing."

The festival lasted a week and finished with illuminations and a grand firework display. There was another, even better, firework display a week later, on the Feast of Our Lady of Sorrows, to celebrate the cessation of a terrible epidemic of cholera, which had raged for over a year in 1836-37, killing some 14,000 persons. This festival recalled to Fellows and Scharf the night of jollity at Venice, to mark a similar deliverance from pestilence.

More fireworks followed on 19 SEPTEMBER, the Feast of San Gennaro, Patron Saint of Naples, when the blood of the Saint, preserved in a phial, is supposed to flow. The tourists attended the ceremony of *Liquefazione*, the miracle announced to the crowds outside by the ringing of church bells and the firing off of cannon.

Fellows was keen for the young men to make the climb up Mount Vesuvius, an experience similar to the ascent of Mont Blanc, which he had achieved when a young man himself. Although the snow and ice were here exchanged for hot grit and lava, the mode of ascent and descent was much the same. Like Alpine climbers, they were attached by straps to their guides and given long staves to help them up; they slid down again, feet first, in the loose stones, just as he had done in the snow. The volcano had erupted in 1839, so the excursion was made with some trepidation. A plume of thick smoke hung over the mountain, lit up red at night by the fire within.

The time spent in Naples was not all amusement, though the archaeological excursions they made were a great pleasure. On SATURDAY, 16 SEPTEMBER, Fellows, Scharf and Rohde Hawkins took a train to visit the ruins of POMPEII[4]. From the well-preserved streets and houses, but lack of people, it seemed to Scharf like a town enjoying its Sunday rest. "Only 'the busy hum of men' is wanting," he said, quoting from Milton. Work was in progress, under Cavaliere Francesco Avellino, Director of the University. Roofs and doors were being put over the painted stucco walls and the mosaics. The great mosaic of *The Battle of Issus*, which Avellino had discovered in 1831, was covered in plaster, preparatory to its being transferred to the National Museum in Naples, where they would see it on their way home.

Five days later, they set off on a three-day excursion south, stopping first to visit the other Vesuvian city, HERCULANEUM. Excavations here had hardly begun. When Vesuvius had erupted in AD 79, Herculaneum had been drowned in molten lava to a depth of forty feet and the modern town of Resina had been built on top of it. Pompeii, on the other hand, had suffocated in hot gases and been covered under only twelve feet of light cinders.

"How great a contrast to Pompeii! There, everything is free and open to daylight, where the visitor walks uninterrupted thro' streets well paved...Here, everything feels cold, dark and enveloped in solid stone...Water trickles down in many places...We were really glad to escape the damp and fumes of the flaring torches and re-enter the carriage." Persons of delicate health and weak lungs were, in fact, strongly advised against going down at all.

The tourists then carried on to SALERNO, which presented a most animated scene, the occasion being the Feast of San Mattèo, St Matthew, the Evangelist. Once again, the night was filled with the noise of laughing people and the inevitable fireworks. "The greatest device was immediately opposite our hotel," Scharf recorded. "A series of figures at considerable intervals discharging rockets etc. at one another" caused great astonishment, hilarity and delight amongst the townsfolk.

The next day, a ride of four hours brought the sight-seers to PAESTUM, over 80 miles away from Naples. This was the ancient POSIDONIA. Three great Greek temples stand here, almost complete to this day, in a flat plain near the sea. Malaria had caused the abandonment of the site in ancient times, and the inhabitants still left for the mountains in summer, as they did in Lycia. The huge Doric temples [6th-5th century BC] are of porous yellow stone, the texture and colour remarkably like the cork copies in the museum at Naples and at the Soane Museum in London, where Scharf had studied. The actual edifices, however, have a grandeur and majesty that the copies totally fail to convey.

The marked *entasis* of the columns, with their excessively narrow necks, under heavy round capitals, make their form inelegant, but the completeness of the buildings, especially the Temple of Poseidon [Neptune], and the solidity of the masses are particularly impressive.

The little party traced the extent of the city walls, a street and the shape of a theatre. Then, in the cool of the evening, they returned to Salerno, to go back to Naples the next day. After one more day of sight-seeing in that glorious city - its history, churches and museums, its animation and its position on the Bay, giving it a glamour that even Rome could not match - it was time to leave.

They packed their bags and shipped home their mementoes and presents to the family. In Malta, Scharf would be leaving his numerous books, guides and maps behind, to be picked up on the way home. Amongst these were catalogues of art collections, John Flaxman's translations of Dante's *Divine Comedy* and Homer's *Works*; the French translation by A. Baron of Thomas Hope's *History of Architecture* in two volumes; Goethe's *Italian Journey* in three volumes; Kugler's *Handbook of Painting*, 1842, for which Scharf would later provide illustrations; several volumes of prints; and, not least, the instructions by C.L. Chevalier for the drawing-aid, the camera lucida, which Scharf was using for the first time, and which would prove to be invaluable for sketching panoramas of the sites in Lycia.

246

II Malta, the Expedition gets under way; Rhodes

MONDAY, 25 SEPTEMBER 1843 - Scharf and Hawkins had gone on board the French sailing-vessel *Minos*, at noon, to take care of the stowing of the baggage, when, to their horror, the vessel weighed and began to chug slowly away from her moorings. Fellows was still on shore, in the custom-house, explaining the reason for the suspiciously large quantity of paper he was taking out of the country. Luckily, the Captain saw a boat put out hurriedly and head for the ship, the loud cries and gesticulations from those on board, taken up by Scharf and Hawkins, who had rushed to acquaint him with the situation. The ship's paddles were stopped and Fellows embarked, to cheers and many protestations of relief and thanks.

Amongst the passengers were the landscape artist William J. Müller and his pupil Harry J. Johnson. It transpired that they were also making for Xanthus. Müller had met Fellows and had shown considerable interest in the artistic potential of Lycia. When he had been engaged by Benjamin Johnson of Birmingham, Harry's father, to take his son, then only 17 years of age, on a long painting journey, Müller decided to take up Fellows's suggestion to stay at Xanthus, while the Expeditionary force could afford them some protection. They would be an independent party, and in no way attached to the Expedition - a source of misunderstanding, as it turned out.

WEDNESDAY, 27 SEPTEMBER - Fellows and his party landed at VALETTA, while the artists continued on to Smyrna, where Müller needed to buy his stores and find a dragoman. For their sojourn of three weeks, Fellows took rooms in the larger Hotel of Dunsford, but in the same street as Mrs. Morrell's establishment. First thing the next morning, he took his assistants to Admiralty House to meet Admiral Sir Edward Owen, perhaps the most important person of the whole enterprise. He was responsible for setting up and equipping the expeditionary force and would issue orders to Captain Warden, who was to maintain communications between Xanthus and Valetta throughout the whole period of the excavations. Admiral Owen expressed great confidence in the Captain's "judgment, his perseverance and resources", and he was not to be disappointed.

Captain Frederick Warden had gained much valuable experience when his ship HMVS *Medea* (4) had been sent to pick up the Marbles in May 1842. He was to defer to Fellows for the selection of antiquities, their mode of recovery and their packing, but to the Admiral for any authorization or sanction which might have been overlooked. He took great personal interest in the work at Xanthus, which was reflected in his actions and in the detailed reports he sent back to Malta. Captain Warden was a jolly-looking, round-faced man with balding red hair and mutton-chop whiskers. He

115. Captain Frederick Warden RN, portrait by Scharf.

248

was popular with his officers and treated his crew well, which they returned with respect and by working with enthusiasm at the site. His salary as Commander was £300:0:9.

A second important member of the force was Dr Alexander Armstrong, co-opted from the *Polyphemus* (1). Besides his medical reports, his brief was to send weekly accounts of the work at Xanthus[1]. These were considered "highly interesting and...most

116. *Captain Warden, officers and seamen.*

creditable to his industry and talents." At the end of the time, Dr Armstrong was able to announce that the general health of the company had been excellent. There had, alas, been one fatality and one case of delirium tremens, but neither directly attributable to the work at the site.

The complement of the *Medea* was to be augmented by officers and men from the Admiral's flagship *Queen* (110)[2], and soon Fellows and his friends were invited to a dinner party on board, to meet the Officers. "All was arranged in the best style," but the band did occasionally drown out the conversation. This was followed by a formal dinner party, given by the Governor, Lt-General Sir Patrick Stuart, where they met several members of the English aristocracy, who happened to be in Malta at the time.

Fellows renewed his acquaintance with Major Yule RE, who took them to see a 'Lycian Tomb', which he had had cut in the cliffs near Valetta in memory of his participation in the first Xanthian Expedition. This well-informed man became their cicerone, and took the visitors round Valetta and into the country on an excursion to the old capital, Città Vecchia [earlier Medina Nobile, now Mdina]. The Cathedral is said to be built on the site of the house of the Roman Governor Publius, who, in AD 60, had looked after Saint Paul and his shipwrecked companions and was converted to Christianity.

They then drove on to see the Grotto where Saint Paul had lived, and the catacombs, an extensive system, much larger than those in Rome. The damp, confined air soon drove them out into the sunshine again, the brightness of the bare rock quite hurting their eyes. The Major informed them that earth had to be imported from Sicily. In modern times, soil is conserved by Law. No wonder Fellows was going to hire the stone-cutters here.

SUNDAY, 15 OCTOBER 1843 - That evening, Fellows with his party, now of ten, including Jackson, the Foreman, the Italian cast-makers and the Maltese stone-cutters, went on board the *Medea*. Her personnel included seven officers and sixty-one seamen and marines from the *Queen*. The *Medea* ranked only as a second-class paddle-steamer, being then ten years old. She was, nevertheless, well adapted for the work on hand. During the period of the excavations, she was to serve as supply ship and receive cases of sculptures and casts, as they became ready. There would be regular contact with the Admiral, through ships calling in at Macry.

MONDAY, 16 OCTOBER - "A.M. 4.10 Lighted fires and up steam. Cast off and proceeded out of Harbour. Up boats." By 7 o'clock, the *Medea's* paddles were turning merrily and by 8.30, she was making "all plain sail" for Rhodes. The civilians spent the day in misery, however, keeping to their beds. Fortunately, by the time they were sailing through the Greek islands, the weather had improved, and they were able to go on deck. The vessel handled well, sailing at 7½ knots, reducing the expected time for the voyage by half - much to Fellows's relief.

FRIDAY, 20 OCTOBER - The *Medea* steamed into the harbour at RHODES at six in the morning and the passengers disembarked. They were to remain here for a few days, while

Fellows and the Captain made a formal call on the Pasha and finalized arrangements with Consul Wilkinson, leaving Scharf and Hawkins to explore the island.

Returning from a walk, Scharf was happy to observe an event peculiar to Rhodes. Arriving at the Gate, he found the drawbridge up, with a crowd assembled, noisily waiting to be let back into the town. Since 1523, when the Turks had conquered Rhodes, every Friday at noon, "the town is cleared of Christians [and Jews] and for half an hour, the gates are fast shut." The Moslem inhabitants went to the mosques for prayer, leaving the ramparts deserted and the places of defence unguarded. Then a trumpet was sounded, the drawbridge lowered and the Gate unlocked. The crowd surged forward and all returned to normal again.

In the afternoon, Scharf took a stroll about the town itself. He was much surprised by its shabbiness and air of decay. The bazaars were in ruins and little business seemed to be being done. There was no traffic and only a few people about. The houses did not have the highly ornamental lattices of the Maltese houses, and, except for the richness of the vegetation, Rhodes compared very badly with that other island.

He risked climbing up the dilapidated Naillac's, or Arab, Tower. From the battlements, a hundred and fifty feet up, he could make out the Turkish coast and a wave of excitement and nostalgia welled up, as he began to think about the months ahead. The square tower, with its fifteenth century carvings and shields stood at the end of a ninety-foot mole. It was further damaged in an earthquake in 1863 and has since been demolished.

The next day, Scharf had an unusual and remarkable experience. He was making some sketches in the courtyard of the Pasha's Palace, when he was sent for by the Pasha himself. He entered the *sofa*, the main chamber, in some trepidation, but was courteously invited to sit next to the Pasha on the *kanepe*. Hassan Pasha had spied him from a window and wanted to know what he was doing. Through an Italian interpreter, Scharf explained his occupation and was more than surprised when he was asked to make a portrait of the Pasha. This was so well received that Hassan Pasha requested him to make a proper painting of it while he was in Xanthus, to be given to him on his way back at the end of the Expedition.

117. Hassan Pasha of Rhodes.

The Pasha is shown as a middle-aged man with a trim black beard. He wears the uniform of the New Regulations - dark navy *setre* with froggings, scarlet *fes* with bright blue tassel - and fingers his *tespih*, worry-beads. When Scharf had finished his sketch, the

Pasha took the pencil himself and drew a portrait of Scharf: not very good, but his round face and spectacles make the head recognizable. Scharf proudly kept this 'portrait' all his life, pasted between the pages of his diary.

Zaman zaman, from time to time, the Pasha had to break off to attend to official matters, messengers and petitioners continually entering the chamber. The Secretary squatted in a corner, writing out the *tezkere*, a permit or a certificate, on thick paper. At last, after the customary cup of coffee, a bemused Scharf returned to his friends to recount this extraordinary adventure.

On SUNDAY, 22 OCTOBER, after Captain Warden had performed Divine Service on board, he and his Officers, Fellows and his team, all called on Consul Wilkinson, who accompanied them to the Palace, in a formal ceremony. As was the practice, Hassan Pasha sat in state with his back to the window, surrounded by his sons, officials and servants, all standing [pl. 150]. The Englishmen sat opposite. After politenesses, Fellows presented him with a handsome telescope with stand.

Hassan Pasha confirmed that the Firman, addressed to his predecessor, Hadgi Ali Pasha, was still valid, and appointed two Cavasses to attend at the site. He reiterated the assurance that cordial relations maintained between the two Governments and wished the Englishmen well in their interesting and important venture. A final exchange of courtesies brought the interview to an end. Early the next morning, the *Medea* sailed for Xanthus, and the Second Xanthian Expedition had begun.

III Xanthus; the encampment, preparations

MONDAY, 23 OCTOBER 1843 - By late afternoon, the *Medea* had dropped anchor off the mouth of the river XANTHUS. The Captain and Lieutenant John Massie of the *Queen* went ashore to reconnoitre. Massie was a fair, curly-haired young man of mild, gentlemanly manners, which endeared him to everybody. He would be in charge of the landforces. His pay was £182:10:0.

The sand-bar, the lagoon behind it, and the marshy nature of the delta created problems at the best of times. That day, the wind was up and the sea very rough. Disembarking either men or stores was out of the question, much to everyone's disappointment. The next day was just as bad and all on board began to suffer severely from the rolling of the vessel in the heavy swell, with land so tantalizingly near.

When disembarkation of stores finally began, the usefulness of the special pontoons, so sadly lacking before, became very evident, as they could pass over the sand-bar, even when fully laden. The Admiral had also commissioned two handcarts for work at the site, which were, likewise, to be of great utility. Thirty camels were hired to carry the heavy loads up to the site. The first items to be brought ashore were for immediate use: tents; bedding; cooking utensils; lamps. Then came the all-important ironmongery for the excavations, as well as ropes, lifting-tackle and grindstone. Iron rations completed this phase.

At this time, there were about twenty families living near the archaeological site in the little village of KOONIK [Kinik], besides a settlement of Chingenese in the myrtle groves to the west. Many of the peasants remembered the excavations of the year before, and murmurs of "Khosh-gheldin" [*hoş geldin*], welcome, were heard on every hand, as little knots of men gathered along the river banks, to smoke their chibouks and gaze anxiously at the proceedings. As more and more people emerged from the great ship lying just out to sea, and more and more strange objects were brought ashore, they were torn between curiosity and fear. Soon, the whole valley had become aware of this 'invasion'.

There were their former English friends, but also so many official-looking men in blue uniforms, with lots of gold braid on their coats and hats; there seemed endless streams of others too, in blue jackets, white trousers and straw hats, who took orders - and what of the men in red coats with swords and guns, drilling and shouting? Then there was the mushrooming of tents and prefabricated huts. It all clearly denoted activity of unprecedented importance.

Before establishing the main camp, a 'Halfway Station' was set up. Lieutenant Henry Temple, a handsome, dark-haired young officer of the *Queen*, was to be in charge here. Though small, the Station played a vital rôle: as signal-station between the camp and the ship; a crossing point; a depôt for stores; a collection-point for crates of Marbles ready for enshipment. The signal-tree was set up and naval sheers [hoist] made fast. A few bell-tents were arranged round a central fire, a source of general warmth, light and meeting-place of an evening. A road was built from here, up to the camp. It was completed within a week, and thereafter put to constant use.

THURSDAY, 26 OCTOBER - Fellows and his staff disembarked and walked up to Koonik to decide the situation for the camp. The old stone granary, which he had occupied the year before, and which had been appropriated by Spratt and his companions later, was still there. This was commandeered to serve as Headquarters. To begin with, the Officers and Fellows's friends had to cram in together, but it was not long before a separate house was constructed for the naval party, leaving Fellows alone with Scharf and Hawkins. Ten prefabricated huts, at £6 each, were set up, enough for all the workforce. When the weather allowed, however, some men would sleep under canvas, giving everyone more room. There was also the Doctor's hospital tent, the blacksmith's forge and the carpenter's workshop. Stores and munitions were kept in locked houses. Thus, "Queen's Town"[1] came into being.

All that was needed was an interpreter. For the time being, they had to do without fresh foods, being unable to communicate with the villagers. Game and wild-fowl came from foraging expeditions into the mountains or to the coast. Three hundred pounds of salt meat had been unloaded and they could bake their own bread. The Officers drank wine, ale and porter, but Fellows had bought a good supply of English tea in Valetta for himself and his two companions. He had also laid in a stock of tallow candles.

For the first two weeks, they all messed together, but Fellows disliked the boisterous jollity of the naval men, their drinking and their smoking, though they were always very sociable and on excellent terms. "We regularly sat down eleven daily, being 9 ourselves and almost always two visitors," Scharf stated. "Our eating store had been most abundant, the meal commencing with rich soup, then Irish stew, cooked meat, roast fowls, etc., pudding or preserve, cheese, and dessert. Breakfast has likewise been attended with boiled rice, cold fowl, pork or chops and toast."

At other times there was jugged hare or roast kid, delicious quails enveloped in bacon, tied up in a large vine-leaf and roasted, pigeon pie, duck and partridge, to alternate with the stringy local chickens. A trip to Patara would result in fish dishes and crab salad. The marshes were full of edible frogs [*Rana esculenta*] and edible snails [*Helix pomata*], marinated, for the more discerning gourmets, while the Cockneys in the company could enjoy their jellied eels and winkles.

More exotic still was porcupine, its white flesh having, not surprisingly, the flavour of sucking pig and was best eaten cold. Bear-meat tasted like fat beef, but was, unreasonably, rejected by several at table, who, on the other hand, found giblet pie, boiled in the crust of an old cheese, quite acceptable. The best meat of all was wild boar. This the Turks would not touch, much less eat, so, when on special occasions Boar's Head graced the Englishmen's table, the villagers would vanish away, leaving the expeditionary party to enjoy their feast in private.

Fresh fruit was the usual dessert, or *kymak* (scum), the curd which forms on top of simmered milk like clotted cream. It was used by the Turks as butter, that commodity imported from Russia. Fellows found it excellent with grape-sugar, "a more agreeable cream than I ever tasted at a London rout," he asserted. In general, he liked Turkish food, it was so wholesome. "Nothing objectionable is met with in it, no garlic of Italy, sour greens of Germany, or unknown compounds of France."

When the Officers had moved out, Fellows had the hut arranged to suit himself. He and Scharf slept on one side, Hawkins

256

118. Xanthus, inside No. 1 Queen's Town.

on the other. All the beds were furnished with Levinge's mosquito-nets and were covered with bright scarlet blankets. Shelves and cupboards accommodated clothes, books and artists' materials, and nails driven into the woodwork did duty as pegs. Wooden benches and trestle tables provided working places and a large fireplace, over which was hung an ancient sculpture of a lion's head, gave comfortable warmth. A branch with real oranges hung

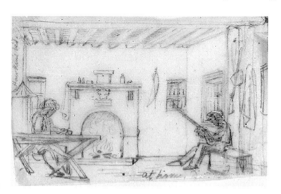

119. Xanthus, 'at home'.

from the rafters, giving fragrance and fresh fruit to hand.

WEDNESDAY, 1 NOVEMBER 1843 - The day was marked by the welcome arrival of Mania, along with the artists, Müller and Johnson, and Nicolo Dopolo, their dragoman. They set up their tent near Fellows's house, with kitchen-quarters for Nicolo. In a short time, "No.3 Xanthian Crescent" had become the focal point for the Officers and men of the Expedition, who were wont to congregate there after work, to drink coffee, smoke, sing and joke together. The peasants, too brought along their musical instruments, singing and dancing for their own enjoyment and that of the English spectators.

Bamboo, gourds, tortoise shells and brass wire were used to construct fiddles, long-necked lutes and mandolins, all decorated in bright colours. Eastern flutes are open-ended and blown from the side of the mouth, which looked strange and uncomfortable. The raucous *zurna*, a short trumpet or shawm, was accompanied by drums, made out of metal or clay bowls covered with skin. Cymbals of beaten metal and tambourines, incorporating coins as the sounding plates, crashed and jingled merrily.

The music was shrill, and lacked the lyric beauty of English airs, but the rhythm was stirring and the wild chant could have a singularly haunting quality. When an expert of the 'spoons' showed the English way of beating the bowls together on the knee and up and down the arms, the Turks were amazed and delighted. They held the bowls in their hands and used them like castanets. Their spoons were wooden, like the Welsh 'love-spoons'; to them, metal spoons with 'springy' handles were unknown.

One night, a gypsy performed the Turkish 'Battle Dance'. He first walked round in a circle, stooping low, his hands almost touching the floor, his thumbs and fingers held out stiffly like a fan. Then the pace quickened. Making writhing movements with his arms and, with great shakings of his shoulders, he accomplished a series of jumps, keeping his legs together, left foot slightly behind the other. The dance finished by his running round and round, his feet always flat, heels to the ground. At the same time, he executed complicated turns and bends of the knee, plunging and thrusting with the body.

258

120. Xanthus, a Turk performing the Battle-Dance.

Greek dancers had a different, more graceful style, which Fellows describes well. "I never was more struck than by the accurate representation of the attitudes displayed in the fauns and bacchanal figures of the antique," he wrote. "The uplifted and curved arm, the bending head, the raised heel, and the displayed muscles - for all the party had bare legs and feet - exactly resembled the figures of ancient Greek sculpture. The snapping finger, in imitation of castanets, was in admirable time to the lute accompaniment...The tradition, if it may be so called, is handed down by the boys dancing for the amusement of the people at their weddings and galas."

It so happened, that they were able to witness another traditional way of celebrating a wedding, which occurred by happy chance on Saturday, 16 December, Scharf's 23rd birthday; coincidentally, on that very day, a year before, the first of the Xanthian Marbles had arrived in London. Müller had heard that a grand wrestling-match was to take place that night in the myrtle groves, where the Chingenese were camped.

259

Nicolo led the way, holding aloft a flaming turpentine torch. The Captain, Officers, artists and marble-hunters followed in single file, making towards the sound of distant drumming. The peace and tranquillity of the starlit night, the wavering torches and the long straggling line of men, wending their way through the labyrinth of trees, produced the eerie effect of being transported into a land of make-believe. Then, all of a sudden, they came upon the source of the noise. The spectacle before them was one never to be forgotten.

"Seated round fires sat in circle, several hundred persons;" Müller told, "their basilisk eyes shining from under their white turbans gave them an unearthly appearance...such a group might have furnished [John] Martin with a subject for one of [his] grand and poetic pictures...The presence of our party was regarded as a compliment [and] we were conducted to a centre place and pressed to sit." Coffee was served, while more and more people crowded into the circle, which had now elongated into an oval, a veritable stadium for the games.

Scharf vividly described the opening rituals. "An old man of fine form, with long beard, and clothed in the most flowing drapery worn by their people, bearing a jar and a wand, advanced

121. Xanthus, the wrestling match, opening rituals.

into the centre, followed by a handsome young man with bare body and limbs. As he knelt, the old man proclaimed aloud the challenge, at the same time covering his head with the skirt of his garment and administering to him some water from the jar, which he rubbed over his body.

"Another young man, his antagonist, approached and after touching him, [received the ablution] and stood a little away from him. Drums and pipes sounded." The contest had begun. Hooking their legs round the other's, grasping, lifting and throwing their opponent, the bout was won, when one managed to place the other on his back. The contestants then collected gifts of half or quarter piastres from the crowd.

122. *Xanthus, the wrestling match, the contest.*

The major event of the evening was a fight between Oiel, chief of the gypsies, and the champion from a neighbouring village. Oiel, a handsome giant of a man, was a friend of Müller's; the challenger, though shorter, was equally muscular. Their lusty struggle lasted an hour. Oiel was finally granted the victory, to great acclaim. The Cavasses made a donation on behalf of the Englishmen, and they took their leave.

Back at Queen's Town, Scharf delightedly regaled Fellows, who had remained behind with Lieutenant Massie, with the details. The colours, the atmosphere, the enigmatic countenances of the dark Chingenese had all bewitched Scharf, and the attitudes of the wrestlers were just like those he had seen in sculpture[2] and painted on ancient Greek vases. Strange that wrestling was so popular amongst the Turks, but had fallen off as a sport in Greece. Mania assured the party that in Smyrna, the contest ended only in the death of one of the contestants, and told of a famous case, a fight between a Negro slave and a convicted man, which had ended in the death of both. The Englishmen were somewhat sceptical, but were prepared to believe in this legacy from the gladiatorial games of Roman times.

The weather was surprisingly fine and hot, for so late in the season. The nights were clear and still, so, as he had done in 1842, after the evening meal, Fellows would often conduct a party to view the tombs of Xanthus. By moonlight, or torchlight, their shapes could be seen more distinctly and the sculptures had a greater depth of focus than in the glare of day. "The light parts shone with peculiar whiteness and the deep mass of trees were only exceeded in blackness by the shadows in the recesses of the ancient walls." The configuration of the site, the theatre in relation to the tall pillar-tombs and the bounding walls, all became more apparent.

Returning homeward, they would hear the laughter and music of the sailors, "a merry set of beings", who were entertaining each other and trying to learn the Greek and Turkish ways of dancing. Out in the fields and down in the marshes, cicadas, grasshoppers and frogs, all set up an incessant chorus of their own, almost outdoing the human voices. The men were singing a parody of a music-hall ditty[2].

> In the days that we went marbling[3],
> A short time ago,
> Our Lads and Joeys [Marines] in their worst,
> Were dressed from top to toe.

We dug and pick'd all through the day,
Upon the ruined hill,
At night we'd mirth and jollity,
For time was at their will.

Chorus   And thus we passed our merry time,
Nor thought of care or woe,
In the days that we went marvelling,
A short time ago.

IV Marble-hunting, November-December 1843

The time had now come to make preparations for the actual excavations. To start with, a detailed plan of the ancient city was required. This was left to Fellows with the able assistance of Rohde Hawkins. Xanthus is on an outcrop, which rises steeply above the

123. Xanthus, panorama looking south.

plain. The Lycian acropolis [c. 200 ft] in the south is where the majority of the tombs and buildings of interest are located; the Roman acropolis [c. 500 ft] in the north, termed 'the Heights', is approached by a series of terraces. Its sides fall precipitously to the river on the north and west. On Hawkins's map, carefully placed arrows indicate the exact direction Scharf was facing, when drawing the tombs and his panoramas of the site.

264

124. Xanthus, George Scharf sketching the Box Tomb.

That was a major task, and not easy. "Walked about the ruins for nearly the whole day, attempting to reconcile myself to some system or general theory, but so much tends to distract and so many differences contradict one another, that to methodize the whole into one arrangement is impossible." He used his camera lucida to help him in this work. By means of a prism, the scene is projected on to a flat plate, enabling the artist to trace the outlines and get relative positions exact.

"The camera lucida renders every curve and peculiarity most admirably, in fact undeniably, and by its use, I have made many more drawings than I could have done otherwise," but out of regard for his eyes, Scharf had to pause from time to time, slowing down progress. The drawings show a greater clarity than before and are more draughtsmanlike.

As well as being a record of the site, these panoramas were probably intended to form the bases for theatrical spectaculars, in the popular manner of the day. Just as Layard's Assyrian discoveries were staged in the 1850s, Fellows's 'adventures' could have been dramatized and given as lectures in front of 'moving panoramas'. For the price of one shilling, all the excitement and atmosphere of exotic places and foreign travel thrilled audiences, who themselves seldom made more than a day's journey, much less went abroad.

SUNDAY, 5 NOVEMBER - Guy Fawkes's Day. Trees and scrub had completely taken over the site, hiding the antiquities and making excavation impossible. They had to be cleared before any work could be done. This day, the operation had an added purpose. In the theatre and down at the Halfway Station, materials for bonfires were piled high, to be lit that night by way of celebration. The Expedition had permission to cut down all trees, except the valuable Valonia oak.

Resin and turpentine from the pines made a fierce and brilliant blaze with much smoke. Looking down from the top range of seats of the theatre near the Harpy Tomb, the effect reminded Scharf of looking down into the crater of Vesuvius. "As fresh boughs were thrown on, the crackle and ascent of sparks was quite magical." The excitement of the onlookers was as intense as the fires, which continued to glow red all through the night.

MONDAY, 6 NOVEMBER - "Today, on returning to lunch," Scharf recorded, "I found our room full of people, which was a complimentary visit from the Aga of Fornas, attended by his suite. He with his secretary occupied Mr. Massie's iron bed, which with my bed serve as day couches. The Aga is a venerable man with full grey beard, long nose and small, quick eye; his complexion pale and his dress simple, being an olive jacket and striped robe, the remainder white." His gold-embroidered turban covered a crimson cap, and a crimson *kuşak* was wound round his waist. The stripes of his robe were red, blue, white and black.

"The secretary was quite the reverse, a little man, black hair and beard, dark brown complexion and large black eyes with wide mouth." He also wore an olive-green jacket, but his turban was plain. The stripes of his robe were a simple blue and white. The Kiara Giaar, the tenant or sub-Aga of Koonik, under the authority of the Aga of Fornas, remained outside the room. He was attired

266

125. Xanthus, visit from the Aga of Fornas.

in a purple and blue robe with a bright orange sash. The uniform of the New Regulations had apparently not penetrated to this distant quarter of the land.

"The rest stood round and lined the room, whilst our officers sat at the table in the middle of the apartment. Mr. Fellows occupied the chair next to the Aga; gravity and pipes were the great features of this interview, which lasted us three hours. He left us as a present, a very handsome young ox."

One of the Cavasses had been sent to show the Firman to the Aga, who was Governor of this district. His personal sanction was necessary, if relations with the villagers were to be cordial and respected. Later in the month, the Governor of Adalia, Mohammet Nezim Kaymakam Bey, made a formal visit to the camp. His titles proclaim him as Deputy to the Pasha, in whose Pashalic the site of Xanthus was located. The river belonged to Rhodes. The work of the Expedition now had the official seal of approval from both Pashas, confirming the wishes of the Porte in Constantinople.

Whilst the Turkish Governor was being entertained, Captain Warden saw to it that the militia- and cutlassmen were drilled and the small-arms men set to fire at targets, in a show of strength for his benefit and to impress the assembled peasants. On board ship, the crews of the 10-inch guns and the 30-pounders were also put on exercise.

More mundanely, the sailors' duties consisted in regular cleaning of the copper and hawses, repairing the rigging, painting the masts and yards, scrubbing their hammocks and clothes. The Captain insisted on a well-disciplined, tidy ship and kept his crew constantly employed. Morale was, in consequence, high and the men both healthy and happy.

WEDNESDAY, 8 NOVEMBER - "Today began our operations in six different places, four gangs being disposed about the site of the previous discoveries, the rest were engaged in the field below at the foot of the arch [Vespasian Arch; AD 80]." Casts were made of the head of Artemis in the centre, and elements of the frieze. The gangs were five men in the charge of an Officer.

126. Xanthus, the Vespasian Arch.

At the beginning, little of importance was turned up. Everybody felt a great sense of disappointmet, and Fellows could scarcely conceal his anxiety. Was all this effort and expense to be for nothing? Patience and perseverance were the watchwords and, sure enough, soon some statues were uncovered, including the body of a female figure, the head and arms of which (excavated in 1842) were already in the Museum. A fine lion was unearthed and some pieces of frieze. Everyone's spirits began to rise and cries of success rang out over the site, as piece after piece emerged from its hiding-place under centuries of rubble and neglect. "Huzza!"

> All hearts are gay, all eyes beam bright,
> If a curio they spy,
> And when a corner stone they sight,
> Their clamours reach the sky.
> With bas-reliefs and statues too,
> We quickly fill the crates,
> The Turks they view this sight so new,
> And wonder fills their pates.

THURSDAY, 9 NOVEMBER - Lord Mayor's Day. Fellows felt the findings already justified his predictions and invited the Officers to a celebration dinner on the double occasion of Lord Mayor's Day and the second birthday of the royal baby, little Bertie (Edward VII). Mania served Boar's Head and the men received an extra tot of rum.

The *Medea* had remained on station off the mouth of the river ever since their arrival, and Captian Warden often walked up to the site, or sent Lieutenant Frederick Stevens of the *Queen*, to enquire if the ship's stores could provide anything to add to the comfort of the Expeditionary party. Now his experienced eye noticed an ominous change in the weather, indicating imminent breakup into storms, perhaps with gale-force winds, so he wisely took his ship to the safe harbour at Macry, round the point to the north-west. "My decision was a judicious one, for it afterward blew very hadr from the southward." The *Medea* was to stay at Macry until the middle of December, when she came round to pick up the first of the crates.

As soon as was opportune, Captain Warden returned to the site, overland, a distance of about 30 miles with a 'stopover' at Minara, to take charge of the cutting of the large Gothic Tombs: the Horse [Payava] Tomb, Fellows's favourite, and the Chimaera [Merehi] Tomb, Scharf's favourite. The Horse Tomb had been left behind, after the first Expedition, being too large to be taken on board ship; the Chimaera Tomb had just been discovered, the lid half-buried in the ground, an earthquake having destroyed the structure, which was lacking the upper chamber, pillaged long ago.

127. Xanthus, the discovery of the Chimaera Tomb.

The beautiful marble lid[1] has a *quadriga* carved on both sides. On the exposed side, one of the horses is unusual - it looks back towards the charioteer like some on the Horse Tomb[1]. On the other side, the horses all look forward, in the more conventional Greek manner. Under their galloping feet, there is an animal,

270

128. Xanthus, the Chimaera Tomb lid.

perhaps a panther, but on the buried side, they are trampling the fabulous Chimaera. The carving is perfectly preserved by the earth, which has conferred an agreeable warm tone to the stone.

The general design is Greek, but the horses with their top-knots are Persian. The warriors wear Greek helmets, but their charioteers wear the Persian (or Phrygian) cap. Both Tombs are perfect examples of Lycian style, incorporating elements from both cultures.

Scharf was charmed by the simplicity of the carvings. "This [lid] alone, I think sufficient compensation for all the trouble and expense hitherto incurred in the expedition," he declared, and the sentiment was echoed by Müller, who wrote: "I am pleased beyond measure that we shall possess it as a national antiquity." *The Times* published a letter from a private correspondent, who singled out the Chimaera Tomb as "one of the most valuable relics of antiquity," and goes on to say: "the whole of the tomb [lid] is as perfect as when first executed, which must have been some thousand years since [4th century BC]." It is more than a pity, therefore, that this lovely sculpture was not on public view for a great many years. The gallery was, however, reopened in 1993, and from it, the sculptures on the Payava Tomb lid can also now be seen.

FRIDAY, 24 NOVEMBER - This day was saddened by the news that a young sailor had died. Samuel Sutton of the *Queen* had succumbed to intermittent fever. Dr Armstrong described him as being of a "weak habit of body and a bad subject for any disease." He had been ill for two days before seeing the Doctor and was then past recovery. His lonely grave, with carved headstone, was sketched by Scharf, a single English tomb amongst the innumerable burial-chambers of the ancient Xanthians.

His was, fortunately, the only death. A few cases of fever did occur, but all the patients recovered. Cuts and bruises and diarrhoea were the usual causes of complaint. Antonio, the cast-maker, was another matter altogether, his illness causing grave disquiet to the Doctor, to the Captain, and to Fellows.

Antonio had caught a severe cold through various wettings and, by early December, his health had deteriorated to the point when his life was in danger. He seemed to recover, but by the end of the year, his health worsened to such an extent that the Doctor advised sending him home. "I have invalided one of the Italian workmen, who had remittant fever," Dr Armstrong reported to Admiral Owen.

He explained that Antonio had led a life of dissipation, which had debilitated his constitution. "A longer residence in this district must eventually be attended with the worst consequences," the Doctor warned. "Under these circumstances, I commended to Capt. Warden that removal to his native clime was advisable...and he has accordingly been sent on board the *Medea* to await a passage to Malta and thence to Italy."

Since alcohol was forbidden to the Moslem Turks, Fellows, who knew of his debauched life, was not unduly apprehensive, believing that Antonio would not be subject to any temptations at Xanthus. The contrary, apparently, applied. "This very want has become his ruin;" the Doctor diagnosed, "the cessation of stimulants, which have artificially supported him, have produced the sad effects now visible upon him."

During DECEMBER 1843, the work of digging and raising fallen blocks of masonry progressed apace, and the cutting of the lids of the Gothic tombs proceeded inch by inch. This was necessary to reduce the size and weight[2]. The Maltese sawyers undertook this task. Four men from the *Queen* also volunteered their services. Fellows, with his usual concern, recommended that their pay be increased to equal that of the Maltese craftsmen, and that every-body should be given compensation for the heavy wear and tear on their clothes.

Cutting was slow work. It took four days to penetrate only two inches into the 'hog-mane' of the Horse Tomb. Equipment had been brought from Malta, but the necessary gritty sand had to be imported from North Africa, the abundant sand at the mouth of the Xanthus, being far too soft for the job. The naval party was now increased by the arrival of Daniel Burch, Boatswain of the *Beacon*, his presence specifically requested by the Admiral, for his expert knowledge in navigation of the Xanthus river. Scharf's services were in demand everywhere. He had to take accurate measurements and record the features of every piece of sculpture, before it was numbered and removed, labelled and encased for transportation.

Marbles began to appear with increasing profusion. On the 5th and 6th, two crouching lions[3] were uncovered near the Lion Tomb[4], which was being excavated. This was a small sarcophagus

129. Xanthus, excavation of the Lion Tomb.

on the top of a 9-foot high monolith. It had once had a cap-stone, like the Harpy Tomb. That had disappeared and the pillar was completely buried in the earth. The sculptures show a recumbent lion, warriors, and a man stabbing a rampant lion in true Persian style. He has a curled wig and the lion has a shaggy mane, also features of eastern sculpture. This Tomb is dated about 560 BC, and is the oldest at Xanthus.

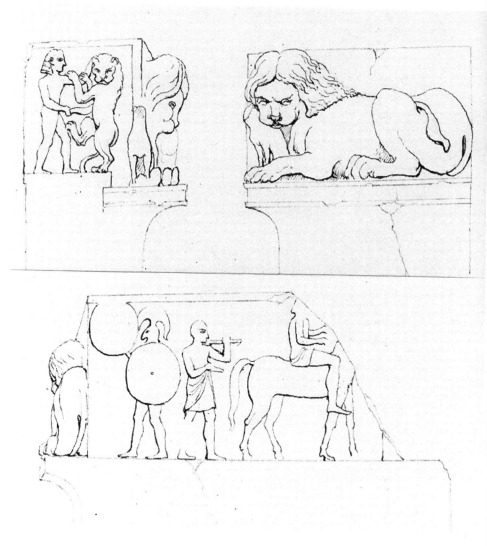

130. Xanthus, Lion Tomb, details of the grave chamber.

On the 11th, a particularly interesting slab from the Ionic Monument came to light. It shows a rider trampling a fallen soldier. There is a naked foot-soldier on one side. He is wearing a Greek helmet and carries a circular Greek curtain-shield. The rider is an Amazon. She is dressed in a short *chiton*, with flying folds, like those seen on the Bassae slabs. Unusually, all the heads are turned to the front. In 1840, Scharf had sketched a similar slab [pl. 109].

By the middle of December, there were enough crates ready for the *Medea* to come round to take off. It took four days to haul them down to the Halfway Station, where they were put on the

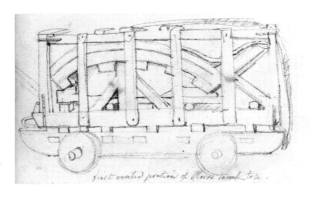

131. Xanthus, the Horse Tomb lid crated.

pontoons to be carried over the tricky sand-bar and out to the ship. Singing made the work go easier.

> All being packed in cases tight,
> And ready for the road,
> The lads in belted harness bright,
> Stand eager for the load.
> Tis then we have a heavy drag,
> Thro' groves and sandy soil,
> But all with spirit do the work,
> And never think it toil.

> *Chorus* And thus we passed our merry time,
> Nor thought of care or woe,
> In the days that we went marvelling,
> A short time ago.

275

V Three cast-making excursions - Pinara; Cadyanda and Tlos; Antiphellus and Myra

One of the chief purposes of the Second Xanthian Expedition was to make casts of inscriptions, and of those sculptures and architectural elements which would be impossible to bring to England. Fellows planned to make 'mock-ups' in the Museum of tomb entrances, incorporating real sculpture and casts. This was a revolutionary idea for museum display, very modern-day in its concept. Alas, as with his other well-thought-out plans, nothing ever came of this splendid idea.

SATURDAY, 11 NOVEMBER 1843 - To the once familiar cries of *"deh! deh!"*, a cavalcade of twelve horses, plus three baggage-camels, moved off to go to Pinara, about 12 miles to the north. They went at the dignified pace of the camels (3 miles an hour), the journey taking nearly six hours, owing to the large number of animals and the fact that the Italians had never ridden a horse before and were terrified.

When they got to the MANGHER CHI, a tributary of the Xanthus, they found the river in spate, the ford four feet deep in water. They had great difficulty in getting across, all got very wet

132. Fording the Mangher-chi.

and one camel lost its footing and was nearly swept away. Antonio, floundering about in his fear, got thoroughly soaked, the start of his illness. Müller and Johnson had also decided to go to Pinara at this time, and they had even more trouble, not finding a crossing-place for some considerable distance.

As was so often the case in this wonderful land, the beauty of the scenery saved the day for the Englishmen. The myrtles were covered with dainty white blossoms, as were the strawberry trees [*Arbutus unedo*], but they had bright orange fruits too, hanging like Christmas-tree baubles and deliciously refreshing to eat. As the sun set, their smooth red trunks took up the glow, deepening to crimson, and their dark glossy foliage turned a dense black.

In the fading light, they began to see the towering rock loom up, but there was no time to stop and gaze at it as before. Instead, they pressed on as quickly as they could and began the ascent to MINARA, while there was still a glimmer of light. The villagers crowded their roof-tops, crying out their welcome, "*hoş geldin!*" The Englishmen did not tarry, however, and rode on up to the acropolis of PINARA. Scharf felt again the excitement and fascination he had experienced in 1840.

"The road up from the village to the ruins was glorious in the extreme; such materials, groupings and effects." When the camels were brought up through the trees by villagers holding blazing torches, the scene was quite unearthly, "their bulky forms and waving dark necks showing in strong contrast against the mass of lights held by guides, who in turn received spots of most brilliant light." The magic of the moment, the distortions and the move-ments, transported him into the realms of theatrical illusion. "Such effects as were produced on different attitudes and varied forms, with all varieties of dress, age and countenance, I shall never forget."

Two days later, Fellows and Mania returned to Xanthus, leaving Scharf in charge, ably assisted by Rohde Hawkins. But they had hardly begun their work, when the storm that Captain Warden had foreseen burst upon them. The rain was so heavy, they were compelled to take shelter in the porches of the tombs. By 10 o'clock that night, a furious thunderstorm had developed. Flashes of lightning lit up the walls of their frail tent, the peals wonderfully prolonged by the echoing mountains. At 3 am, "a tremendous blast of wind, with lightning and thunder, started us from our beds, which were floating in water, the ground soaked...At this time, a shout from the other tent of Müller and Johnson told us that it was entirely blown down, and we felt our own was likely to undergo the same fate. Accordingly we dressed in haste and heaped the things as nearly as possible together in the middle of the tent, mine having been tolerably packed the night before from motives of prudence.

"We rushed up at random to the cottage above us, pausing momentarily for the assistance of the tremendous flashes of lightning...In the cottage, whither the Italians had already taken refuge, [it] was far from waterproof, indeed the floor was one pool of water, excepting just in front of the fire. Through the smoke and wall-chinks behind, the lightning burst vehemently...At daybreak the rain ceased; we returned in curious plight to our tent, and to our great comfort, our baggage was found uninjured. The bedding etc. was most wetted...We had tea, hot, very hot, and sat upon the centre pile of things, singing, in a kind of thankfulness, songs, merry ones too."

FRIDAY, 17 NOVEMBER - The casts[1] of the City reliefs [pl. 73] inside the portico of the City Tomb were finished before breakfast. Attention then turned to the frieze and pediment over the doorway [pl. 74]. An old Turk provided a roughly constructed ladder and helped in erecting a scaffolding of tree-trunks. The work went well, but when Antonio attempted to cast the Ox-horn Crest [pl. 72], which Fellows found so interesting, the mould fell to pieces and he had to do it all over again. Regrettably, he had indulged too much in strong liquor in the hope of allaying a fever, after his drenching on the way, and again in the storm.

The other two artists spent their days painting the landscape as a setting for the antiquities, rather than the tombs themselves. Müller declared Pinara to be one of the grandest subjects for the pencil he had ever seen. He was intrigued by the warm, rich colour of the worked stone, at variance with the cold grey of the natural limestone. He speculated on the use by the ancients of a wax polish, giving the sculpture a finish and acting as a preservative. He had heard about the Painted Tomb at Myra, and firmly believed that the Greeks had painted all their buildings. This had been done in ancient Egypt and in Mexico, in modern times in India and in China, so why not in ancient Lycia?

"If well done," he argued, "it blends and harmonizes the building with the surrounding scenery. What can be worse than a new, glaring, staring white building?" he asked. "The subject of paint, as applied to embellish buildings, is one that deserves the attention of our architects," and soon the polychromatic interiors in the Gothic-Revival style would overwhelm Victorian England. For the exteriors, bright red brick and terra-cotta against white stone dressings was eye-catching enough. Neoclassical buildings, like the new entrance wing of the British Museum, remained, however, starkly white.

While Antonio was labouring at the casting, Scharf busied himself drawing another grand panorama, the Pinara rock as seen from the Turkish burial-ground. It took him nearly a week to trace accurately the hundreds of little dots, which are the entrance holes to the rock-tombs. The camera lucida allowed him to do this. The cemetery appears in the foreground. The graves are marked "with stakes of wood, on which were flying flags of various colours...from the veil or turban": white from the women, the

133. Pinara, panorama from the Turkish cemetery.   279

colours from the men. They reminded Scharf of the funeral fillets of the ancients, "so often repeated on the vases and alluded to by ancient authors." He also observed that an article of the dead person's clothing, usually a pair of shoes, was carefully laid on the grave.

THURSDAY, 23 NOVEMBER - Scharf had sent the measurements of the casts back to Xanthus, and now camels brought the six crates required. Much arguing and cursing ensued in loading them onto the great beasts, which gurgled and snarled their objections the while. Scharf felt dreadfully sad to be leaving this wonderful city. He had enjoyed himself here so much; the place was so full of interest and the villagers so kind and hospitable. He had loved Pinara from the first, but then he had not seen Xanthus, nor Antiphellus, nor Myra, nor Arycanda. Now, he could make a fairer judgment - and it was the same as before, this was definitely *his* favourite city.

The caravan set off at half past twelve, the villagers once more crowding their roof-tops, but this time calling *"güle güle!"*, go smilingly, waving their hands and watching as the procession wound its way down from the acropolis and out into the plain, Scharf turning round to wave back until they disappeared from view and the great rock became an indistinguishable mass, blending into the obscurity.

Dusk had fallen by the time they came to the rope-and-pontoon ferry at KESTEP [Eşen], about halfway to Xanthus. When they finally got back, it was to learn the satisfactory news that all was well at the camp, and that several interesting new sculptures had been discovered.

The second cast-making excursion was a much larger undertaking, beginning with a voyage to Macry. They would be away for ten days, over the Christmas and New Year period, bringing back memories of those far-off days in Rome in 1839/40.

MONDAY, 25 DECEMBER 1843 - Christmas Day. Captain Warden read the Service on board the *Medea*. This was not the fine spectacle of High Mass in Rome with the Pope officiating, but it was a moving ceremony, nevertheless. To mark the occasion, Scharf declaimed Milton's *Ode on the morning of Christ's nativity*. This was followed by Christmas Dinner in grand style.

The next morning, the ship passed into Macry Bay. The day was marred by the administration of thirty-six lashes on a seaman for smuggling liquor. The Captain's Log records only two other cases when punishment was meted out: once for drunkenness on duty; once for theft - a splendid record of good behaviour and discipline.

Two days later, Fellows, with Scharf and Hawkins and the *formatori*, disembarked to go overland to Cadyanda and, later, on to Tlos. The *Medea* sailed to Rhodes to exchange the crates of Marbles and casts on board for coal and provisions brought over by the Maltese barque *Bouverie*. She had left Valetta on the 13th and was now at anchor in Rhodes harbour. This was an opportunity to start poor Antonio and his boy on their homeward journey. While at Rhodes, the Captain was able to convert bills-of-exchange into coin. He also obtained further supplies of fresh vegetables, bread, and tea for the company. By the 30th, the ship was safely back in Macry Bay.

Before Fellows and his party could leave, Mania had to go across to Levisse to procure horses for the excursion. While waiting, the Englishmen walked again among the tombs of TELMESSUS. Nothing new caught their eyes, so Scharf settled himself down to paint the beautiful scene. "The view of Macry itself, looking down from the Theatre [pl. 53] is superb. There is great effect with the rich and varied colour from the distant mountains. The red hills springing from the green plain, and leading the eye to the immense heights of purple and snow, which are the supports and barriers of Caria, surpass in richness anything around Xanthus."

He also drew the huge Doric Tomb of Helen [5th century BC] described and pictured by Clarke[2] on his travels in 1801. It was a tremendous size, the sides were blocks of stone 25 feet square and 4½ feet thick. Its 'Carian' lid was one immense stone. These, alas, were too good to escape the notice of builders in the modern age, and this remarkable relic of antiquity has been totally demolished.

In Scharf's picture, he shows two Turks on a hunting foray. One has a double-barrelled gun, the other holds the cage of their decoy bird, a red-legged partridge [*Perdix rufus*]. Sometimes quails were used too. The birds were taught to call, attracting a rival, which was shot from behind cover. Turks did not shoot birds on

134. Telmessus, Helen's Tomb.

the wing. In fact, they were inclined to believe this accomplishment of the Franks, to be a piece of magic. Birds were also netted, a very ancient practice, as attested to by a sculpture drawn by Cockerell near Kakava - meaning 'partridge country'. It shows a naked youth holding a net, under which a bird is cowering.

By 11 o'clock, the party was on its way to HOOZUMLEE [Üzümlü], the town at the foot of the escarpment, on the top of which the ancient city of CADYANDA is situated. The weather was hot and clear and a goodish road took them through the coastal marshes. As they began to ascend into the mountains, it degenerated into a rough track. This was the pretty scenery seen behind Macry, the red earth contrasting gaudily with the sombre firs and evergreen trees and bushes.

Early in the afternoon, the small cavalcade reached the little town, where the Englishmen received an elaborate welcome of recognition by the same kind Aga [pl. 58], their interested host of

282

1840, who made them comfortable in his *konak*. While enough light remained, the cast-making party rode on up to the top of the mountain to reconnoitre the site, the first city truly in Lycia that Fellows had discovered on his second journey to that province.

From this vantage point, they could look down on to Hoozumlee below. The town was quite large with a mosque and a single minaret. Each house had its own enclosed garden and the land round was divided into fields and plantations. In their eagerness, the cast-makers began clearing away the vegetation, the villagers soon joining in, to expose the broken tombs.

"The site presented...is as novel as it is grand, [owing to] the effect of these masses of rock, displaced by volcanic convulsion. Each mass is of rounded form and containing a Lycian tomb; some are even torn in two, showing the inside of these recesses in a most curious manner. One is actually thrown upside down. Close by, and a little in advance, on the slope of a ravine, is the 'Thrown-down Tomb' [Hector's Tomb; pl. 59]."

The next day, Raffaelle and his boy Tomaso, began the cast-making. Several willing Turks offered assistance, while the Aga and his retinue watched as the moulds were made and left in the

135. Cadyanda, casting Salas's Tomb.

sun to dry. Casts were made of the sculptures on the lids and sides of both Salas's and Hector's Tombs. Fellows confidently asserted: "The casts of these, I doubt not will be valued as important illustrations" of Lycian culture and art. This would have been even more the case today, as the badly damaged originals are now almost worthless from an artistic point of view. Unfortunately, all but one (Salas's death-banquet [3]) of the casts have vanished through the passage of time. Scharf's drawings, however, present a clear record of these lovely and important sculptures.

136. Cadyanda, Salas's Tomb, detail.

By SATURDAY, 30 DECEMBER, the work was finished and the party moved on. They rode east, down a ravine clothed in Holm oaks and myrtles to the Xanthus valley. At the head of this ravine stood sentinel, a tall, square column with Lycian letters on it like the Inscribed Stele at Xanthus. It was 10 feet high, on a base 3 feet deep, the remains of a pillar-tomb. Unhappily, this has since broken up.

At the river, they turned south to their old friend, the BRIDGE at SATALA-COOE, where they crossed, and continued along the eastern banks to DOOVEER. The new Aga had transferred residence to the castle above, in the ruins of ancient TLOS. There, Fellows's party found the artists, Müller and Johnson, already installed. The Aga had greeted their arrival "with much brusqueness, and without the smallest show of hospitality." Scharf described him as uncivil, a "large, gross, sensual-looking man, surly and with a gruff, loud voice."

Ignoring his official duty to provide accommodation for strangers, the Aga had boorishly continued to smoke his pipe and pointed rudely to a hovel on the other side of the courtyard. Nicolo had remonstrated and cajoled, till he obtained an empty room for the artists and himself. Another was eventually found for the cast-making party. At last, the Aga relented to the extent of leaving a loaded pistol and a sabre in their rooms for their defence, a usual gesture of hospitality.

SUNDAY, 31 DECEMBER - *Şeker Bayramı*. Sugar Feast; the Lesser Bairam. Perhaps the Aga's churlish behaviour could be accounted for through hunger. It had been the final day of the month-long fast of *Ramazan*, and he was probably in no mood to receive visitors. This morning, his conduct was more correct. He handed out presents and provisions to his people in the tradition of the Day and also gave the English parties a sort of 'haggis', which came in aptly for their New Year celebrations.

All day long, men and boys could be seen returning home from their flocks, carrying a lamb or a kid across their shoulders, looking like subjects from an ancient frieze or antique sculpture, the animal destined to be dispatched at their doors after the time-honoured custom.

137. Man carrying a fat-tailed lamb.

138. Xanthus, sacrificial procession frieze.

MONDAY, 1 JANUARY 1844 - New Year's Day. Fellows now returned to Xanthus, leaving Scharf once again in charge of the cast-making. Raffaelle began on the base of a sculptured pedestal with reliefs of fighting, and views of the ancient city of Tlos carved on it. He then turned his attention to the Bellerophon sculpture [pl. 71]. "As each piece [four in all] was completed, it was lowered by a rope to Thomaso, who carried it upon his shoulder to our house," to dry out in front of the fire. This procedure seriously incommoded the Aga, who followed them everywhere and always occupied their room on their return.

Ousted from there through lack of space, he repaired to Müller's room. He sat silent, smoking, apparently deep in thought.

286

Finally he divulged the subject of his reflections. He was pondering on the real reason why these Englishmen were here and at Xanthus. He was quite unable to comprehend that they could have come just for pleasure and study. He dismissed the notion as totally untenable. There must certainly be a much more serious motive behind it all.

To leave home and country, wife and family, travel thousands of miles to an unknown land, just for that? No, it must be, could only be, in the hope of finding gold, which as everyone knew was concealed in the tombs. Were not the men at Xanthus taking some stones back to England? Müller protested, but could not shake his conviction. Finally, Müller conceded that Nicolo was right when he asserted that "the stones were to be taken home to build a *handsome house* for the Queen."

One night, Tlos was subjected to the speciality of the country, namely a tremendous thunderstorm. The Aga, who was, of course, seated with his guests, got up hurriedly and rushed off to his own part of the castle. Vivid lightning illuminated the habitation and crashing peals of thunder reverberated all around, accompanied by a deluge of rain. Needless to say, water poured into the rooms and very soon everything was soaking wet. Part of Müller's abode blew down and makeshift repairs had to be effected by tearing up the floor-boards. In each room, there was a huddle of people vainly trying to keep warm and dry round the fire.

Suddenly the Aga reappeared in Müller's room. In he stalked, together with his retinue, who "arranged themselves all in a row, and *let off the steam* from their damp clothes" in front of the fire. This giant of a man, over six foot tall, flanked by attendants all in sopping vestments, cut a rather ridiculous figure, much to Müller's amusement. Keeping a straight face nevertheless, he administered solace in the shape of fresh pipes and calming coffee. It would seem, that the castle had once been struck by lightning, wrecking the stables and killing some horses, a calamity which could easily be repeated.

The storm delayed the departure of Scharf's party, and decided Müller on remaining a little longer, having lost so much drawing time. When Scharf did get away, it was hotly debated whether to risk crossing the Mangher, where they had had such trouble on the way to Pinara, or to go back upstream the six or seven miles, to cross by the Satala Bridge. They finally opted for the ford and luckily had no difficulty in getting across.

On their way south, Scharf was greatly surprised to find himself hailed in Italian. The shout came, in fact, from a Frenchman. He invited the strangers into his house, cut out of the living rock. The arched chimneypiece, the seats, cupboards and niches were all hollowed out of the mountain. His bed occupied a recess on one side, the kitchen on the other. With rugs covering the earth floor and with numerous cushions, he had made his "haunt of boars and jackals" really very snug.

Over coffee, he told his story: his employer, a German, lived in Smyrna, and he himself had lived in Asia Minor for the past six years. He had purchased a large tract of land, the area of a ride of one-and-a-half hours, for only TL14 (14 gns). He also owned some Yeeilassies to the north. Scharf described him as "the very picture of a squalid Frenchman". His low opinion of the French was shared by Fellows, whose experiences had caused him to write frankly: "I cannot like the middle classes of the French nation, particularly in travelling and in rough weather; they have little idea of cleanliness, never shaving or dressing, and often exhibit all that is disgusting in the epicure, added to the German unmannerly mode of eating."

At half-past two, the party came to the MANGHER CHI, which descends a gorge in the mountains and spreads over a broad expanse of stones in a series of deep streamlets. They were home at Xanthus by four. Müller and Johnson returned a few days later, having run out of paper.

Tlos was *his* favourite city. He had found the fortress-like situation much in accord with his ideas of Romantic landscape, for "nature in her wild moods, her savage beauty" was for him far more "sketchable" than the grim antiquities at Xanthus, laid bare to the glare of the sun. He had also conceived a sneaking regard for the dour old Aga. After the initial setback, Müller was not sorry to keep his company and to listen to his tales and beliefs. One such concerned that mysterious place, Yeddy Cappee, where one of the passages of the ancient Roman building, which caused so much fear in the minds of the ignorant Turks, was blocked at the end by a large stone, with 'cryptic' writing on it. Behind was, of course, a treasure-house of gold.

"*Bir varmış, bir yokmuş*," - Once upon a time, the Aga began, two Turks resolved to steal the gold. They had started to remove the stone, but a terrible fate awaited them. The Keeper within, a Giant wearing chains of gold, had struck them dead on the spot, in spite of the amulets and talismans they carried. Their black slave had witnessed the scene and run off to report the matter.

Bir az evvel - a little while ago - the present Aga, well armed and supported by a large retinue, had bravely been to see this baneful 'cave', and heard the Giant inside counting his golden coins. He then slyly asked Müller to persuade the sailors from the Expedition to blow the stone right away. It would not require more than two camel-skins of powder, and they would be rewarded with one third of the treasure. Or, indeed, Müller himself, a person who clearly possessed magic powers - for did he not strike fire from the walls? - could surely spirit the stone away.

Müller then asked the Aga to show him the place, but the next day, the Aga was not to be found, nor the next, or the next. "Here was a great Turk, armed to the teeth...afraid to go and point out a hole in a building, not half a mile from his house," Müller laughed. He and Nicolo boldly ventured into the passage themselves, but when they neared the end, Nicolo, much impressed by the Aga's tale, took to his heels, leaving Müller alone with the Giant. He found the stone with some 'magic' writing on it, and did in fact hear the metallic clink of something dropping.

His logical explanation was that the stone was only a piece of ancient marble with an inscription on it and that, when it was moved, it had let a blast of mephitic air escape, killing the Turks. The dropping noise was simply water seeping through the limestone of the mountain. As for his own magic powers - he used non-safety, phosphoric matches, which he struck on stone to light his pipe[4].

The last cast-making excursion was the most ambitious, involving a large party, and lasting nearly two weeks. On SATURDAY, 17 FEBRUARY 1844, a warm, cloudless day, Fellows and his team; Mania; the *formatori* and carpenters; with Edward Hore, Mate of the *Queen*, to take charge, started for the coast at KALAMAKI, Fellows seizing the occasion to make a courtesy call on the Aga of Fornas.

A boat was moored ready, furnished with rugs and cushions, and a four-hour voyage brought them to ANTIPHELLUS [Kaş]. While the *formatori* made casts of a long bilingual inscription, Fellows searched amongst the ruins on the beach for others, but found nothing new. Since his previous visit, the modern town had swallowed up many of the remains. Two years earlier, Spratt had counted only eight houses, but now they lined the beach. Using his camera lucida, Scharf made another sketch of the lovely slender Gothic tomb, drawn by Fellows in 1838 [fig. 13], so much more elegant than the usual squatter forms of that area. Two days later the party set off again.

TUESDAY, 20 FEBRUARY - "Beautiful clear weather. At ten, we went on board. Our hopes for a land breeze at noon failed and we were compelled to depend mainly on rowing, which is but slow work...Instead of four hours, we lay almost motionless, not even in sight of KAKAVA [Kekova, ancient DOLICHISTE; Greek, longest], but just before sunset, making use of a faint breeze, we passed inside, between that island and the mainland," yet another bad voyage. But worse was to come.

With no hope of getting to their destination that day, Fellows decided to go on shore here for the night. Mania was sent to the Greek custom-house to seek lodgings. "In an instant, he rushes out with violent exclamations and begins to beat his legs; they were without exaggeration covered with fleas - and he had not been in two seconds. This gave great fright to Fellows and Hore, to whom I had lent my bed, finding fleas tortured him more than myself." There was no other possible house, so, the night being calm and mild, they opted to sleep on the beach.

A tent was set up with an extra awning, rugs and benches were taken from the boat, and a lantern hung from a spar. "The bivouac on the beach, our fires lighted in recesses of ancient tombs, the assemblage of Turks, with ourselves stretched on a mat with cloaks, canteen, traps, etc., were really combinations worthy of a picture," and so saying, Scharf made a quick sketch of the scene. Fowls, milk, eggs and bread were kindly brought for them and it soon felt quite comfortable, more than would have been said of the flea-ridden house for all its walls and roof.

290

139. *Kakava, bivouac on the beach.*

In the morning, they went up to see the Byzantine fortress on
the top of the hill, proposed as an alternative resting-place the
night before, but that had only bare castellated ramparts and no
roof at all, being a total ruin. The village is now called KALE
(Castle). Late Greek and Roman sarcophagi littered the shoreline.
On one, they found the ancient name, APERLAE. The Turkish
name, Kekova, derived from the abundance of partridges [*keklik*]
which ran, about the ruins calling [*kekelik*, stutter].

A three-hour row brought the party to their final destination,
the mouth of the river DEMRE, the ancient MYRUS. It was
banked up by sand and the passengers had to be carried ashore.
The boat was beached and the cast-making group straggled the
long three miles to the site, passing a well-preserved late Roman
house tomb of the Corinthian Order on the way. Its arches of fine
masonry rise to 40 feet. Its forbidding foursquare solidity deserves
the local name, Karabucak - Black Tower.

At MYRA, the Englishmen were given lodging with the Greek
priest. The room was on the upper floor, reached by a ladder. With
their own beds, mats, tables and chairs, books and personal
belongings, it soon took on the aspect of home. The Priest contributed more rush-bottomed chairs and the carpenter built another
table.

291

From the window, they looked down upon the roof of the Church of Saint Nicholas[5]. To Scharf, the place was just like a khan, rooms round a quadrangle, but with the little church in the middle rather than a kiosk. The courtyard was paved with round black and white stones. There was a small column, perhaps an ancient Greek altar, where a fire was lit on the Festival of Saint Nicholas (5 December) "to light the groups of dancing votaries. At other times, it seems the favourite seat of our priest."

The interior of the church was quite plain. Scharf looked behind the iconostasis (sanctuary screen) and "was surprised at the collection of things in such a place: upon a broken table were thrown old clothes, a bason, gourd, a set of pictures nearly effaced by kissing - 7 rotten with worms. Some shabby candle spikes and broken lamp glasses were mingled with old books and palm branches. Among these glittered a coffee pot, a richly chased silver censer, and a rolled up surplice, embroidered."

Regarding the ceremony, he wrote: "The hum of service going on in the little church of our courtyard, is heard morning and evening...On approach, this murmur assumes the sound of a rapid gabble." Fellows was not impressed by the Orthodox service either. "In the Greek church, the dresses are more splendid than the Romish;" he commented, "but the whole effect is quite in contrast. In this church there is not the slightest semblance of devotional feeling." He did not see an uplifted eye or any attitude of adoration.

He describes the priests as "ordinary-looking men of the world; they sing the service in merry time, in a common but rather nasal tone, and look about them as if they were in the crowded streets instead of a place of worship." Spratt had written of "mummery" in this church, and when he and his companions had neither crossed themselves, nor joined in the kissing of the icons, the priest had enquired whether they be Christians at all.

The priest himself was not old, but his deportment was "undignified; he smokes incessantly and, as he passes along, touches the objects nearest to him like little boys at home." After the middle of May, the poor man was left entirely on his own, all the villagers going to their Yeeilassies, on account of the unhealthiness of the place, the heat, and the overwhelming number of mosquitoes and gnats.

140. Myra, the Greek priest.

"A large black fly also appears at that season, which stings the cattle; at its approach, they are described running as if mad into the mountains," Fellows reported with feeling, being a martyr to insect bites himself. During their stay at Myra, both he and Mate Hore complained bitterly of "animal attacks".

293

THURSDAY, 22 FEBRUARY - "Sunless day. Immediately after our early breakfast, we all proceeded to the [Painted] Tomb, in fact the chief object of our present excursion. Without loss of time, operations of plaster were commenced and three large pieces were finished by sunset." While Raffaelle and his assistant, Paolo,

141. Myra, Raffaelle making casts at the Painted Tomb.

were thus engaged, Scharf began a drawing of the eastern group of rock-tombs[6], again making use of his invaluable camera lucida. Fellows had already painted the western group [pl. 90]. The tombs are mainly of the window type but some have gable ends and pediments. In one, Scharf drew the grand sculpture of a lion attacking a bull in true Persian style. This sculpture has now fallen away through decay, but fortunately his sketch survives. Inside the portico are sculptures showing a death banquet and the curious figures of the Artemis of Thera [ancient Kalliste - Greek, beautiful - now Santorini, in the Cyclades].

142.
Myra, rock-tombs,
the eastern group.

Later on, he went to sit in the Roman theatre. The wind got up and he felt as if he could be blown away. Nevertheless, it was lovely sitting there, so early in the season, yet surrounded by the flowers of an English garden in high summer. The showy heads of camomile plants and bright orange marigolds contrasted with the spikes of delicate mignonette and bold purple lupins, along with the deep blue of borage and alkanet, all growing at random amongst the seats. Beyond, he could see the glittering waters of the sea.

"It is a glorious place for the romantic mind," he mused. "Nature's ruin here is very probably more excitive [sic] of admiration than the pristine, gorgeous icons and trim of the Roman peoples...Some parts remind one of the bygone time; others so perfect that one might expect the rush when the play is over." The soffits and cornices showed rich carvings and ornamentation, but were in a very unstable state. "The centre door of the proscenium has jambs of enormous scale...The whole is shaded by a magnificent castor-oil plant."

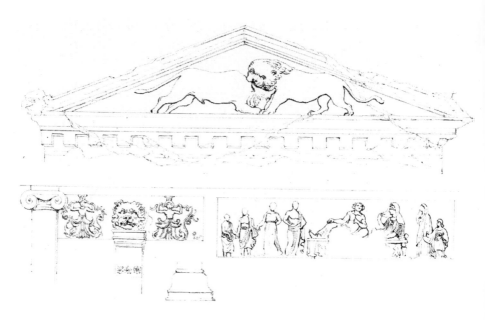

143. Myra, Bull and Lion pediment and Artemis frieze.

MONDAY, 26 FEBRUARY - "Beautiful day, seaward intensely bright. I painted two casts from inside the [Painted] Tomb, so as to be a facsimile of the colours upon them." Fellows had published a colour plate [pl. 92] of these figures in his *Account*. A reclining man, like Hector at Cadyanda, holds aloft a *rhyton*, a Persian ritual vase associated with funerary banquets, a convention to show the deceased was in the state of happiness[7]. He is semi-nude, the drapery is purple; his couch is yellow, with a design picked out in red. On the wall opposite, his wife sits with her hand-maiden. She wears a red dress and purple mantel. Her head-veil is

296

yellow. Her maid also wears yellow. There is a youth, probably her son, naked in heroic style, but with an Asiatic topknot left on his shaven head. Their background is blue, the man's, red.

Between them, on a central panel, there was a chubby little naked boy, holding a *strigil*, a Classical body-scraper, in his hand. His background was also red. Some twenty years later, he was sawn off by a Greek and taken away to Athens. Today, the colours have all but disappeared too.

Fellows, Hawkins and Hore took a "walk" - more of an hour-and-a-half's scramble really - along the shore to SURA, discovered by Spratt in 1842. It had been famous for its Temple to Apollo Surius and his fish oracle, but they found no relics of significance amongst the boulders. When they got back to Myra, it was time for Fellows to make arrangements for their return voyage.

FRIDAY, 1 MARCH 1844 - The party sailed down the ANDRAKE river to landlocked ANDRIACE [Andrake]. "At the bar, we leapt out and rambled on the sands [re-embarking] at the end of a set of craggy rocks that ran far out like a promontory, along which we scrambled. At sunset we were off the land, at sea and our sails filling gloriously in the breeze. [It] was so strong and favourable that we determined to use it and pass Castelorizo and continue our course for Patara." Too good to last - and had they not a 'Jonah' on board? The 'strong and favourable breeze' turned into a gale, making landfall at KALAMAKI almost impossible.

It was after midnight, when they finally got ashore. Taking a hasty repast of arrowroot to calm their queasy stomachs, they set out to walk up to the camp, hoping to get there in time for breakfast. "We took almost an hour to get to FORNAS [about 1 mile], where the people were in bed, and between yawning and stupidity could not understand our want of a guide along the mountains to KOONIK; the marsh they said was still too full of water. The moon was bright and the walk pleasant.

"Unfortunately, the worst road and that most covered with thickets fell to our lot between her going down and day break. The morning rose damp and wet. At some Yoorook huts we procured milk and fresh bread and arrived at home long before horn-blow", in time for breakfast after all.

Scharf rounds off his account with the satisfactory report that all were well and that only three more crates had to be got down river. The crates from Myra arrived by camel the following day.

VI Marble-hunting, January-February 1844

SATURDAY, 6 JANUARY 1844 - "The ploughing season has now begun and we are already inconvenienced by the people stopping up our paths by fences of thick brushes and stones...The Kiara Giaar sent a threat that he would destroy our path across his district, which we bade him do at the peril of being carried at once prisoner to Adalia by our Cavass."

It had been stipulated that the paths should remain open and that the people would be remunerated at the rate of about 20k. [4s.] per field. The Kiara Giaar was the only person to object, claiming TL10 [over £10] reimbursement. The Aga of Fornas was consulted, and he decreed that, as punishment for his outrageous demands, he should receive no payment whatsoever. This decision was to have its repercussions later on.

The weather at the beginning of the month was showery, slowing down the work. The air was mild, however - the temperature rising to the mid-60°s F - but the continual rain turned the roads into quagmires and the river Xanthus began to rise ominously. The *Medea* was forced to remain in the shelter of Macry Bay and the *Bouverie* in harbour at Rhodes.

TUESDAY, 16 JANUARY 1844 - The arrival of the survey vessel *Devastation* (6)[1], on her way to Malta with dispatches from the Capital, caused quite a stir in the camp. She had been ordered to call in at Xanthus to pick up any cases ready. They would be kept in dry store at Malta. There was a sudden spurt of activity by all hands, in an effort to get the cases down to the river mouth, in spite of the adverse conditions. Two days later, however, the ship was obliged to seek safer anchorage at Macry, leaving the larger Tombs behind. At Macry, the crates on board the *Medea* were trans-shipped, and the *Devastation* sailed.

SUNDAY, 21 JANUARY - "Tremendously wet, awful storms and continued darkness." Lieutenant Massie had never known the pressure so low in the Mediterranean. The glass had sunk to two points lower than at the time of 'the Great Storm of Liverpool'. In

298

the night of 7/8 January, 1839, a storm had passed in a broad swathe across Ireland and on to Liverpool and Manchester, extending as far as Scotland. Shipping in the Mersey had been destroyed and over a hundred persons drowned. Elsewhere, property and trees were swept away, people and animals killed and many fires started, the destruction similar in scale to that caused by the storms of 1987 and 1990.

At Xanthus, a tremendous hurricane blew. "Devoted this keep-at-home day to working at the Pasha of Rhodes's portrait...Whilst at dinner," Scharf wrote, "we were alarmed by much shouting and running and intelligence was brought that the river was overflowing the fields just under us. By the light of the moon, we saw the water pouring over from the ditch and in a few minutes, the field was a sheet of water, in which the new moon and stars were beautifully reflected.

"A general consternation prevailed among the people; the sailors proceeded different ways to render assistance. Men and boys running to and fro with torches driving cattle, and the cries of fear from the women and children heightened the excitement of the scene." The Expeditionary party in the safety of the high ground of the acropolis hill began to be seriously worried for those in the low ground of the plain at the Halfway Station. Luckily no one came to any harm.

Two days later, the storm returned with a vengeance. The rain was incessant and the river again burst its banks. "We were awakened by the cries of shouting people. The flood had increased tremendously, every field visible from [our] elevation was deep in water, [which] rushed and foamed with terrible fury. Cattle were seen swimming in all directions and children and men wading about endeavouring to recover them, or, at least, prevent their being carried away by the main course of the river. [Seaman] Curtis and 3 marines ventured from the Station, where even in the house is water 1 ft. deep."

This was enough for Müller, in whose opinion the inundations rendered the scenery "only suitable to the study of a deluge picture". He and Johnson packed their things, put up a notice "To Let" on No.3 Xanthian Crescent, and departed for England, travelling via Rhodes, Smyrna, Malta, Italy and France. Lycia had not lived up to his expectations. Nor had Xanthus. Müller had incorrectly imagined that he would count as part of the Expedition and felt resentment when he realized that this was not the case.

Müller writes sadly of his farewells to his friends the Ching-enese, and tells how Oiel, hearing of his going, galloped down to the river and swam across, despite its foaming waters, to smoke a last pipe with him. Nevertheless, when Müller exhibited his paint-ings[2] in London, they brought him great acclaim. Nor is he forgotten. In the autumn of 1991, an extensive exhibition of his works was put on at Bristol Art Gallery, his native town, and several of his Lycian paintings were included.

Notwithstanding the terrible weather, some important finds were made. Little by little, the mosaic pavement of the Roman baths was exposed, bringing to light a beautiful coloured mosaic of Leda and the Swan. At a later date, the extensive complex had,

144. Xanthus, Leda mosaic.

apparently, been converted into a monastery. The walls had been stuccoed and painted, traces of red remaining. There was also a sunken area, perhaps a courtyard with a well, on the same lines as the Church and Monastery of St Nicholas at Myra.

On MONDAY, 22 JANUARY, a fine figure of a Sphinx[3] (one of a pair) was found on the acropolis. She was of the Oriental type with a female head and breasts, on a lion's body, with folded wings. The Egyptian type was never to be seen in Turkey. She is facing left. Pairs of Sphinxes[3], facing each other, were the frequent decoration in the 'gable-ends' of Gothic tombs.

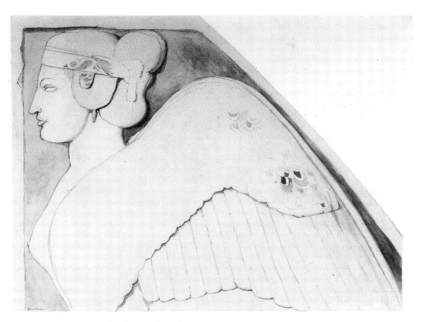

145. Xanthus, the 'coloured' Sphinx.

"Blue seems to have covered the whole background, the hair is yellow and the head-band and several parts of the wings, crimson. The top, flat part of the wings are patterned with different coloured scales with white edges. Some two or three appear black." Scharf published a coloured sketch of this interesting sculpture[4]. There is no undercarving on the wings: the feathers were added in paint. Even with foreknowledge, it is hardly possible to see any traces of colour today, so a colour photograph of Scharf's painting near the sculpture would add greatly to its interest.

301

Shortly after, another coloured sculpture[5] was found. "It is in a pedimental form and richly coloured. A fluted Ionic column supporting a Harpy in a short garment with sleeves, and a sitting figure with a wand on either side." Scharf's painting of this shows that one of the figures was wearing red, the other yellow. The Harpy and column were also red and the background, as generally the case, was blue. At the time, this and the Sphinx were described as "brilliantly coloured", but no colour can be seen on it today. Again, a coloured reproduction would add knowledge and enhance the display.

146. Xanthus, the Harpy on a column relief.

"Other slabs with cocks and hens have come to light[3]." The fighting cocks have long legs, like those still bred in Turkey for sport. The best came from Rhodes; exceptionally good specimens were sent as gifts to the Sultan. They are of Persian origin and were introduced into the country about 500 BC.

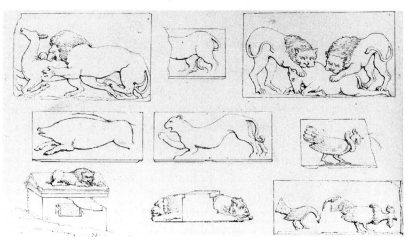

147. Xanthus, animal slabs and the Lion Throne.

302

Excavations round the base of the Inscribed Stele[6], which Raffaelle was casting, uncovered the top of the monument, proving it to be the shaft of a pillar-tomb. Portions of the frieze and cap-stone were also uncovered. This was a wonderful find, for marks on the surface indicated that there had been something, perhaps statues, on the very top.

On FRIDAY, 11 JANUARY, to Fellows's deepest satisfaction, a large foot in a sandal, 11 inches long, with part of a leg was discovered, still attached to a piece of cap-stone. Renewed efforts were made, and just over a week later, like a miracle, the other foot and the rest of the cap-stone were uncovered. This Stele had always exerted a powerful fascination over Fellows, and now its true importance was revealed.

148. Xanthus, Raffaelle casting the Inscribed Stele.

In a reconstruction, Professor Demargne[7] showed that, beneath the cap-stone, there had been sculptured friezes with kneeling bulls at the corners, a Persian motif. On the cap-stone itself, there had been the Satrap Kherei, guarded by springing lions, in the Oriental manner, and a warrior standing to one side. Kherei, a bronze statue, had been seated in majesty on his 'lion-throne' [pl. 147; bottom row, centre], a strange "ugly" stone with the forequarters of a lion on either side, which Fellows had discovered in 1842. Its importance was now made clear, but it was to cause Fellows much anguish when it was wantonly cut by the designer at the Museum. The stone is still on display[8], but its relevance is not made clear as the reconstruction is not shown.

149. *Xanthus, the Inscribed Stele reconstruction.*

The weather had seemed to have improved, when, without warning, on TUESDAY, 6 FEBRUARY 1844, a hurricane struck, carrying the Doctor's tent away, as well as the outhouses and the beams of the portico to Fellows's house. It soon blew itself out, however, and then it really was spring. "There is a freshness in the morning air to which we have lately been unaccustomed," Scharf wrote in lyrical mood. "The late rains have washed the old leaves off the branches displaying so much better the objects of antiquity, which in summer-time lie quite concealed. The Theatre to this time was beautifully open, but fresh buds are covering many trees. The Storax[9] buds already, the wild almond is in beautiful [bloom]. The evergreens: Charubus[10], Oak, Olive and small leaved plants are changing their leaves. Small flowers of various colours spangle the ground, but are lost in the comparative size and brilliancy of the anemones. The bright purple and orange crocus or hyacinth is fast disappearing before a smaller yellow flower of the same character."

SATURDAY, 10 FEBRUARY - HMVS *Virago* (6)[11] arrived from Malta bringing dispatches, stores and equipment, including two spars to replace the broken ones of the shears at the Halfway Station. She also brought letters from home, Scharf's dated 15 December 1843. For Fellows, there was a copy of Dickens's new story, *A Christmas Carol*, published in time for the festive season.

Work at the site was renewed with fresh impetus and during the next few days all the cases of Marbles and casts were transferred to the Station and then on down to the mouth of the river.

> Whilst thus employed, Burch cries: Come my boys,
> Come give her steerage way,
> A bridge is nigh and none too wide,
> Haul, haul away I say.
> Then off we go; what cheer ye ho,
> Her helm she answers well,
> Another rally thro' the grove,
> And then we'll have a spell.
>
> Then having stood 10 minutes good,
> They start with strength anew,
> And trotting on so cheerily,
> They soon the station view.
> Then being there arrived at last,
> Our Luff [Lieut. Massie] thus to them spoke,
> Come quick the cases bundle off,
> You've time to have a smoke.

305

VII   Last days at Xanthus; Rhodes

WEDNESDAY, 6 MARCH 1844 - The final crate of the Chimaera Tomb was taken down river and everybody began to pack his "traps and curios", ready to embark for Malta before long. Scharf "ran" everywhere, saying Goodbye to his now familiar surroundings, to the tombs he had sketched with such diligence and to the theatre where he had sat watching the Bonfire Night blaze, all those months ago. It was impossible to think that he would never see them again.

Two days earlier, the Aga of Fornas had arrived in great state to the sound of drums and *zurna*, to settle some debts and pay his respects to the Englishmen and wish them well on their return to their native land. On the Saturday, Fellows, his friends and the Officers had all dined together and spent a last jovial evening in each other's company.

WEDNESDAY, 13 MARCH - An unlucky date, and an unlucky day. The Captain sent a pinnace and two cutters to tow the pontoons out to the *Medea* with the entire workforce. Fellows and Scharf said Goodbye to Rohde Hawkins, who was staying behind for a few days, before going south to Patara and then on to Smyrna. He would make his own way home via Athens, Italy and Germany to complete his studies. He was to arrive in London in September.

To start with, all went splendidly. "By daylight, we were all down at the river by the Mosque and embarked in the pontoons. Lieutenant Massie addressed the men in a short and pithy speech before shoving off and we passed down the river gaily, free from grounding on any flats or shallows, avoiding bushes at all sharp turns of the river and in fact every kind of danger, generally incidental to the voyage."

The shore was spotted here and there by groups of people waiting to see them pass, waving and crying out "O-ourlah" [*uğurlar olsun!*], Goodbye, have a safe journey! The dogs, Lion, Calabash and Jumbo, which had attached themselves to the party, chased along the bank, barking furiously. "On passing where the Station was planted, the signal-tree alone remained, not a vestige of the house existed beyond thatching, which was scattered about the ground." The signal-tree was collected later. The tools had been distributed to the villagers and for them the presence of the Expeditionary Force was already a thing of the past.

By this time, a wind had sprung up. The boats had just passed the treacherous sand-bar, when disaster struck. A strong wave broke over the cutter, driving it into the shore, where fortunately all the passengers were able to jump out. But the pinnace towing the other pontoon was thrown back onto it, damaging both boats, which capsized. Mate Hore and three men were washed overboard; one was nearly drowned. "He sank twice!" Scharf wrote in horror. Everyone finally reached the shore safely and the boats were beached.

But for Scharf, there still remained cause for alarm - his soaked paintings. "The sketches were thoroughly saturated, the colours had run from one to another and the gum-water [a fixative] over my pencil-outlines helped them to adhere one to another." All his work and effort over four months ruined. "By timely opening and separating them, I have prevented any material injury to them. They were all spread out on the beach and fortunately the wind had abated during that time." What a relief!

Captain Warden watching through his telescope, waited until he was satisfied that all the men were safely on shore, before sailing off to Macry to ride out the gale there. The Officers persuaded Fellows and Scharf to return to the site, leaving the other castaways to fend for themselves. Great was the astonishment of Hawkins and Mania, when their erstwhile companions suddenly reappeared at Xanthus. They told their sorry tale and were made warm and welcome at what had lately been No.1 Queen's Town.

The following day, the wind was far too strong for the *Medea* to return, so all remained where they were. Mania was sent down to the beach with provisions for the company bivouacked there. With true naval ingenuity, the boats had been upturned and with two tents and awnings and the benches, the men had made themselves tolerably comfortable. The Captain in his report of the incident praised his men and especially the Officers, who had slept in the open themselves, with all the seamen under cover.

FRIDAY, 15 MARCH - The Ides of March; another ominous date. The weather was glorious and, hoping to get off that morning, Fellows and Scharf had returned to the bivouac. The *Medea* had returned and most of the men were already on board. There was no possibility, however, for further embarkations, so, after a short walk, they joined the remainder under the upturned cutter.

SATURDAY, 16 MARCH - "We crossed the sand-bar drily, with care and with no loss of time. On going to the ship, we passed the pontoon with [Lieut.] Temple going to fetch the shears and the last of the light crates." The seven crates containing the Horse and Chimaera Tombs had again to be left behind, as they were too big to go down the hatchways and Admiral Owen had ordered that nothing should be transported as deck cargo[1].The great HMSS *Warspite* (50)[2] was even now on her way to collect them - or so they were told.

Charles Fellows did not go on board till mid-morning. He had returned to the ruins, to make his farewells in private. Hawkins and Mania had now departed and the ancient city of Xanthus was once more silent, peaceful and deserted, just as it had been when he had first set foot here on that fateful spring day, six years earlier. Only now the city was full of ghosts - those of the present for the moment transcending those of antiquity.

It seemed only yesterday that he had first beheld this place, yet since that time, he had paid a second visit here with his two youthful assistants - and had led two Government Expeditions. Can it really have happened? Was it really so? Looking round he could scarcely believe it. True, the site had been cleared of much of the encroaching vegetation and of the rubble of ages. Scattered pieces of sculpture had been removed. Nevertheless, Xanthus appeared much as it had done all those years before. True, the Harpy Tomb now lacked its frieze (replaced by casts in 1957), and the Horse Tomb was reduced to its podium. But all the other striking features remained.

Fellows felt a deep sense of thankfulness. His dream of preserving examples of the beautiful art of this unique place had been realized. Through his energy, a valuable contribution would be made to the knowledge and enjoyment of future generations. But, on this bright morning, he was gazing for the very last time at XANTHUS - *his* favourite city. There would certainly be no more return visits, no more Expeditions. Fellows could, nevertheless, anticipate years of work ahead: books to write and collaboration with young Scharf on the diagrams and illustrations needed; discussions to hold with antiquarians and epigraphists; labels to compose and explanations to give as to the significance of each object, each inscription, each cast; close liaison with the Museum to ensure that the Marbles were exhibited to their best advantage.

Now, however, it was time to say those farewells - farewell to the friendly people of Koonik; farewell to the magic of Xanthus; farewell for ever to that antique land of Lycia.

Captain Warden was himself quite moved by the occasion. He fully understood Fellows's emotion and his need to spend a little time by himself in that place which had come to mean so much to him. "It must be very sad for him," he wrote sympathetically to the Admiral, "in spite of his success in the discovery and the collection of valuable Marbles for the Nation, to say farewell to Xanthus for ever...[He] literally knew every stick and stone. It is easy to imagine him, alone, on the Heights, taking a last long look and then, turning his back on the site of all his dreams, so lately full of people and bustle, now deserted and still, knowing he would never go there again...

"Thus terminated the Expedition of which I may say with the Authority of Mr. Fellows that the objects of it have been completely obtained and carried out to the full extent originally contemplated...The Officers, one and all, have done the most ample justice to your expectations and to mine...and each in his station has fulfilled the hope expressed by you..."

Fellows was also quick to let Admiral Owen know of the complete fulfilment of his hopes, and to voice his praise of Captain Frederick Warden's management of the whole undertaking. "It rested with you, Sir, to make the various appointments and to these we are indebted not only for the success of the expedition, but for the perfect harmony and good feeling which has prevailed throughout every class amongst us."

Fellows commended each of the Officers by name and re-marked that the men had all worked well and willingly. He ends his letter by assuring the Admiral "that the full objects and anticipations of the expedition have been accomplished, and that our satisfaction will be shared by the Trustees of the British Museum as well as all interested in Ancient Art."

The *Medea* first returned to Macry to take on water. While waiting, who should they find in the square, but Hawkins and Mania! Now it was Scharf's turn to be surprised and to listen to *their* sorry tale. It transpired that the disgruntled Kiara Giaar, in revenge, had bribed a party of gypsies to lie in wait to rob and murder them - or so it was rumoured. Discretion prevailing, they loudly announced their departure to Patara, but rode off smartly in the opposite direction. The young men all dined together to laugh over their separate escapes and recall the happy time spent at Xanthus. Then for the third time, the friends shook hands, wished each other good luck, God speed, and a safe return to

150. Captain Warden, Fellows and Scharf say Goodbye to the Pasha of Rhodes.

310

England. Hawkins and Mania rode off and the others went back on board the ship.

TUESDAY, 19 MARCH - "a.m. 12.15. Weighed and proceed out. Reduced speed of Engines...to allow pontoons to tow with ease. 8.40. Came to...at RHODES. Sent the two larger Pontoons on shore." Captain Warden, Fellows and Scharf, with Consul Wilkinson in attendance, paid a formal call on Hassan Pasha to acknowledge, on behalf of the British Government, the facilities and protection he had afforded the Expedition and to enable Scharf to present him with the finished portrait [pl. 117]. Coffee and pipes accompanied the proceedings, the Captain pluckily joining the Pasha in the pleasures of the chibouk. Hassan Pasha congratulated the Englishmen on the success of their undertaking and wished God's blessing on each one. *Allah mübarek etsin!*

In less than an hour and a half, the audience was concluded. "11.15. Weighed and proceed out [to Crete]. P.M. Force 7. Sail."

VIII   The voyage back to Malta

For the voyage to CRETE[1], well over 200 miles to the south-west, the passengers - as usual - were in for a miserable time. The barometer fell and the sea grew very rough. The vessel rolled fearfully and, although the island came into sight at dawn, the *Medea* took all day to reach it, and was then forced to lie pitching and tossing in deep water outside the harbour all night. Early next morning, THURSDAY, 21 MARCH 1844, she ran for the BAY OF SUDA [Soudha], splitting her fore-topsail as she did so. By 11 o'clock, the vessel was, thankfully, at anchor, but she would have to wait three days for repairs to be made.

The following day, a large party disembarked to walk across the neck of the headland to the capital, CANEA [Khania]. The road was straight and level. Out in the country, the wild lavender, the aromatic cistus bushes covered with large crimson and white flowers, the tall spiky aloes, all seen against a background of snow-topped mountains, were a most glorious sight. The white minarets of Canea gleamed brightly in contrast to the sandy colour of the local brick.

They found the town full of Turkish soldiers looking rather sheepish in the new uniforms of the Nizam Djedid. "The fez is thrown far back on their shaven forehead, often displaying the fancy patterned skull-cap beneath, which looks the whiter in contrast with the deep brown of their almost negro features. They wear tight jackets of deep blue with a small order or insignia hanging at the collar under the chin; they vary, but the star and crescent is most common. The trousers of the same material as the jackets are loose over the hips and give a clumsy appearance to the whole figure."

Although most of the inhabitants were Greeks, the shop-keepers were nearly all Turks. There were many Arabs to be seen too. The Turkish language was scarcely understood, except in Canea. The Englishmen paid a fleeting courtesy call on the British Consul "who sustained the shock of an interview well." They then

312

did some shopping for Souvenirs. Lieutenant Massie bought himself an expensive fez for 10 shillings and, for a further outlay of half a guinea, a complete smoking establishment - long-stemmed chibouk, amber mouthpiece, clay bowl and metal dish - together with a quantity of the finest Latakian tobacco..

SUNDAY, 24 MARCH - "Divine Service, 9.30. P.M. 12.25. weighed." Their departure was given an extra dimension by virtue of the band music from on board a Turkish ship, which was entertaining Mustafa Pasha of Candia [Crete] and all the resident consuls. As the *Medea* paddled slowly by, the guests crowded the rail to wave them *bon voyage*.

The morning was fine and the glass rising. With a strong wind in their favour, they made "all plain sail", the ship speeding along at 7-9 knots. A splendid crossing was in prospect. But such luck could not possibly last: the wind veered round and set dead against them. This time it was the wind which registered Force 7-9. The foretop sheet was lost and the ship began to roll.

Scharf wrote miserably: "After Sunday, I kept my bed, the ship rolled awfully and today, in ploughing the waves against the wind, her bowsprit was almost entirely in the water. The noise with which every timber and beam groaned and cracked was nearly lost in the crashing of utensils, rattling of books and shelves, on rolling about (to the extent of their lashings) tables, chairs, sofas, etc. Three times when dozing, I was thrown forcibly from my bed on to the floor, having lost my hold. I could not read, hear, talk or think, and lay in a kind of unprofitable stupor. The glass sank, and stopped at the north-east wind.

"MONDAY was all rain and wind. TUESDAY night was a tremendous hurricane, and our speed was reduced to 4 knots. We were disappointed in hopes of seeing Malta on Tuesday morning and a southwest wind kept us back on WEDNESDAY afternoon. However, at sunset land was visible and after much difficulty, and almost without hope, we entered VALETTA harbour at 11 o'clock [pm]. We slept quietly and in gratitude for our escape." The *Medea* was moored to a buoy downstream and, by midnight, Captain Warden had run up the yellow Quarantine Flag.

THURSDAY, 28 MARCH - "Directly after breakfast, we left the ship for the Lazaretto [at Fort Manoel], where we have comfortable, clean apartments and are accompanied by Jackson [foreman], Raffaelle and Paolo [*formatori*]. The other 3 Maltese [sawyers] are in another portion of the Quarantine. Thus the ship is once more without civilians."

The Lazaretto of San Rocco had been established by the Knights of St John in the mid-seventeenth century. It was last used in 1936 and is now a tourist attraction. It was "one of the best conducted and most agreeable of all similar institutions," according to that indispensable guide for tourists, Murray's *Handbook*[2]. "It is under the direction of Mr. Casolini, who appears to make it his sole object to add as much as possible to the convenience of its inmates."

The passage continues: "A restaurateur lives within the walls...and the travellers are supplied with every comfort attainable...at an expense, which is moderate compared with the misery and charges of most other establishments of the same kind in the Mediterranean. The bastions of Fort Manoel allow its inmates to have the privilege of air and exercise to a degree unknown elsewhere."

The innkeeper, Giacchino Eriquez, charged 1s.2d. for an English breakfast with 2 eggs; 1s.8d. if meat was served as well. Dinner of soup, two courses, vegetables and fruit, etc. cost 3 shillings; 4s.4d. for extra vegetables and salad. The Guardian's fee was 2s.6d. a day. Extra beds, bedding, linen and furniture could all be hired at 8 pence a day.

While Fellows and his party were immured - for only seven days - the *Polyphemus*[3] sailed with the good Doctor on board. He had called in at the *Parlatorio* (visitor's room), to bid Fellows and his friends Goodbye, and they expressed their heartfelt thanks to him for his care of the party and his keen interest in the work at Xanthus. Several other Officers, the Captain and the Admiral visited the Lazaretto to see Fellows and put him in touch with the outside world.

The *Medea* had been warped into Isola Creek, where she was tied up to undergo a thorough overhaul, cleaning and repairs. The powder and shells were landed at the Magazine and the Xanthian Marbles discharged into HMS *Queen* (110), the Admiral's own ship. On MAUNDY THURSDAY, 4 APRIL, 1844, the party obtained their *Pratique*. The Maltese workmen went to their own homes and passages were sought to England for Jackson and to Rome for the *formatori*.

Fellows and Scharf, once more on their own, repaired to their old haunt, Mrs. Dunsford's. They were to stay another ten days in Valetta, awaiting the arrival of the *Warspite* with the last of the Marbles. They would then start their journey home, this time travelling via Sicily, Italy and Paris. That evening, the Expedition was rounded off with a formal dinner party in their honour on board the *Queen*, as guests of Admiral Owen.

Earlier in the day, Scharf had noticed a woman, clothed entirely in white, with thin boots on her feet and a sort of sack with eye-holes on her head. Heavy chains shackled her ankles and she held out her gloved hands in supplication. She was doing penance. "They say this extraction of penance is frequent in Malta, but is sometimes modified by an open money-box being placed in the hands, which as soon as it accumulated a certain sum from compassion, freed the penitent."

Maundy Thursday, Good Friday, and until 10 o'clock on Saturday morning, church bells were silent, but from the belfries a kind of huge rattle was constantly ground. "The vulgar explanation is that they are 'grinding Judas's bones' by way of execration," Scharf was informed.

GOOD FRIDAY, 5 APRIL - "I was attracted by the music into St. John's church, where a very rich service was being performed." A gold crucifix was uncovered and raised in reference to the Day of the Suffering. Then, "the effigy [of Christ] was taken down, laid on a cloth on the ground and mourned by all the priests; the Miserere was beautifully sung, and being ended, the figure was carried with great care and pomp, with a canopy and tapers, besides extra attendants, and placed in a side chapel, typical of the entombment. Now candles were lighted and all golden ornaments deprived of their black mufflings. In Italian churches at this period," Scharf adds, "it is usual to tear or separate a large black curtain with reference to the rent of the veil of the Temple."

After dinner, he and Fellows went to the Strada Mercante to witness the Good Friday procession. "The pomp consisted in various stupendous groups [of figures], representing the seven stages of the Passion," each scene carried by men in black, except the last, when they wore purple. Pairs of churchmen and candle-bearers walked between each group. The procession was preceded by a long crimson banner and a band playing a solemn march with muffled drums. Then came the clergy. It ended with the figure of Christ, profusely decorated, laid out on a sumptuous catafalque under a canopy, followed by the empty Cross. About twenty penitents brought up the rear.

EASTER SUNDAY, 7 APRIL - "All the streets were in a bustle, men walked about with fire-brands." The effigy of Judas was burnt and a large group of "Christ coming out of the Tomb with frightened soldiers" was paraded about. Finally it was "run home", up the hill of St Elmo. All the children carried Easter eggs and new dolls to commemorate the day.

The two travellers treated themselves to a special Easter dinner. Four years before, incredibly, they had feasted on roast lamb, cooked by Mania, at Xanthus; now they were awaiting the arrival of the last of the treasures from that site, before continuing their journey to England and home.

EASTER MONDAY, 8 APRIL - "Tremendously wet, worked at home."

TUESDAY, 9 APRIL - This day began happily with the exciting news that the *Warspite* had arrived, but the mood soon turned to one of dismay, when, on going alongside, it was discovered that the seven crates of Marbles were not on board. Captain Lord John Hay had called in at Macry and had been informed that the *Medea* had just sailed. He had not gone over either to Xanthus, or to Rhodes.

Admiral Owen was greatly displeased by his lack of initiative and sent orders that he was to return there immediately. He sent Lieutenant Temple and four men from the *Queen* with him to superintend the recovery of the crates, which were safely brought away to Malta. The last shipment of the Xanthian Marbles arrived in England on 14 December 1844.

After the vexations of the morning, Fellows and Scharf were happy to spend one last evening in the company of Captain Warden, Lieutenant John Massie and their fellow Officers in the wardroom of the *Queen*. It repeated the social evenings and the celebrations that had characterized their time together at Xanthus. Their merry songs delighted the other Officers, who had been invited to share this farewell party.

> And fill a glass to every lass,
> And all our friends so dear,
> And with them many a happy day,
> And many a happy year.
> We'll give the *Queen* with all our hearts,
> And may her people be,
> Supporters of our country's cause,
> And merry too as we.

Chorus   And thus we passed our merry time,
> Nor thought of care or woe,
> In the days that we went marbling,
> A short time ago.

IX Homeward bound

MONDAY, 15 APRIL 1844 - The day was spent making official calls and saying Goodbyes. Müller and Johnson had just arrived in the Lazaretto, so Fellows and Scharf went to see them in the *Parlatorio*. They called on the Governor of Malta, Sir Patrick Stuart, on Captain Warden, and, of course, on the sympathetic champion of the Expedition, Admiral Sir Edward Owen. Lastly, they made the rounds of the ships in harbour: the *Vesuvius*; the *Devastation*; the *Queen*; and their trusty old work-horse, the *Medea*. She had done her task so well. A few years later, in 1850, she attained brief fame as the vessel which brought the famous Koh-i-nor Diamond to England. Both the Diamond and a model of the ship were put on show at the Great Exhibition of 1851. Then, in 1867, after thirty-four years of service, the *Medea* was finally broken up.

At 7 o'clock in the evening, Fellows and Scharf boarded the Neapolitan packet *Francesco Primo* for their voyage to Naples, via SICILY. A twelve-hour crossing brought them to SYRACUSE, where they spent a whole day at leisure. The city, dating back to the 7th century BC, is built on the off-shore island of Ortygia. The travellers were keen to see how the Cathedral [7th century AD] had been constructed by in-filling between the Doric columns of the ancient Greek Temple of Athena [5th century BC]. The very ornate eighteenth century façade creates a strange contrast with the austere thick columns of the Temple, which can be seen all along the north side.

Passing the water-gardens on the quay - unique as the only place where papyrus [*Cyperus papyrus*] grows wild in Europe - the tourists walked along the causeway to the mainland, to visit the ancient ruins of NEAPOLIS and explore the *Latomie*, quarries from whence the stone was taken. They tried out the famous acoustics of the 'Ear of Dionysius' where his spies were said to be able to eavesdrop on the plottings of political prisoners immured in the cave below. Fellows then bought some antique coins for his collection and they rejoined the ship at dusk.

318

It took all night to steam up the coast to MESSINA, where they had to leave the ship for the night. On FRIDAY, 19 APRIL, the *Francesco Primo* at last docked at NAPLES. With only two days to rediscover the atmosphere and the treasures of this city, first in importance was to see the Pompeian mosaic, *The Battle of Issus*, now installed in the National Museum. Their old friend Cavaliere Avellino took them personally to view it and allowed Scharf to make a drawing. Years later, father Scharf made a ten-foot-long enlargement of it, as well as the other sketches done at Pompeii and Herculaneum, for his son's lectures at Liverpool.

The scene depicts the great battle of 333 BC, when Alexander the Great defeated the Persian King, Darius Codomannus. King Darius is shown wearing the imperial *kidaris*, the characteristic Persian headdress, and he looks just like the Satraps portrayed in the 'City' frieze of the Ionic Monument and on the side of the Horse Tomb [pl. 85] of Xanthus. The mosaic would certainly not have been out of place there, they all agreed, especially as Alexander had camped at Xanthus.

TUESDAY, 23 APRIL - "Father's birthday, many happy returns to him." A gruelling thirty-six hours of continuous travel brought them to ROME. As at Naples, there were only two days to revisit old haunts and favourite works of art. In this, Scharf's "City of dreams", how could he best use the precious hours?

To begin, he went for a third time to the Trinità dei Monte church to see the *Descent from the Cross* by Daniele da Volterra, "which they conceal so much from strangers." Perseverance prevailing, he found it near the High Altar, but the composition and the colours were obscured in the darkness. This painting was considered to be one of the finest in the world, but it had been badly damaged in an attempt to remove it to Paris during the Napoleonic Wars.

Scharf went back to the Vatican Museum and, of course, into St Peter's. There he saw two new objects to claim his attention: a statue and a mosaic. The statue "called S. Paul (from the catacombs) is curious and well wrought. It is life-size and certainly resembles the old portraits in early paintings; he also holds a book, but I could not learn the period of his Christening, nor if the book was always in his hands." Scharf doubted the authenticity of this statue. "I suspect him to be a converted pagan" was his shrewd guess. The "singular mosaic painting" shows the face of Christ - very unusually - in profile.

After arranging places in a conveyance to Florence, Fellows called on Lawrence Macdonald. He wanted to enquire after the unfortunate Antonio and tell the sculptor personally of the success of the cast-making operations. The next day, they went to see John Gibson, another famous sculptor, who had made his home in Rome. They viewed his latest works in his studio and then spent the evening together at his house.

The subject of polychromy was the chief topic of conversation. Gibson dearly wanted to revive this ancient practice. In 1847, Queen Victoria, though with some misgivings, was to allow him to introduce a little colour to her portrait bust for St George's Hall, Liverpool[1]. Gibson's most famous statue, known as *The Tinted Venus*[1], coloured in the Greek manner, caused an outage when it was displayed in 1862. Prince Albert had been greatly in favour of coloured statuary, but biased public opinion considered it eccentric and vulgar. The Venus was only lightly tinged, her hair yellow and the edge of her drapery bordered in red and blue. Nevertheless, this brave attempt to educate the public was a total failure. The fashion for Classical art had, by that time, been displaced by the High Church and Gothic Revival Movements, together with Victorian prudery concerning the nude figure, where nakedness seemed accentuated by colouring.

Five-and-a-half days of almost non-stop travel northwards along the APENNINES was now in prospect. At TERNI, there was just time to see the famous *Cascata del Marmore*, where the river Velino falls over 500 feet "in headlong recklessness", a favourite spectacle in the Romantic Age. Then, on MONDAY, 29 APRIL, Scharf made a dash for ASSISI.

"Rose at half past two and started alone in a small express carriage for Assisi, which I entered just as the sun rose upon the tower of the great Convent. Here I saw everything that I so longed to see and so little expected a few days ago." "Running" from one to another, he visited all the churches with their glorious mosaics and Giotto frescoes. "It is a duty long impending, performed," he was able to say. By 7.30, he had rejoined Fellows in the coach.

They continued their tortuous way to PERUGIA, where they saw the big Etruscan Gate and the other celebrated antiquities of that enigmatic people, then on to Lake Trasimeno and the frontier between the Papal States and the Grand Duchy of Tuscany, about halfway on their journey. A paul [5d.] satisfied the customs men, who left their baggage untouched. It was WEDNESDAY, 1 MAY 1844, before the tired Englishmen reached the fair city of FLORENCE, for a restful five days.

Fellows spent the time with his many friends, residents there, while Scharf, in his energetic way, took full advantage of this bonus visit to a city he thought never to see again. It also gave him the opportunity to view two things that were not to be seen on the previous occasion: a portrait of Dante and a painting by Raphael.

When the Grand Duke, Leopold II was in residence, he kept the Raphael in his bedroom. But as he was away from Florence, it was deposited in the Palazzo Pitti for the public to see. The so-called *Madonna del Gran Duca* is about two feet high, a "fine rich-toned picture, mellowed yellow by age...The entire tone of the drapery has acquired a greenish tone especially the blue," Scharf noticed.

The Dante head was a fresco in the Bargello. The Chapel had at some time been divided into an upper and a lower chamber and white-washed, covering some frescoed heads, reputedly by Giotto, including his self-portrait. The heads had been found by three men, Baron Kirkup[2], Henry Wilde[3,] and the friends' cicerone of 1839, Aubrey Bezzi[4]. Dante was wearing a red robe over a green undergarment. This 'Revolutionary' green was ordered to be painted over in a less provocative chocolate brown. The damaged face was also over-painted, injuring it still further. Kirkup bribed the custodian to let him stay in the Chapel all night, to make a copy before 'restoration'. The fresco now bears very little resemblance to the original. Scharf was to publish an outline of the face in a translation of the *Divine Comedy*[5] and in Kugler's *Handbook*, 1855[5].

MONDAY, 6 MAY - At 7 o'clock in the evening, the two indefatigable travellers took their places in Oresi's Diligence, a new service to BOLOGNA, scheduled to take only sixteen hours. They could then remain there a whole day, before embarking on another three-day journey north. Snatching what sleep they could while the coach trundled relentlessly on across the Lombardy Plain, they arrived in good shape for their last sight-seeing stay of three days in Milan, before the final stage of the journey home began in earnest.

MILAN was then part of the Austrian Empire, but it had been under Napoleon's rule from 1796 to 1815, and still looked remarkably French. In society, French was the language spoken; in the shops, the goods were Parisian. Napoleon had laid out the Place d'Armes [Piazza d'Armi] with the magnificent Triumphal Arch [Arco della Pace], reminiscent of its counterpart in Paris. Scharf admired the streakiness of the marble - much deplored by others - considering the colours to act as a foil to the pure white of the sculptures.

He was less approving of the Duomo, however. Begun in 1385, it had only been finished in the Napoleonic period, and then rather hurriedly. Scharf was critical of its multi-styled façade, censuring the whole as "wretchedly inconsistent, and in bad taste; modern windows, Gothic pinnacles and niches, square panes, oriel windows, battlements and Palladian doors with reversed brackets, to say nothing of large and small figures and all kinds of reliefs brought together, produce a defect perceptible to every minute observer." Then, the Cathedral could indeed be minutely examined from across the Piazza, devoid not only of traffic, but without the huge equestrian statue of King Victor Emmanuel II, erected in 1896.

Like all tourists to Milan, they went to see the "wreck" of Leonardo's *Last Supper*. "Woe for its condition. Not a firm line is left, two heads are quite lost and all hands destroyed...All the background ruined by water streaming down it besides cracking. The general impression of the picture is dullness, dirt and grey. There is not a glowing colour in it...The lower part quite lost; the cloth has lost all its pattern." Scharf knew the painting well from a very good copy in the Academy in London, which had been made before much damage had befallen the original.

Now the journey home was to be one remorseless trek - through SWITZERLAND, then on, day and night, across northern FRANCE - a whole week of exhausting travel, to arrive in a cold, rain-soaked PARIS. It could not have been more miserable.

322

Fellows decided that to stay at the renowned, and expensive, Meurice's Hotel (still one of the best) was called for. Here, he enjoyed the comforts of the public rooms, while young Scharf made one last effort at sightseeing.

MONDAY, 20 MAY - In the morning, he drove to the Exhibition of National Industry in the Champs Elysées, but "after being sent from door to door in the mud, found that the King [Louis-Philippe] was expected and therefore no persons, not even foreigners, could be admitted." Foreign tourists were usually given preference over local people, when occasion demanded. So, after a melancholy 'lounge' along the banks of the Seine, Scharf returned to the hotel, to await the diligence to the coast and the Channel steamer.

THURSDAY, 23 MAY - Home again, safe and sound! They had been away almost ten months. George could now assure his excited parents that the Expedition had been a complete success and the journeys through Europe another wonderful experience. Mr Fellows had praised his management of the casting operations and had been well pleased with his outlines and panoramas. He also told them of Fellows's many kindnesses towards the men and of their happy relationship with the naval officers.

On SATURDAY, 6 JULY 1844, the first consignment of the Marbles arrived at the British Museum. Packed in amongst them were presents for the family: geological specimens for father Scharf; Turkish bows and arrows for Henry; costumes and trinkets for his mother and aunt Hicks; musical instruments for himself. A fine Turkey rug bought at Macry was unrolled and immediately spread on the floor in a place of honour.

During the next few years, Fellows and Scharf were to be much occupied by the results of the enterprise. Through Fellows's family connections, George received a commission from a Mr S. Wright, a relative of Jones Loyd, the Nottingham banker, for two oil paintings, *The Harpy Tomb at Xanthus* and *The Horse Tomb at Xanthus*, which were exhibited at the Royal Academy in 1846. He had two others hung that year, besides two the year before. He also prepared many illustrations for the book proposed by the Museum.

Fellows devoted his energies to the arrangement of the Marbles, though this was not really his responsibility. He was concerned, because the Museum's scheme totally failed to make the historical statement he had aimed for in making the collection: a unique opportunity lost. Nor did they publish the book, in spite of the recognized importance of these works of art.

Interest in the Marbles began to decline, and after his death, Fellows's name was forgotten. In recent years, he is again quoted in connection with Xanthus, but his achievements as explorer of Caria and Lycia and his discoveries of many other ancient cities besides Xanthus are ignored. Worse, his rôle as Director of two Government expeditions is distorted and falsified. George Scharf does not even merit a mention.

At present, the Xanthian Marbles are scattered in six separate rooms, so visitors to the Museum today are not able to view them as a special collection from Xanthus, and few will be aware of the history and purpose of the acquisition of these unique antiquities.

POSTSCRIPT

I   The Xanthian Marbles

"The acquisition of the Xanthian Marbles for the British Museum is a subject of rejoicing for all scholars and lovers of ancient art." This was the enthusiastic opinion of one art historian in 1843[1]. "Too much credit cannot be given to Mr. Fellows for his zeal and perseverance in finally securing these interesting objects," he declared.

"All honour be to him," quoth another, "to whose disinterested and patriotic exertions we owe the possession of these marvellous works! To few men is granted at once to immortalize themselves and enrich their country; and Mr. Fellows will reap his best and only recompense in the grateful and perpetual remembrance which will for ever link his name with these national treasures." 'Grateful and perpetual remembrance'? - would that it were so.

The Trustees conveyed to Fellows their "grateful acknowledgements of his active, judicious and disinterested services, as well in making the proper arrangements for the last expedition to Xanthus, as in giving at great personal sacrifice, the advantage of his constant superintendence to the operations carried on in Lycia." They confirmed that the intentions of the Trustees had been satisfactorily accomplished, and that the Museum had been enriched, both as regards to "the extensive series of curious and valuable Marbles and Casts", as by the illustrative drawings of scenery, sculpture and architecture, "so admirably executed under Mr. Fellows's directions by Messrs. Scharf and Rohde Hawkins."

As a token of their esteem, a complete set of twenty-two volumes of the Museum's publications on antiquities was presented to Fellows. He presented the Trustees with models of the Horse Tomb and the Ionic Trophy Monument, which were placed by the objects themselves.

325

Fellows modestly declared: "Personally I am amply rewarded for my devotion of time to the expedition in Lycia by seeing safely deposited within our national Museum the results of my researches." This he meant sincerely. He confidently anticipated that much important knowledge would soon be obtained through them, and was proud to assert that for early Lycian sculpture "the collection has no parallel in any European museum" - nor has it today.

At St James's Palace on 5 MAY, 1845, Sir Charles Fellows received the accolade from Queen Victoria in recognition of his initial enterprise and his skilled management of the two Government expeditions to Xanthus. Thus, the whole saga of Fellows's travels of discovery in Turkey was brought to a most satisfactory conclusion.

Less satisfactory was the question of a publication. Edward Hawkins, Keeper of the Antiquities urged the Trustees that an illustrated account of the work of the expedition and explanations of the Marbles collected should be published as soon as possible, "in order to meet the expectations of the public". The quantity and types of illustration were discussed and Scharf began to prepare some. It was suggested that Fellows's 'Memoirs' should form the preface and a run of 1,000 copies with 90 plates was considered. To this end, Fellows sent a factual account of the excavations, with details of the tombs, inscriptions and casts.

All these plans came to nothing, however, and, in fact, the only book to come out was a folio volume, entitled *Lycia, Caria, Lydia*, of eight lithographs by Scharf, which he dedicated to the Trustees. A separate octavo pamphlet by Fellows, published by John Murray in 1847, furnished the introduction.

II The Lycian Room at the British Museum, 1848

The collections of the British Museum were expanding rapidly and a new building was urgently needed. The architect was Sir Robert Smirke. When he retired in 1845, the plans were completed by his brother Sidney. The figures in the pediment over the main entrance are by the sculptor Sir Richard Westmacott, and once had an 'ancient Greek' blue background. The new Entrance Hall was opened in 1847, and the great South Front in 1848.

It is in the Neoclassical style, very popular when the building was designed in 1823, but already becoming outmoded by the new Gothic style, epitomized by the Houses of Parliament (1849-60). In a letter to a friend, Müller voiced a contemporary view. "The new part of the British Museum...will not add to our architectural adornments;" he wrote, adding, "I think it is built to keep the Academy and National Gallery in countenance."

When, in 1848, the Xanthian Marbles and the casts were displayed all together in the 'Lycian Room' in the West Wing, the

151. British Museum, Lycian Room foundations.

327

collection was received with great enthusiasm. The Marbles were universally acknowledged as the finest and most interesting of the antiquities in the Museum - in truth, anywhere, for that matter.

Two springing lions flanked the entrance. Behind them, opposite to each other, were the cast of the Inscribed Stele and the Harpy Tomb frieze, raised high on a false pillar. Beyond, facing

152. British Museum, the Xanthian Room just opened.

each other, were the Horse Tomb and the Chimaera Tomb lid, placed on its lower chamber. At the back of the Room, were some columns, friezes and a pediment from the Ionic Monument, not yet reconstructed, the Nereids standing in line leading up to it.

There were also the models of the Monument and of the Horse Tomb, Scharf's drawings and panoramas, and Hawkins's architectural plans. Other Marbles, such as the animal slabs from

328

the city wall, the Sphinxes and the inscriptions, were mortared into the side walls of the Room, and the coloured casts and the architectural casts were disposed here and there. In all, an astonishing wealth of actual sculpture and peripheral informative material was on display for the use of scholars and the public. But alas, despite the plans, measurements and estimated weights supplied by Fellows, the Room was found to be far too small, and certain arrangements and the changes made to some of the objects did not please him at all.

The positionings of the Marbles had been placed in the hands of Sir Richard Westmacott[1], an old man, following the out-of-date traditions of an earlier era. His old-fashioned plan was based solely on creating what he considered to be an artistic and picturesque effect, regardless of the important criteria of age and provenance of the objects concerned. And he was not above altering them, either, to bring about a balanced composition, or 'improving' them, to make them look 'perfectly Greek'. He split up cohesive elements of architecture, and introduced pieces that had no connection with Lycia. Edward Hawkins was given no say in the matter whatsoever. "Many evils suggest themselves as arriving from this system," Fellows predicted.

Fellows was conversant with the more modern practices followed at Munich. He wanted the Marbles and casts to be shown in relation to each other and to the region as a whole, in a chronological sequence, ranging over six centuries, illustrative of the historical changes in Lycia. He took an active interest in what was going on in the Gallery, and made frequent representations to the Trustees, to object to mistakes. He got no satisfaction from them, however, nor could he voice his objections to Westmacott himself. He was never available. "Decidedly, I will not be a party to misplacing anything I have seen in the country," Fellows staunchly maintained.

The top of one monument had been placed on the top of another; a raking cornice, showing the angle of the pediment of the Ionic Monument, had been set horizontally, to form a shelf. Fellows could not condone such inaccuracies. Then there was the case of what he termed an "unsightly" stone [pl. 147, centre bottom], but which was, nonetheless, an extremely important one.

A tenant had been cut off, destroying its significance. "Fifty years hence, the cutting off of this will be quite forgotten, and we shall not know why it was placed in the Museum," he prophesied.

"It is the cap-stone of a monument forming a lion seat; the lions are on either side, and the seat is in the centre between them; underneath was a tenant, or projecting square, showing that it had been put on the top of a monument. On examining the monument near [the Inscribed Stele], I found that there was a hole on the cap, corresponding with this...In order to make it rest on the floor, this indication has been cut off." He was justifiably outraged by this wanton destruction of evidence. "It ought not to have been removed," he stressed again.

Fellows was well aware that, by the standards of the day, the lion-seat - and many other of the Lycian sculptures, such as the 'shaggy' lions - were considered aesthetically unattractive. The 'problem' of the Marbles was that there seemed to be great difficulty in accepting them as 'Lycian' Greek rather than 'pure' Greek. As such, they were conceived to be "not of such exquisite beauty as those of the Elgin and the Townley collections, [though] there is no want of elegance, and character in them." Even the artist, Müller, condemned them as "novelties" and opined that "they must be looked on more as antiquarian curiosities than models in sculpture" - as if that were the only criterion by which to assess their value.

Another fault that Fellows pointed out was that the Harpy Tomb frieze was positioned too high to be seen properly, yet that height was wrong if taken as a reconstruction. He had wanted a viewing-gallery built, but it was now too late for that. "This monument is esteemed so important by the archaeologists of Europe, that it is the most important in the collection, yet it is placed in the least important part of the room," he lamented. A great many treatises had been written on it - by French and Italian scholars, and especially by Germans. "I have been informed by two of the authors," Fellows told the Trustees, "that their sole motive for coming over to England was to see that monumnt. One was from Berlin, and the other from Bonn."

The one from Bonn was, more than likely, Georg Friedrich Grotefend, the linguist, whose translations had brought Fellows's investigations to the notice of German scholars; there had been many visitors from Berlin. As early as the summer of 1844, the archaeologist, August Emil Braun, had visited Fellows specifically to view the Marbles and find out about Lycia at first hand. The following summer, the Marbles had attracted several more visitors from Berlin, including the classical scholars, Carl Wilhelm Goettling and his friend, Theodor Panofka.

These learned men had spent much time studying the antiquities of Greece, Sicily and Italy. Panofka had founded the annual *Winckelmannsfest* in Berlin, at which papers were read in his honour. He took a great interest in the Lycian sculptures, calling on the Scharfs to look through George's notebooks and his portfolio of drawings. In 1848, Scharf junior was to provide the illustrations for *Manners and Customs of the Greeks*, an English translation of Panofka's major work.

In fact, during the 1840s and 1850s, dozens of artists, architects, and archaeologists journeyed from the Continent to study the new antiquities. Scharf had sent a number of Lycian views to Munich and Fellows's friend, Professor Thiersch, even came over to examine the Marbles for himself and compare their arrangement with the chronological system followed for the sculptures in the Glyptothek.

The Marbles attracted visits also from men distinguished in other fields, including the geologist Leopold von Buch; J.F. von Leibig, the chemist; and J.S.H. Kiepert[2], the cartographer, who worked for the archaeologist of Pergamon, Karl Humann. Yet for all this interest abroad, in the Museum, Fellows's guidance was unsought.

As discoverer of the ancient city of Xanthus, and explorer of the whole province of Lycia, Fellows "fancied" he should at least have been consulted over the way the objects were displayed. "I was intrusted...to select such objects as would best illustrate the art of the Lycians," he reminded the Trustees, and rightly pointed out that his motives for that selection could only be explained by himself. He made the heartfelt observation that, if consulted now, whilst he was still alive, the Museum could take advantage of his special knowledge.

During an Investigation set up in 1848, the whole question was gone into. Fellows deplored the want of a scientific plan: no attempt at a classification, either chronological or geographical, had been made. He told the Trustees that he had been five or six times to Munich to see the chronological disposition of those sculptures and to consult with his learned friends in the art world there.

He could assert that in the "illustration of the history of art, scarcely a Museum in Europe contains a specimen of sculpture of known country or date. These sculptures are the Egina[3] at Munich, the Selinunte[3] at Palermo, and now the Nineveh in Paris[4] - the Vatican has none. In our Museum," he proudly asserted, "we have the sculptures of the Parthenon, Phigalia [Bassae], the tomb of Mausolus, the Ionic Monument from Xanthus, the Lycian and the Nineveh sculptures. With this advantage," he declared, "much is expected from us by the Archaeologists of the Continent." In Fellows's opinion it represented a unique opportunity for a scientific arrangement to make "our National Institution of Instruction the envy of all others."

Fellows's vision for museum display far outstripped the notions of the conservators of his day and is more appropriate to modern times. Since rock-tombs are the leading feature of the province, but are impossible to transport away, he proposed building mock-ups of the rock architecture and had had measurements taken for that purpose. Casts made on the Second Expedition were to be set into the replicas. Nothing of this was ever done, nor was a reconstruction of the Ionic Monument attempted.

Another well-considered suggestion was that casts, painted in facsimile, should be made of once-coloured sculptures, and placed beside them[5], thus preserving the brilliancy of the originals. He wisely stated: "If we look forward 50 or 100 years, it would be the means of registering information which the living can only give now." But this, like Fellows's other dreams concerning the Xanthian Marbles, was doomed to vanish, as a mirage, in the heat of contention.

III The past, the present - and the future?

The wrangle over the Lycian Room continued for a considerable period. After Edward Hawkins's retirement in June 1860, at the age of 80, the Department of Antiquities was split up into several new ones, bringing inevitable changes. Over the years, a number of rearrangements and relocations have been made, and the quantity of exhibits reduced. The public continued to admire the Xanthian Marbles for a long time, but, little by little, interest waned, as other rare and impressive objects from distant places made their appearance. The problems of space grew ever more acute. Time and wars left their scars. In 1878, the Lycian Room ceased to be.

Most of the Lycian casts have now disappeared, as have Fellows's models and most of Rohde Hawkins's drawings and reports. Scharf's many sketches, outlines and water-colours do, however, still exist[1] - as do many by Fellows himself[1]. The tombs and sculptured slabs from Xanthus are now shown in a more chronological manner - but they are located in various rooms on different floors, along with objects from other countries. The visitor to the Museum is thus prevented from relating one monument with another, and is frustrated in attempts to compare and follow the changes in style through the centuries.

In the case of the Nereid Monument, its close proximity to the Elgin collection encourages the uninitiated to jump to the wrong conclusions. Its prominent position conflicts with the fact that its form is the least representative of Lycian tomb architecture and, were it possible to see it in conjunction with the other Lycian tombs, rather than adjacent to the relics of so famous a temple as the Parthenon, the public would be less likely to misinterpret what they see. It would be a distinct advantage, if a scale model of the complete structure, including its base, were again placed here to aid in its understanding. In this age of rush and crowds, and education through video and television, visual impact is more important than any label, no matter how informative, which

153. Sir Charles Fellows, portrait by John Wood, 1850.[2]

hurrying tourists and school parties have no time to read, and a mass of feet cover over the notices on the slabs let into the floor.

If the Xanthian antiquities and remaining casts could only be reassembled all in one view, in a new Lycian Room, they would surely create as much interest today as the Xanthian Marbles did a century and a half ago. Through a compact display, this unrivalled collection from this unique area of ancient culture and art might once more attract the attention and prominence it so richly merits.

An arrangement could still be attained in keeping with Fellows's idea of chronological sequence and fulfilling his modernistic approach. Photographs of Scharf's drawings, especially of the coloured sculptures, and models of the tombs ought to be added. Portraits of the worthy Captain Frederick Warden, of the artist Sir George Scharf, as well as that of the champion of ancient Lycia and discoverer of Xanthus itself, Sir Charles Fellows, should grace the room.

Charles Fellows had the vision of enhancing the National Museum by bringing learning and beauty from a far land to the consciousness of the world. His was the dream, the reality should for ever be "a subject of rejoicing".

Chapter Notes

Introduction
Chapter I The Xanthian Marbles

1. Plaster casts of the Xanthian Marbles taken from the price list of Messrs Brucciani & Co., 1910. Harpy Tomb friezes, £11:4:0; one slab, £3:0:0 - Horse Tomb lid and sides, £54:7:0 - Lion Tomb friezes, £5:10:0 - Ionic Tomb friezes from 11s.6d. to £3:0:0 per slab; Nereid, £9:0:0 - Wall slabs, £1:7:0 each; cocks and hens (9 slabs), £5:10:0 - Relief of two figures with Harpy on a column, £1:6:0 - Bilingual inscription, £1:2:0 - Inscribed Stele, £25:0:0. Casts of all the Elgin Marbles were available: a slab of the frieze at 16 shillings; a metope at £3:10:0; pedimental figures up to £19:0:0. The head of the Horse of Silene cost 16 shillings. It is still available today [1993] in resin - priced at £675·00. Orders may also now be placed for a plaster cast of a hen slab from Xanthus at £60·00 [p&p £35·00] and a choice of three slabs from the Parthenon frieze at £275·00 each [p&p £80·00].
2. See Part One, Chapter II, note 1.

Chapter II Sir Charles Fellows

1. The Fellows family lived on High Pavement, Nottingham. From 1966 to March 1993, the house became the Nottingham Record Office.
2. A history of the first ascents of Mont Blanc was published by the author to celebrate the bicentenary. *The Alpine Journal*, 150-159; 1986.
3. *Arms* recorded at Heralds' College: Per pale azure and sable, a fesse dancettée ermine between lions' heads erased, each within an annulet or. *Mantling:* Azure and argent. *Crest:* On a wreath of colours, in front of a lion's head erased sable, charged with two barrulets dancettée, three annulets fessewise or. *Motto: Confide recte agens* - Doing rightly be confident.
4. Fellows's 'Milton's watch' and those bequeathed by his second wife are in the British Museum. Lady Fellows's paintings of his collection are in the Royal Institution.
5. The colossal figures and other sculptures from Layard's enormous Assyrian collection, Rooms 16-26, 89, etc. Sir Austen Henry Layard: *Nineveh and its remains, etc.,* 1849, 2 vols. Some illustrations are by George Scharf junior.
6. Mausoleum Room 12, also Rooms 9, 78, 81, and Main Staircase. See also Part Two, Chapter V, note 1. Casts at Oxford [O˙] and Cambridge [C˙]. Sir Charles Thomas Newton: *A History of Discoveries at Halicarnassus, Cnidus, and Branchidae, etc.* Vol.1: Plates [lithographs from photos], 1862; Vol.2 in 2: Text, 1862-63.

˙O - Oxford, Ashmolean Museum Cast Gallery, St John Street (behind the Museum)
˙C - Cambridge, University Museum of Classical Archaeology, Sidwick Avenue

7. Column drums etc. from the Temple of Diana, Ephesus Gallery 82 [basement];O; C. John Turtle Wood: *Discoveries at Ephesus*, 1877.
8. Harry John Johnson (1826-84), son of Benjamin Johnson of Birmingham. Friend of David Cox; pupil of Samuel Lines and W.J. Müller. Member of the Institute of Painters in Water-colours, 1870. Exhibited at the RA.

Chapter III Sir George Scharf

1. Phillip Henry Stanhope (1805-75), 5th Earl, the former Lord Mahon. Entered Parliament, 1830; held office. Published historical works. President of the Society of Antiquaries, 1846; Chairman of Trustees of the NPG, 1857. A copy of his bust (1854) by Macdonald [see p.242] stands in the Gallery's entrance hall.
2. The Worthies depicted are: Edward VI (63); William Wilberforce (3); Elizabeth, Queen of Bohemia (71); William Paulet, Marquis of Winchester (65); Sir Joshua Reynolds (41); Nell Gwyn (36); Mrs Elizabeth Carter (28); Chancellor (Judge) Jeffreys (56); Mrs Siddons (50); General Wolfe (48); George Frederick Handel (8); Henry Ireton (33); John Foxe (24); Cardinal Wolsey (32); Sir Walter Raleigh (7). [NPG acquisition numbers.]
3. A sketch-book of cartoons is conserved at the Centre for Kentish Studies, Maidstone. It includes a cartoon of the many portraits of Mary, Queen of Scots, with Scharf himself as the headsman, ready to wield the axe.
4. Scharf's portrait by William Edward Kilburn, a noted London daguerreotypist. This process, invented by a Frenchman, L.J.M. Daguerre, in 1839, gives a unique mirror-image of the subject. It became extremely popular for portraits, at one guinea each.

Part One
Chapter I Fellows plans his excursion

1. *Revelation* I, v.11 - the Seven Churches were at Ephesus, Smyrna, Pergamus, Thyatira, Sardis, Philadelphia and Laodiceia.
2. Aegina Marbles [c. 500 BC] in the Glyptothek, Munich; O; C.
3. Bassae Marbles [5th century BC] from the Temple of Apollo Epikourios, near Phigaleia, acquired in 1815, Room 6 (mezzanine); O; C.
4. Charles-Félix-Marie Texier (1802-71), French archaeologist. *Description de l'Asie Mineure faite par ordre du Gouvernement Français de 1833 à 1837 et publiée par le Ministère de l'Instruction publique*, Paris, 1839-49, 3 vols. See also Part Four, Chapter I, note 1.

Chapter II Travels

1. "I have made use of the ancient names of places, as being the best known to English readers, from association both with classic and sacred history. When I have used the modern Turkish names, I have endeavoured to represent the sound of the word." *Fellows*. His scheme has been adhered to; today's Turkish names are included for the benefit of holiday-makers. The Turkish letter c has the sound dj; ç is ch; ş is sh; ğ is an aspirated gh.

In Fellows's day, Latin names were always used for places of antiquity. Inscriptions were in Greek, even when the buildings were Roman.

2. Antiquities were not protected by Turkish law until 1976.

3. Godfrey Levinge, a friend of Fellows's, had travelled via the Seven Churches to the Holy Land. Fellows recommended the use of the invention, which he perfected, of a calico sheet with a muslin top, sewn into a tube and drawn together by a string. It could be hung up from a nail in the ceiling. The occupant could undress within it and also sit up to read or write, completely protected from mosquitoes and other insects. Fellows considered it a life-saving device. Published in Fellows's *Journal*, 1839 and Levinge's *The Traveller in the East, being a guide, etc.*, 1839.

4. Altar of Zeus from Pergamus, reconstructed in the Pergamon Museum, Berlin; O; C.

5. Assos frieze, in the Louvre, Paris; O.

6. When Mustafa Kemal Paşa came to power in 1923, he made many changes and reforms, including the transfer of the capital to Ankara, the use of the Roman alphabet and the abolition of the fez. There was an exchange of Greek and Turkish people between the new Republic and the islands and countries formerly part of the Ottoman Empire. In 1935, he obliged everybody to take a surname, styling himself Atatürk, Father of the Turks.

7. Throughout the text, wherever possible, the present tense has been used for antiquities still in existence - at the site, or in a museum.

8. In 1842, Fellows sent the BM 40 bird-skins and reptiles, and 27 segmented worms; in 1843, he sent 8 mammals, 10 birds, 38 reptiles, 3 fish and 15 segmented worms. He also sent shells and sponges from Sicily, and over 200 insects from Britain.

9. The names Ephesus and Aiasalook both infer 'Place of the Moon', Aiasalook being also a confusion of *Agios Theologos*, pronounced by the Greeks *Aios Scologos*, the epithet given to Saint John. According to tradition, it was here that he wrote the *Revelation*, the *Fourth Gospel*, and the *Epistles*. He brought the elderly Virgin Mary to live near Ephesus. Saint Paul lived here for three years.

10. *Pistacia lentiscus* is the gum-mastic; *P. vera* gives the edible pistachio nut. *Cistus creticus* is the gum-cistus; *C. villosa* is the probable source of myrrh. *Styrax officinalis* is the gum-storax, used for perfumes and incense. It exudes gum from incisions made in the branches. Liquid-storax, a resin, comes from *Liquidambar orientalis*.

Chapter III The outcome

1. See Postscript, Chapter III, note 1.

2. *Beacon* (6 guns); survey-vessel, built 1823; 378 tons. Commander, Thomas Graves, appointed 1841; pay, £300:0:9 + £1 a day extra, as Surveyor.

3. Francis Street led off the east side of Tottenham Court Road, between Nos 191 and 192. Collard's piano business (Charles Collard was the Scharf's landlord) was at No.195, next to F. Heal & Son, feather-bed manufacturers.

4. Philip Hardwick (1792-1870). His best known works are the Goldsmiths'

Hall and the now modernized warehouses at St Katherine's Dock. His 'Doric' portico to Euston Station was demolished in 1961-62.

5. Fellows had the first floor bachelor apartment (1 of 5); Henry Crabb Robinson, the diarist, lived above. No.30 became the Institute of Chemistry of Great Britain, and is now the Royal Society of Chemistry, London University.

6. William Clarkson Stanfield (1793-1867), marine and landscape artist, scene-painter at the Drury Lane and Covent Garden Theatres. His works can be seen at the National Maritime and V & A Museums.

7. George Scharf junior: *Recollections of the Scenic Effects of Covent Garden Theatre during the season 1838-9*, 1839, 42 plates.

8. In 1838, Henry Scharf (1822-87) took a position at the [Royal] College of Surgeons drawing articulated skeletons, initially for two years at one guinea a week. He was a skilled draughtsman, but always preferred his hobby of acting, which he took up professionally in 1842.

9. The diaries of George Scharf senior, Mrs Scharf and her sister, Miss Mary Hicks, are conserved in the Heinz Archive and Library of the NPG. The diaries of George Scharf junior concerning his travels with Fellows are in the Department of Manuscripts of the British Library. When quoting from them, his spelling has been modernized and some punctuation added.

10. J.W. Goethe *Italienische Reise*, Weimar, 1816/17; Engl. transl., 1962.

Part Two

Chapter I The journey out

1. Fellows's mother was acquainted with Byron's mother and the Fellows family visited at Newstead Abbey. Charles Fellows admired the poet's works and some of Fellows's sketches were used to illustrate Byron's *Childe Harold* and T. Moore's *Byron's Life*. Two of Fellows's brothers were pall-bearers at the poet's funeral.

2. Giovanni Aubrey Bezzi was exiled from Italy on account of his connection with the political plot of Silvio Pellico, dramatist and Carbonaro. Bezzi lived for a time in Torquay; exhibited at the RA, 1850-53. There are some of his works at Chatsworth, Derbyshire. See also Part Four, Chapter IX, note 4.

3. In 1840, the aspiring young actor, Henry Scharf, went to see Kemble, aged 65, in his final rôle as Mercutio, at Covent Garden Theatre.

4. Scharf was to provide 120 illustrations for *The Poetical Works of John Keats*, 1854.

5. Townley Room 84 (basement); O; C. Charles Townley's collection was acquired in 1802.

6. Pope Gregory XVI was elected in 1831. Civita Vecchia held allegiance to the Pope. It became part of the unified Italy in 1870.

Chapter II Malta; Smyrna

1. The Austrian Empire extended to the sea at Trieste and stretched all down the eastern Adriatic coast. Trieste was taken by Italian troops in 1918.

2. *Devletlü, inâyetlü, iffetlü* [illegible word] *efendimiz hazretleri. Bundan akdem İngiltere ceziresinden eski devletlerini taharrileri icün beyzâdeleri üç aded refikı ile vurud etmiştir.*

Chapter III Lydia

1. *Kazan*, a cauldron, was the symbol of the dreaded Janissaries [*yeniçeri*], soldiers of the Old Regime; disbanded in 1826. They beat the vessels to arouse fear and also used them as begging-bowls.
2. George Scharf senior (1788-1860), born at Mainburg, Bavaria. His 'zoo' lithographs were sold at the Gardens and proved a great success. Sets were bought by the King of Prussia; the Queen of Bavaria; by Queen Adelaide, wife of William IV; and by the Duchess of Kent for her daughter, Victoria, later Queen. Postcards can be bought at Camden Public Library, Charing Cross Road. Scharf senior also made popular prints of young chimps and orang-utangs in dresses; of the first four giraffes ever to be brought to England, with their Nubian attendants, (1836); and of the baby giraffe, born in 1839.

Chapter IV Caria, NE

1. Laocoön group in the Vatican Museum Rome; O; C. Scharf's favourite sculpture. At that time, it was universally admired as the finest work of antiquity, greater even than the Apollo Belvedere, Vatican Museum, Rome; O; C.
2. Venus de Milo, in the Louvre, Paris; O; C.
3. Karamania was the name given to the whole of the southern regions; from Karaman, a great Turkish Prince; in the Middle Ages, his city, Karaman, was the capital of Turkey. By the 1830s, the name had fallen out of use. Captain Beaufort (1774-1857) entitled his book of the survey: *Karamania, or, a brief description of the South Coast of Asia-Minor, etc.*, 1817. Francis Beaufort entered the Navy in 1787; Lieutenant, 1796; Post-Captain, 1810. Hydrographer of the Admiralty, 1829-55. Retired, Rear-Admiral, 1846. KCB, 1848; FRS, 1814; FRAS; FGS. Scale of Wind-force, 1806; adopted by the Admiralty, 1838.
4. Cadmus, King of Phoenicia, imported the initial alphabet of 16 Phoenician letters into Greece.

Chapter V Caria, SW

1. The Mausoleum, one of the Seven Wonders of the World, was built for King Mausolus by his wife, Artemisia, in 353 BC. It had 36 columns under a high stepped-pyramid, surmounted by a *quadriga*. There are plaster models of both the Mausoleum and the Mylasa Tomb in the Soane Museum, London. See also Part Three, Chapter I, note 2.
2. Richard Pococke (1705-65) became Bishop of Ossory just before his death. His travels took him to Egypt and the Levant. *Description of the East*, 1743-45, 2 vols in 3.
3. Richard Chandler (1738-1810). D.D, 1773. He published several works

on antiquities. *Richard Chandler. Travels in Asia Minor and Greece*, Oxford, 1775-76, 2 vols; edited and abridged by Edith Clay, 1971.

4. John Morritt (1772-1843) was the owner of the celebrated painting, the 'Rokeby Venus', by Velasquez, now in the National Gallery. *A Grand Tour...1794-96*, published in 1914.

5. There had been three Temples to Zeus at Mylasa and, until about 1750, an almost perfect Temple of Augustus and Rome [c. 12 BC], destroyed to build a mosque.

6. *Edictum de pretiis*, fixing maxima for prices and wages. Colonel Leake (1777-1860) published *An Edict of Diocletian, etc.*, 1826, as *A Sequel* to his *Journal of a Tour in Asia Minor*, 1824. Part of another copy of the edict has recently been found at Aphrodisias. William Martin Leake, Classical topographer and numismatist, spent 1799-1800 in Turkey; with W.R. Hamilton [see Chapter VII, note 9], 1801-02 surveying Egypt. In Greece, 1805-07. His antiquarian collections went to the BM and to Cambridge University. Lt-Colonel, 1820; FRS, 1815; FRGS. Member of the Society of Dilettanti, 1814.

7. Daedalus, a Greek inventor, father of Icarus. He created the Labyrinth to house the Minotaur of Crete.

8. John Martin (1789-1854), known as 'mad Martin' for his eccentric character. Exhibited at the RA. His paintings were very popular at that time, but are scarcely known today; there are some in the Tate Gallery.

9. The new Aga would build himself a new *konak*. When a Turkish house was left unoccupied, it was not taken over by another owner, but left to decay.

Chapter VI Lycia, NW

1. Daniel Sharpe (1806-56), geologist, archaeologist, philologist; FRS, 1850; President of the Geological Society, 1856. Killed by falling from his horse. He transcribed Fellows's collection of Lycian inscriptions.

2. The chief cities of the League were Xanthus, Patara, Pinara, Tlos, Myra and Olympus.

3. *Myrtus communis*, the 'Daphne' of Classical mythology. It was sacred to the Goddess of Love. Queen Victoria carried some in her wedding bouquet. See also Chapter VIII, note 4.

4. Dr Wilde, to become Sir William Wilde (1815-76), a Dublin surgeon; travelled as far as Egypt. *Narrative of a Voyage to Madeira, etc.*, Dublin, 1840, 2 vols. He was the father of the dramatist, Oscar Wilde.

Chapter VII Lycia, The Xanthus valley

1. Formerly called Koca Çay (Old River), now Eşen Çayı, the river of Eşen, then called Kestep. Neither name establishes the river's connection with Xanthus, located near its mouth. *Çay* also means 'tea' - the English (Chinese) 'cha'. "The river Xanthus is one of the most powerful, wild, and unmanageable streams I ever saw, the volume of water is very great ... The stream runs probably at the rate of five miles an hour." *Fellows.*

2. Thomas Burgon, numismatist, collector, merchant of Smyrna, had a

terracotta of Bellerophon killing the Chimaera, which Scharf drew. It retained traces of paint. The collection was bought by the BM in 1842. The restored group is in a case in Room 5. The cast of the Tlos sculpture is in the Museum store. For other casts from Lycia, see notes for Part Four.

3. See Part One, Chapter II, note 10.

4. *Certonia siliqua*, the Locust Tree, or St John's Bread; Leguminosae, the Pea family. The pods are the 'husks' of the Parable of the Prodigal Son, and the 'locusts' eaten by John, the Baptist. When dry, they twist, giving rise to the Turkish name *keçiboynuzu ağacı* - Goat's-horn tree. The pulp makes a substitute for chocolate; the seeds are edible. They are the origin of the jeweller's 'carat' [Greek, *kerato*, horn]. Scharf always called the Carob 'charubas' [Arabic, *kharruba*].

5. *Quercus macrolepsis (aegilops)*. The acorn-cups [Greek, *valanos*] are used in the dyeing trade, imparting the characteristic sweet smell to Turkish leather.

6. Hugh Edwin Strickland (1811-53), naturalist. He accompanied W.J. Hamilton, geologist, to Asia Minor in 1835-36. His bird collection went to Cambridge University. *Memoirs of Hugh Edwin Strickland, M.A.*, 1858, by Sir William Jardine.

7. Quay or landing-place in Turkish is *iskele*. The kingfisher is called *iskelekuşu [kuş, bird]*. Strickland was especially interested to see the rare species, *Alcedo Smyrnensis*, the great Bengal kingfisher, the last recorded specimen having been shot by the botanist William Sherard (1659-1728), while Consul at Smyrna (1702-16/17). One was shot in 1841, while the *Beacon* was at Macry. The great Bengal kingfisher is twice the size of the English 'Halcyon' (*A. atthis*), its bright plumage more like that of its relative, the bee-eater.

8. The Satrap on a slab from the lower frieze of the Nereid Monument wears the royal *kidaris* and sits under an Oriental ceremonial umbrella. Room 7, on the wall opposite Room 8.

9. Rosetta Stone, Room 25. Discovered in Egypt in 1799; brought to England by W.R. Hamilton, antiquary, Secretary to Lord Elgin; BM Trustee; father of the geologist, W.J. Hamilton. The stone has three inscriptions - the Egyptian characters, Egyptian script and Greek letters - thus giving the key to the interpretation of Egyptian hieroglyphics. As Trustees, Hamilton with the Marquis of Northampton promoted the acquisition by the BM of antiquities from Xanthus.

Chapter VIII Lycia, S

1. *Coins of ancient Lycia ... with an Essay on the relative dates of the Lycian Monuments in the British Museum*, 1855. Plate 88 shows Apollo's lyre, bottom right; the *triquetra*, rows 1 and 3; row 3, left, head of the God Pan. Other coins show lions, wild boars, etc.

2. George Scharf senior died from bronchitis in November, 1860, at the early age of 72. Fellows had died just four days before, aged 61.

3. Scharf made several drawings of the groups of tombs, and of particular tombs and sculptures.

342

4. *Daphne gnidium*. The garden plant is *D. mezereum*.
5. 'Letter from Mr Cockerell', in Robert Walpole's *Travels in various Countries of the East*, 1820, pp.524-525. Charles Robert Cockerell (1788-1863), architect of the Bank of England, and of University buildings in Oxford, Cambridge and London. His Neoclassical style was based on his studies in Greece and Asia Minor. Professor of Architecture at the Royal Academy, 1840-57; first President of the RIBA, 1860.
6. Fellows retired to West Cowes, the home of his second wife. He took an active part in raising the standard of agriculture on the Isle of Wight.

Chapter IX Lycia, the interior

1. Although put to many uses, the Lycian tombs were never made into homes, perhaps through superstitious fear.
2. Glaucus, a King of Lycia; grandson of Bellerophon.
3. See Part Four, Chapter I, note 1.

Chapter X Return to Smyrna

1. *Kuruş*, piastre; 100*k*. = TL1. One Turkish Lira was worth just over £1.
2. Until about 1838, the great bustard [*Otis tarda*] of the Cursores group was a native of the plains of southern and eastern England. It was coursed by greyhounds for sport and was much prized for its meat.
3. Hierapolis, Greek for 'Sacred City', confounded with Hiera [Roman, Juno], Goddess of Marriage, wife and sister of Zeus [Jupiter]; or, Hiera, wife of Telephus, son of Hercules, King of Mysia (northern Asia Minor).
4. Sardis was the first city to produce gold coins. There is gold jewellery from Sardis in the Archaeological Museum in Smyrna.
5. The Double Temple of Artemis and Zeus or, more probably, Faustina, at Sardis. Cybele, a Phrygian Mother Goddess equated with Artemis [Diana], Goddess of Fertility. She was also worshipped at Ephesus and Aezani.
6. Diana of the Ephesians, *Acts*, XIX, v.23-41.
7. Legend tells how, about AD 250, seven Christian youths, persecuted by the Romans for their religion, were walled up in a cave, fell asleep, and woke up 200 years later to safety in the time of Theodosius, a Christian.
8. J.P. de Tournefort, French botanist and plant collector, described the Gate of Persecution in his *Relation d'un Voyage du Levant*, Paris, 1717; English translation, 1741.

Chapter XI The voyage to Athens

1. Detailed accounts of the Lazaretto at Syra are given by the author in *Pratique* X (3/4): 55-58; 1984 and *Medical History* 28: 73-80; 1984.
2. 'A List of Plants collected...between...February and June, 1840', by David Don, in Fellows's *Account, etc.*, 1841, pp.286-294. New species: *Veronica cuneifolia*; *V. grandiflora*, now *donii*; *Phlomis lycia*; *Pinus carica*, now *pyrenaica*.
3. 'Charioteer' [Venus] and Victories sculptures, in the Acropolis Museum, Athens; O; C.

4. Aristion stele, in the Acropolis Museum, Athens; O; C (with coloured version).
5. 'A History of the Characteristics of Greek Art by George Scharf FSA', in Christopher Wordsworth's *Greece - Pictorial, Descriptive, and Historical,* 1882, pp.1-87.
6. Ludwig Ross (1806-59). German Classical philologist and antiquarian. His Scottish grandfather was a doctor in Hamburg. Spent many years working for King Otho in Athens. Travelled in Ionia, Caria and Lycia; excavated in Greece, Rhodes and Cyprus. Met Fellows in London, 1845; discussed inscriptions at Xanthus. Ended his long suffering from a painful spinal disease by opening his veins in a warm bath. *Reisen nach Kos, Halikarnassos, Rhodos und der Insel Cypern.* Halle, 1852.
7. 'On the Polychromy of Sculpture: being recollections of remarks on this subject by C.O. Müller, at Athens, in 1840', by George Scharf junior, in *Museum of Classical Antiquities* I: 247-255; 1851.

Chapter XII Homeward bound

1. Robert Hesketh seems to have had a different arrangement with Fellows from that of Scharf, giving him more independence and allowing him to keep his drawings and plans.
2. The Temple of Aphaea, then known as the Temple of Jupiter Panhellenicus, on the island of Aegina.
3. The iron *flèche* was added to Cologne Cathedral in 1860, the twin spires not until 1880.
4. There was custom duty to pay on 16 lbs of books printed before 1801 @ £1 per cwt; 14 lbs of books printed after 1801 @ £2:10:0 per cwt; 84 prints @ 1d. each; 24 lbs of sweets @ 6d. per lb.; plus packing, freighting and sundry charges to the agent, Mr Northwood.

Chapter XIII At home

1. Illustrations by George Scharf senior, see plates 3; 151; 152.

Part Three
Chapter I Preliminaries

1. *Vesuvius* (6), survey vessel; built 1840; 970 tons; 220 HP. Commander, Erasmus Ommanney, appointed 1841; pay £300:0:9.
2. Sir Stratford Canning (1786-1880), Ambassador at Constantinople. He became known as 'The Great Elchi' [Turkish, *elçi*, ambassador]. In 1846, he acquired the stones (the frieze of the Mausoleum), extracted from the walls of the Sultan's Palace, formerly of the Knights of St John. Room 12, with some of Newton's huge haul from Bodrum.

Chapter II The work

1. Prof. Pierre Demargne (b. 1903), Légion d'honneur, Membre de l'Institut

de France, began on-going excavations at Xanthus in 1950. He dedicated volume I, *Les piliers funeraires* of his definitive work: *Fouilles, etc.*, to "*la mémoire de nos predecesseurs*" - Charles Fellows and the Austrian epigraphist, Otto Benndorf (1838-1907). With the architect, George Niemann (1841-1912), he excavated the site in 1881. See also note 9 and Bibliography.

2. Slabs from the Nereid Monument, now in the Museum at Antalya.

3. Nereid Monument, Room 7.

4. Sir Charles Fellows: *Account of the Ionic Trophy Monument excavated at Xanthus*, 1848. He describes its initial appearance: "not a marble fragment of the superstructure...remained upon its base" and, in his typically circumspect way, called his reconstruction "daring and perhaps incautious". Fellows, nevertheless, declared his laudable intentions: "to register my evidence...and to court discussion."

5. Benjamin Gibson, antiquarian, lived in Rome with his brother John, the Neoclassical sculptor. 'On the sculptures of the Ionic Monument at Xanthus, discovered by Sir Charles Fellows', in *The Museum of Classical Antiquities* I: 131-155; 1851.

6. Harpy Tomb, Room 5; frieze, O; C.

7. Horse [Payava] Tomb, Room 10 (behind the Nereid Monument).

8. T.A.B. Spratt and Edward Forbes: *Travels in Lycia, Milyas, and the Cibyratis, in company with the late Rev. E.T. Daniell*, 1847, 2 vols. Thomas Abel Spratt (1811-88), hydrographer and surveyor. Entered the Navy, 1827, Lieutenant, 1841; Captain, 1855; CB, 1855; FRS, 1856. Vice-Admiral, 1878. Lieutenant's pay, £182:10:9.

9. J. August Schoenborn discovered the site of Trysa at Gölbasi in 1841. The reliefs [4th century BC] were excavated in 1881 by O. Benndorf and G. Niemann for the Kunsthistorisches Museum, Vienna; O. See Bibliography.

10. Later in 1842, the first tourists arrived: Sir Thomas Phillips, Welsh coal-mine owner, with his artist, Richard Dadd, having met Lieutenant Spratt. In May 1843, Dadd became insane, spending the rest of his life in an asylum. See also part Four, Chapter I, note 1. In the autumn of 1843, Charles Somers, Viscount Eastnor, later Earl Somers (1819-83), stayed in 'Fellows's' hut on his return from a tour with Layard. Somers was an artist, pioneer photographer and noted arboriculturalist. MP, 1841-47. Trustee of the NPG, 1860; of the BM, 1874.

11. Fellows's catalogue is conserved in the BM, Department of Greek and Roman Antiquities.

12. *Medea* (4), paddle-steamer; built 1833; 835 tons. Commander, Frederick Warden, appointed 1840; pay, £300:0:9. See also Chapter III note 12. Steam took the vessel in and out of harbour, but sail was used for the main voyage. It was faster than paddles and the weight of coal precluded its use for long passages.

Chapter III The sequel

1. *Monarch* (84), screw-steamship; built 1832; 2786 tons. Commander, Samuel Chambers, appointed 1840; pay £700:0:4. 540 officers and men; 60 boys; 150 marines.

2. Walcheren Island off the Dutch coast was the scene of a disastrous expedition during the Napoleonic Wars. Of a force of 40,000 men serving under Lord Chatham, 7,900 died and 15,000 were disabled by a malarial fever, indigenous to that place.

3. *Cambridge* (78), screw-steamship; built 1817; 2139 tons. Commander, Edward Barnard, appointed 1840; pay, £600:1:6. 445 officers and men; 60 boys; 150 marines.

4. Charles Fellows: *The Xanthian Marbles; their acquisition and transmission to England*, 1843.

5. Elgin Marbles, Room 8; O; C.

6. Caryatid Room 9 (behind the Nereid Monument); O; C.

7. Sir Edmund Walker Head, art historian. '*Observations on the Xanthian marbles*', in *The Classical Museum*, 1844, pp.222-230.

8. In 1850, Henry went to America, returning only briefly to England in 1860, to see his dying father.

9. Charles Fellows: *The inscribed monument at Xanthus, recopied in 1842*, 1842.

10. Thomas Cubitt (1788-1855), builder of Belgravia, Bloomsbury and Pimlico; also the front of Buckingham Palace (architect, Edward Blore) and, to Prince Albert's plans, Osborne, Isle of Wight. Involved in establishing the Great Exhibition, 1851. He died, a rich man, at his estate, Denbies, near Dorking, now the largest vineyard in Britain. His Will was the longest, copied onto 36 skins of parchment.

11. Sir Edward Campbell Rich Owen GCB, GCH (1771-1849). Entered the Navy, 1775; Captain, 1779. Distinguished service in the Napoleonic Wars. Vice-Admiral, 1837; C-in-C, Mediterranean, 1841-46; Admiral of the Blue, 1846. His papers are conserved in the PRO, Kew.

12. Frederick Warden (1807-69). Entered the Navy, 1820. Commander, 1838; Captain, 1845. CB, 1855. Received public thanks from the Admiralty and the BM Trustees for his part in the Second Xanthian Expedition. His Log and papers are conserved in the PRO, Kew.

13. The camera lucida, invented in 1806, was a portable instrument about a foot long with a prism on an extending arm. Used for copying both landscapes and Old Masters. It superseded the cumbersome camera obscura, which, like early photographic apparatuses, needed a tent. Scharf's own camera lucida is conserved in the NPG Archive.

14. Amongst other items, Scharf took: 1 pair boots (12s.); 1 pr shoes; a travelling-cap; 2 stocks and 1 satin neckerchief; 4 prs gloves (1s. 3½d. a pair); 4 prs white and 2 prs worsted stockings; 1 pr muffettes; 1 pr braces; 2 blue and 2 white shirts plus 3 fronts; 4 collars; 1 cotton night-cap, 1 worsted ditto; 2 night-shirts; 1 silk waistcoat (1 gn-£1:10:0); 1 kerseymere ditto (12s.-16s.); 2 flannel ditto; 1 dress coat (2 gns); 1 pr buckskin trousers (16s. 6d.); frock coat, trousers and waistcoat (£4-£5); jacket, trousers and waistcoat, all lined (£2:15:0); 1 pr drawers [protective over-trousers; long shirt-tails did duty as pants]; pilot coat (£1:4:0-£2:15:0); capote (2 gns-£2:10:0); 6 handkerchiefs; 1 towel. His dressing-case cost 13 shillings, Fellows's leather 'Tourist Companion' with silver toiletries, cutlery, and medicines would have cost him 5 guineas.

Part Four

Chapter I The journey out

1. Charles Texier was sent by the French Ministère de l'Intérieure to Magnesia-ad-Maeandrum to collect the frieze. His excavations of the Temple, in October 1842, were witnessed by Phillips and Dadd.
2. Cardinal Albani built the Villa to house his collection. It is no longer open to the public. The 'Leucothea' (O; C) is described by J.J. Winckelmann (1717-68) in his *Monument Antichi Inediti, etc.*, Rome, 1767, 2 vols. He was fatally mugged at Trieste. See also Postscript, Chapter II, note 1.
3. Under the influence of his wife, Ferdinand's rule became progressively oppressive, provoking revolts. In 1848, he bombarded Messina, earning the nickname *Re Bomba*, King Bomb.
4. George Scharf junior: *The Pompeian Court in the Crystal Palace*, 1854. He also published *The Greek Court*, 1854, and *The Roman Court*, 1854. He would have studied the cork model of Pompeii at the Soane Museum.

Chapter II Malta; Rhodes

1. Sir Alexander Armstrong (1818-99). Entered the Navy, 1842. Promoted 1849; 1866; 1871. Military KCB, 1873; FRS. Received official thanks for his 'sanitary arrangements' at Xanthus. During the excavations of the 1950s, Prof. Demargne made great use of his reports, conserved in the PRO, Kew.
2. *Queen* (110), screw-steamship; built 1839; 3099 tons; 500 HP. Flagship of Admiral Owen. Commanded by Captain George F. Rich, appointed 1841; pay £799:19:2. 724 officers and men; 66 boys; 160 marines.

Chapter III Xanthus

1. Scharf's oil, *Our village at Xanthus during the expedition of 1844*, was hung at the RA in 1845. 'Queen's' Town refers to the ship, not Her Majesty.
2. There is a relief of wrestlers and musicians [c. 525 BC] from Xanthus in the Istanbul Museum.
3. A parody of the popular song, *In the days when we went gipsying, a long time ago*, written and sung by Edwin Ransford to music by N.J. Sporle. The Sailors' Song is in Scharf's diary; Ransford's song is in the BL, Music Library.

Chapter IV Marble-hunting I

1. Chimaera [Merehi] Tomb lid, Room 11 (gallery above the Payava Tomb, behind the Nereid Monument), recently reopened to the public.
2. The *Medea* was only a small paddle-steamer and Admiral Owen wisely ordered that, for safety's sake, no deck-cargo should be carried. Manpower and tackle were limited. This was the first expedition of its kind and established basic procedures. The Assyrian sculptures, brought to England a few years later, were also cut.

3. Lions, the Nereid Monument Room 7.
4. Lion Tomb, Room 79 (basement).

Chapter V Three Cast-making excursions

1. City Tomb cast from Pinara, Room 80 (basement).
2. Edward Daniel Clarke (1769-1822), traveller and collector of coins, antiquities and minerals. LLD, 1803. *Travels in various countries of Europe, Asia, and Africa*, 1810-23, 6 vols. The Doric Tomb (Helen's Tomb) is described in vol.2, 1812, and by Dr Wilde [see Part Two Chapter VI, note 4]. Through an inscription, it was dated c. 360 BC.
3. Bellerophon cast from Tlos, in the Museum store.
4. The story is quoted in *Memoir of W.J. Müller*, 1875, by N.N. Solly.
5. Saint Nicholas (4th century AD), born at Patara, buried at Myra. In 1087, his body was carried off to Bari, Italy. During the Greek War of Independence, more relics were taken to Russia. Czar Nicholas I sent a gaudy picture of the Saint in exchange. The body was said to have been floating in myrrh. *Meira* is a holy oil used in the Armenian Church; *merhem* in Turkish means salve or ointment.
6. Scharf's oil, *Tombs in the face of the rock at Myra*, was hung at the RA in 1845.
7. There is a similar scene in the *cella* frieze of the Nereid Monument. The man has a full 'Persian' beard. Room 7, opposite the Monument.

Chapter VI Marble-hunting II

1. *Devastation* (6), paddle-steamer; built 1841; 400 HP. Commander, Hastings R. Henry, appointed 1841; pay, £300:0:9.
2. Müller had five Turkish paintings hung at the RA in 1845; Johnson had one, and another in 1847. Some of Müller's work is in the Tate Gallery. His beautiful oil , *Tomb in the Water, Telmessus, Lycia*, hangs in the Dining Hall of Royal Holloway and Bedford New College, Surrey.
3. 'Coloured' Sphinx, pairs of sphinxes, animal wall slabs, Room 5.
4. See Part 2, Chapter 11, note 7.
5. 'Coloured' Harpy-on-column, Room 80 (basement).
6. Inscribed Stele cast, in the Museum store.
7. Inscribed Stele, reconstruction in *The Illustrated London News*, 5 October 1963, p.512-513. The frieze is in the Istanbul Museum.
8. Lion Throne, from the Inscribed Stele, near the Lion Tomb, Room 79 (basement). It has no connection with the Lion Tomb. The reconstruction of the Inscribed Stele is not shown. See Fellows's remarks, pp.329-330.
9. See Part One, Chapter II, note 10.
10. See Part Two, Chapter VII, note 4.
11. *Virago* (6), steam-vessel; built 1842; 1060 tons; 300 HP. Commander, George G. Otway, appointed 1843; pay, £300:0:9.

Chapter VII Last days

1. See Chapter IV, note 2.

2. *Warspite* (50), steamship; 1890 tons. Captain, Rt Hon. Lord John Hay CB, appointed 1841; pay £499:18:4. 393 officers and men; 47 boys; 60 marines.

Chapter VIII The voyage to Malta

1. Crete [Candia] was then part of the Ottoman Empire, returned after ten years of rule under Mohammed Ali Pasha of Egypt. In 1841, there was an insurrection. Crete became Greek in 1913; population exchange, 1923.
2. Murray's *A Hand-Book for travellers in the Ionian Islands, Greece, Turkey...Malta*, 1840. It quotes paragraphs from Fellows's *Journal*, 1839; the itinerary in Asia Minor is based on his 1838 journey.
3. *Polyphemus* (1), steamship; built 1840. Lt-Commander John Evans, appointed 1841; pay £200:15:0.

Chapter IX Homeward bound

1. Gibson's statue of Queen Victoria in the Guard Room of Buckingham Palace was also once slightly tinted. A second version of 'The Tinted Venus' is in the Walker Gallery, Liverpool; a plaster version is in the new Sackler Gallery of the RA, London.
2. Seymour Stocker Kirkup (1788-1880), artist and leader of the literary circle in Florence. British Consul. Created *Cavaliere* ('Baron') for his part in the recovery of the fresco heads. He possessed a portrait of Dante 'signed' by him from the 'spirit world'. It later passed to Dante Gabriel Rossetti, the Pre-Raphaelite painter and poet. When aged 87, 'Baron' Kirkup married a lady of 22.
3. Richard Henry Wilde (1784-1847), American poet and Dante scholar; Congressman. Settled in Florence, 1835; died of yellow fever in New Orleans. Buried there; re-interred in his garden in Augusta, 1854; reburied in Poets' Corner, Augusta, 1856.
4. Aubrey Bezzi instigated the recovery of the fresco heads in May, 1839, estimating the cost at 250 francs (about 53 guineas), which just sufficed for the work. See also Part Two, Chapter I, note 2.
5. One of Scharf's illustrations for Dante's *Divine Comedy*, 1854 and for Kugler's *Handbook of [Italian] Painting*, 3rd ed., 1855. His outline also appeared in volume 1 of *A New History of Painting in Italy*, 1864-66, 3 vols, by J.A. Crowe and G.B. Cavalcaselle. The Italian came to London as a political refugee and was taken up by Scharf, who gave him work enlarging the drawings for his lectures. Strangely enough, in 1867, Cavalcaselle was to take up the post of *Ispettore* at the Bargello Museum.

Postscript
Chapter I The Xanthian Marbles

1. See Part Three, Chapter III, note 7.

Chapter II The Lycian Room

1. Sir Richard Westmacott (1775-1856), sculptor. Studied in Rome under the Neoclassical sculptor, Antonio Canova. RA, 1816; knighted, 1835. He retained the eighteenth century ideas advanced by J.J. Winckelmann regarding the aesthetic qualities of Greek sculpture - 'noble simplicity and calm grandeur' - which influenced generations of artists and art historians. Westmacott was not on the Museum staff; called in to arrange the Townley and the Elgin Marbles, then considered the acme of perfection.
2. See Bibliography.
3. Aegina Marbles and Selinunte (Selinus) sculptures; O; C.
4. The French archaeologist, Paul-Emile Botta (1802-70), Consul at Mosel, 1842. Unsuccessfully excavated at Kuyunjik; in 1843, excavated northeast of Mosul finding Khorsabad, believed to be Nineveh. *Monument de Ninive*, etc., Paris, 1847-50, 5 vols. Layard excavated sites at Nimrud (the biblical Calah) and later, successfully, at Kuyunjik, the true Nineveh. See Introduction, Chapter II, note 5. The Khorsabad bulls were acquired for the BM by Major, later Sir, Henry Rawlinson, Consul at Baghdad, in 1849; Room 16.
5. Colouring of casts has been done at the Cambridge Museum of Classical Archaeology. See Part Two, Chapter XI, note 4.

Chapter III Past, present - and future?

1. A book of sketches and wash-drawings done in 1838 by Fellows (used in his *Journal*, 1839) and sketches by him and Scharf done in 1840 (used in Fellows's *Account*, 1841) is in the Wellcome Institute for the History of Medicine, London. Scharf's water-colours and sketches done in 1840 and 1843-44 are in the Heinz Archive and Library of the National Portrait Gallery. Other drawings by Fellows and Scharf are in the British Museum, Department of Greek and Roman Antiquities, formerly the Department of Antiquities.
2. The oil painting by John Wood of Sir Charles Fellows in court dress hangs in the Board Room area of the British Museum.

Bibliography

For Fellows's books and contemporary works, see text and Chapter Notes.

Akurgal, Ekrem, *Ancient civilizations and ruins of Turkey*. Engl. trans., Istanbul, 1969; 4th ed., Istanbul, 1978.

Bean, George E., *Aegean Turkey*. London, 1966; reissued 1989.

Bean, George E., *Turkey's Southern Shore*. London, 1968; reissued 1989.

Bean, George E., *Turkey beyond the Maeander*. London, 1971; reissued 1989.

Bean, George E., *Lycian Turkey*. London, 1978; reissued 1989.

Benndorf, F.A. Otto, *Das Heroon von Gjölbaschi-Trysa*. 3 parts, in *Jahrb. kunsth. Samml. Allerh. Kaiserhauses*, Bd 9, 11, 12: 1889, 1890, 1891.

Demargne, Pierre *et al.*, *Fouilles de Xanthos, etc*. Paris, 1958-92 [continuing].

Haynes, Sybille, *Land of the Chimaera*. London, 1974.

Metzger, Henri, *Anatolia II*. Engl. trans., Geneva, 1969.

Niemann, George, *Das Nereiden-Monument in Xanthos. Versuch einer Wiederherstellung, etc*. Vienna, 1921.

Perrot, Georges and Chipiez, Charles, *Histoire de l'art dans l'antiquité*. Paris, 1881-1914, 10 vols.

Perrot, Georges and Chipiez, Charles, *History of Art in Phrygia, Lydia, Caria, and Lycia*. Vol. 5, 1890; Engl. trans., London, 1892.

Reisen im sudwestlichen Kleinasien. [Illustrated with heliographs of the sites.]
  Bd 1. Benndorf, Otto and Neimann, George, *Reisen in Lykien und Karien*. Vienna, 1884.
  Kiepert, Heinrich and Niemann, George, *Erläuterungen zu der dem Werke, Reisen in Lykien und Karien...beigefügten Specialkarte*. Vienna, 1884.
  Bd 2. Petersen, Eugen and Luschen, Felix von. *Reisen in Lykien, Milyas und Kibyrates*. Vienna, 1889.

Stark, Freya, *Ionia, A Quest*. London, 1954; reissued 1988.

Stark, Freya, *The Lycian Shore*. London, 1956; reissued 1989.

Stark, Freya, *Alexander's Path from Caria to Cilicia*. London, 1959; reissued 1991.

Zahle, Jan. *Harpy-monumentet i Xanthos. En lykisk pillegrav*. Copenhagen, 1975.

Zahle, Jan. *Arkaeologiske studier i lykiske klippergrave og deres relieffer*. Copenhagen, 1983.

Archaeological Sites

Archaeological sites in Turkey

Aezani
Alabanda
Alexandria Troas
Alinda
Antiocheia
Antiphellus
Aperlae
Aphrodisias
Araxa
Arycanda
Aspendus
Assos

Cadyanda
Calynda
Caystrus
Corydalla
Cydna

Ephesus
Euromus

Gagae

Hierapolis

Isium

Labranda
Laodiceia
Letoum
Limyra

Mylasa
Myra

Nicaea
Nysa

Olympus

Patara
Pergamus

Perge
Philadelphia
Pinara
Podalia
Pydna
Pyrrha

Sagalassus
Sardis
Selge
Side
Sidyma
Stratoniceia
Sura

Telmessus
Thyatira
Tlos
Trabala
Tralles
Troy

Archaeological sites in Europe; *see also* Antiquities in Europe; Malta

Athens
Herculaneum

Neapolis
Ostia Antica

Paestum
Pompeii

Index

Troy - Truva 26
Turgutlu, *see* Cassaba

Uç Göz, *see* Tralles
Uslann 140-1; *see also* Cydna
Üzümlü, *see* Hoozumlee

Valetta; Malta 56-7, 215, 226, 232, 234, 238, 246, 247-50, 298, 305, 313-8
Venice 204-5
Volterra 52

Walls, City 33, 44, 73, 79, 81-2, 87, 88, 91, 97, 112-3, 124, 125, 133, 135, 136, 138, 141, 154, 159, 160, 162, 164, 168-9, 172, 186, 219, *112*
Warden, Capt., Frederick, RN 232, 238, 247-9, 250-1, 253, 254, 260, 268, 269-70, 280-1, 306, 307-8, 309, 311, 313, 314, 316, 318, 335, 345, 346, *248, 249, 311*
Westmacott, Sir Richard (sculptor) 234-5, 327, 329, 350
Wilde, Dr. William (Irish surgeon) 116, 179, 341, 348
Wilkinson, G. (British Consul, Rhodes) 175, 176, 232, 251, 253, 311, *311*
Wilkinson - (son) 217, 219, 233
Winckelmann, Johann Joachim (German antiquary) 35, 242, 331, 347, 350

Xanthian Marbles i-ii, 1-2, 4, 7-8, 13, 47, 177, 212, 214, 216-7, 226-31, 233-6, 238, 248, 259, 305, 308, 309, 314, 315, 316, 323-4, 325 *ff.*, 336, 342, *214, 328*
Xanthus 2, 5-6, 19, 20, 38-43, 124, 142-8, 216, 218, 262, 264-5, 267, 308-9, 341, *cover, 39, 143, 220, 264, 265, 268, 270, 273; see also* Firman; Koonik; Rivers
Xanthus, First Xanthian Expedition 1, 6, 7, 47, 176-7, 214-36, 249-50, 326. Camp 218-9, 230-1, 233-4, *218*; Equipment 215, 218, 231; Provisions 215, 219; Deaths 226, 233-4, 249
Xanthus, Second Xanthian Expedition 1, 7, 232, 237-8, 247-9, 250-1, 253, 254-311, 315, 326; *see also* Cast-making. Camp, Queen's Town 255-8, 262-3, 266, 268, 280, 304-5, 306, 307, 347, *257*; Halfway Station 255, 266, 275, 299, 305, 307, 308; Equipment 239, 254, 255, 305, 307, 308; Provisions 254, 255-6, 305;

Death 272; Sailors' song 262-3, 269, 275, 305, 317, 347; Wrestling match 259-62, 347, *260, 261*
Xanthus, antiquities; Baths 300-1; Leda mosaic 300, *300*; Box Tomb 142, *cover, 265*; Chimaera (Merehi) Tomb 147-8, 270-1, 272-3, 306, 308, 328, 347, *270, 271, 328*; Harpy-on-column 302, 336, 348, *302*; Harpy Tomb 1, 2, 40, 143-4, 147, 199, 211, 229, 230, 234, 235, 236, 237, 242-3, 308, 328, 330, 336, 345, *39, 41, 144, 265, 328*; Harpies 143, 236, *40, 144*; Horse (Payava) Tomb 1, 2, 42-3, 142, 144-6, 147-8, 211, 229-30, 234, 235, 270-1, 272-3, 308, 319, 328, 336, 345, *42, 145, 146, 229, 275, 328*; model of 325, *334*; Inscribed Stele 42, 146, 148, 227-8, 230, 237, 303-4, 328, 330, 336, 348, *227, 303, 304, 328*; Lion Throne 304, 329-30, 348, *302, 304*; Ionic (Nereid) Monument 1, 2, 138, 148, 220-5, 228, 230, 234, 235, 328, 329, 333, 345, 348, *221, 222, 334*; models of 225, 325, 328, 333; friezes of 1, 2, 138, 221-5, 227, 230-1, 269, 275, 319, 336, *224, 286*; lions of 269, 273, 328, 330, 348; Nereids 221, 223, 225, 227, 236, 328, 336, *225*; Lion Tomb 1, 2, 40, 142, 147, 229, 273-4, 304, 336, 348, *40, 273, 274*; Sphynxes 301-2, 329, 348, *301*; Theatre 143, 266, 305, *39, 265*; Vespasian Arch 268, *264, 268*; Wall Slabs 228, 230, 234, 235, 302, 328-9, 336, 348, *228, 302*

Yanar Dağ (Burning Mountain) 165-6
Yeddy Cappee - Yedi Kapı (Cadyanda) 124, *111*; (Tlos) 131, 288-9
Yeeilassies (highland pastures) 173-4, 180-2, 233, 288, 292
Yeerah - Geyre, *see* Aphrodisias
Yehnejah - Yenice 76, 77
Yoorooks (nomads) 184, 187, 297
Yule, Major, RE 232, 249-50

Zend (ancient Persian) 6, 106; *see also* Persians in Lycia
Zeus (Jupiter) 86; Altar of 24, 338; Temples 30, 91, 94, 95, 96, 341, 343
Zhumarlee-cooe - Çumali 85, *85*
Zoorigees (grooms) 69, 83, 84, 183, 184; *see also* Cavalcades

362